NEW STUDIES IN I

Series editor: D. A. Carson

All things new

REVELATION AS CANONICAL CAPSTONE

Brian J. Tabb

Apollos

IVP Academic

An imprint of InterVarsity Press
Downers Grove, Illinois

APOLLOS (an imprint of Inter-Varsity Press)
36 Causton Street
London SW1P 4ST, England
ivpbooks.com
ivp@ivpbooks.com

InterVarsity Press, USA
P.O. Box 1400
Downers Grove, IL 60515, USA
ivpress.com
email@ivpress.com

InterVarsity Press® is the book-publishing division of InterVarsity Christian Fellowship/USA®, a movement of students and faculty active on campus at hundreds of universities, colleges, and schools of nursing in the United States of America, and a member movement of the International Fellowship of Evangelical Students. For information about local and regional activities, visit intervarsity.org.

Inter-Varsity Press, England, originated within the Inter-Varsity Fellowship, now the Universities and Colleges Christian Fellowship, a student movement connecting Christian Unions in universities and colleges throughout Great Britain, and a member movement of the International Fellowship of Evangelical Students. That historic association is maintained, and all senior IVP staff and committee members subscribe to the UCCF Basis of Faith. Website: www.uccf.org.uk.

The publisher and author acknowledge with thanks permission to reproduce the following: Table format adapted from NIV Zondervan Study Bible edited by D. A. Carson. Copyright © 2015 by Zondervan. Used by permission of Zondervan. www.zondervan.com.

First published 2019

Set in Monotype Times New Roman
Typeset in Great Britain by CRB Associates, Potterhanworth, Lincolnshire

USA ISBN 978-0-8308-2649-0 (print)
USA ISBN 978-0-8308-5500-1 (digital)
UK ISBN 978-1-78359-915-8 (print)
UK ISBN 978-1-78359-916-5 (digital)

Printed in the United States of America ∞

InterVarsity Press is committed to ecological stewardship and to the conservation of natural resources in all our operations. This book was printed using sustainably sourced paper.

British Library Cataloguing-in-Publication Data
A catalogue record for this book is available from the British Library.

Library of Congress Cataloging-in-Publication Data
A catalog record for this book is available from the Library of Congress.

P	21	20	19	18	17	16	15	14	13	12	11	10	9	8	7	6	5	4	3
Y	36	35	34	33	32	31	30	29	28	27	26	25	24	23					

For Jeremiah, Julia, Judson and Jonah

Contents

Series preface

New Studies in Biblical Theology is a series of monographs that address key issues in the discipline of biblical theology. Contributions to the series focus on one or more of three areas: (1) the nature and status of biblical theology, including its relations with other disciplines (e.g. historical theology, exegesis, systematic theology, historical criticism, narrative theology); (2) the articulation and exposition of the structure of thought of a particular biblical writer or corpus; and (3) the delineation of a biblical theme across all or part of the biblical corpora.

Above all, these monographs are creative attempts to help thinking Christians understand their Bibles better. The series aims simultaneously to instruct and to edify, to interact with the current literature, and to point the way ahead. In God's universe, mind and heart should not be divorced: in this series we will try not to separate what God has joined together. While the notes interact with the best of scholarly literature, the text is uncluttered with untransliterated Greek and Hebrew, and tries to avoid too much technical jargon. The volumes are written within the framework of confessional evangelicalism, but there is always an attempt at thoughtful engagement with the sweep of the relevant literature.

Someone who makes a study of such things once assured me that the Puritans wrote far, far more commentaries on the Book of Revelation than on any other book of the Bible. Interestingly enough, very few of them have been reprinted in our age, despite the resurgence of many other Puritan writings. I have since learned that similar statistics could be amassed about several other historical periods. This suggests two things: first, interest in the Apocalypse is perennial; and second, relatively little of all this industry will stand the test of time. So what are the prospects for Dr Brian Tabb's *All Things New*?

I'd say they are very good indeed! If this world staggers on for several hundred more years, during this time serious readers will return to Dr Tabb again and again. Not only does he write with clarity and deceptive simplicity, but *what* he writes will prove enduring. He belongs to that biblical-theological school which, without forcing the evidence, eagerly probes how the trajectories of Scripture come together in Scripture's last book. As Richard Bauckham has taught us, the Book of Revelation is the very culmination of prophecy – and Dr Tabb is eager to work this out. In a book like Revelation, full of symbols that have little resonance with our world, Dr Tabb brings them to life once again. And he does this in a context that ties the themes of the book to some foundational Christian convictions. Take, and read.

D. A. Carson
Trinity Evangelical Divinity School

Author's preface

This book had its genesis in 2013, when Don Carson invited me to contribute notes on Revelation for the *NIV Zondervan Study Bible*. Many of the tables in this book have been adapted from my earlier work in that volume and are used with the publisher's permission. I am grateful to Don and Philip Duce of Inter-Varsity Press for accepting this work for inclusion in the New Studies in Biblical Theology series and for their careful editorial labours. Thanks also to Rima Devereaux, who oversaw the production of the book, and to Eldo Barkhuizen, who copy-edited the manuscript.

It is a great privilege to serve on the faculty of Bethlehem College & Seminary under the leadership of President Tomlinson. I have had the privilege of working through the Greek text of Revelation with several classes of students, whose questions and insights have sharpened my own understanding of the book. I am grateful to my colleagues Andy Naselli, Chris Bruno and Matthew Westerholm, and my teaching assistant Matt Denzer and a number of my students, who graciously read portions of the manuscript and offered valuable feedback. Our librarian, Barbara Winters, also provided wonderful assistance securing needed books and articles.

Two of my former professors, G. K. Beale and Craig Koester, significantly influenced my approach to and love for the book of Revelation, first through their teaching and more recently through their writings. C. S. Lewis (1961: 40) once wrote, 'My own eyes are not enough for me, I will see through those of others.' This need to see with other people's eyes is particularly acute when studying the Apocalypse, so I am grateful that my teachers have written outstanding commentaries, which I reference frequently throughout this study.

I give thanks to God for my beloved wife, Kristin, who offered great encouragement and helpful feedback on this project. My children, Jeremiah, Julia, Judson and Jonah, bring great joy to my life, and I pray that they may worship God and hold fast to his trustworthy Word. I dedicate this book to them.

Soli Deo gloria.

Brian J. Tabb

Abbreviations

1Q28b	*Rule of the Congregation* (Dead Sea Scrolls)
1QM	*War Scroll* (Dead Sea Scrolls)
1QS	*Rule of the Community* (Dead Sea Scrolls)
1 En.	*1 Enoch*
2 En.	*2 Enoch*
3 En.	*3 Enoch*
2 Bar.	*2 Baruch*
4 Bar.	*4 Baruch*
4Q252	*Commentary on Genesis A* (Dead Sea Scrolls)
4Q405	*Songs of the Sabbath Sacrifice* (Dead Sea Scrolls)
4Q523	*4Q Jonathan* (Dead Sea Scrolls)
AB	Anchor Bible
ACCS	Ancient Christian Commentary on Scripture
AOTC	Apollos Old Testament Commentary
Apoc. Ab.	*Apocalypse of Abraham*
ArBib	The Aramaic Bible
BBR	Bulletin for Biblical Research
BDAG	W. Bauer, F. W. Danker, W. F. Arndt and F. W. Gingrich, *A Greek–English Lexicon of the New Testament and Other Early Christian Literature*, 3rd edn, Chicago: University of Chicago Press, 2000
BECNT	Baker Exegetical Commentary on the New Testament
BETL	Bibliotheca ephemeridum theologicarum lovaniensium
Bib	*Biblica*
BibInt	*Biblical Interpretation*
BNTC	Black's New Testament Commentaries
BR	*Biblical Research*
BSac	*Bibliotheca sacra*
BST	The Bible Speaks Today
BZNW	Beihefte zur Zeitschrift für die neutestamentliche Wissenschaft
CBQ	*Catholic Biblical Quarterly*
CTJ	*Calvin Theological Journal*

CTR	Criswell Theological Review
CurBR	*Currents in Biblical Research*
d.	died
EKKNT	Evangelisch-katholischer Kommentar zum Neuen Testament
ESV	English Standard Version (2016)
ET	English Translation
EvQ	*Evangelical Quarterly*
HCSB	Holman Christian Standard Bible (2003)
HDR	Harvard Dissertations in Religion
Hebr.	Hebrew
Herm., *Vis.*	Shepherd of Hermas, *Visions*
HNT	Handbuch zum Neuen Testament
ICC	International Critical Commentary
JBL	*Journal of Biblical Literature*
JECS	*Journal of Early Christian Studies*
JETS	*Journal of the Evangelical Theological Society*
JSJSup	Journal for the Study of Judaism Supplement Series
JSNT	*Journal for the Study of the New Testament*
JSNTSup	Journal for the Study of the New Testament Supplement Series
JSOT	*Journal for the Study of the Old Testament*
JSOTSup	Journal for the Study of the Old Testament Supplement Series
Jub.	*Jubilees*
L&N	*Greek–English Lexicon of the New Testament: Based on Semantic Domains*, J. P. Louw and E. A. Nida, New York: United Bible Societies, 1988
LAB	*Liber antiquitatum biblicarum*
LNTS	Library of New Testament Studies
Luther	Luther Bibel (1912)
LXX	Septuagint
MT	Masoretic Text
NA[28]	*Nestle-Aland Novum Testamentum Graece*, 28th edn, Stuttgart: Deutsche Bibelgesellschaft, 2012
NASB	New American Standard Bible (1995)
NDBT	*New Dictionary of Biblical Theology*, ed. T. D. Alexander and B. S. Rosner, Downers Grove: InterVarsity Press, 2000
Neot	*Neotestamentica*
NET	New English Translation (2005)

NETS	New English Translation of the Septuagint (2007)
NIBCNT	New International Biblical Commentary on the New Testament
NICNT	New International Commentary on the New Testament
NICOT	New International Commentary on the Old Testament
NIDNTTE	*New International Dictionary of New Testament Theology and Exegesis*, ed. M. Silva, 2nd edn, 5 vols., Grand Rapids: Zondervan, 2014
NIGTC	New International Greek Testament Commentary
NIV	New International Version (2011)
NIVAC	New International Version Application Commentary
NKJV	New King James Version (1982)
NLT	New Living Translation (2015)
NovT	*Novum Testamentum*
NRSV	New Revised Standard Version (1989)
NSBT	New Studies in Biblical Theology
NT	New Testament
NTL	New Testament Library
NTM	New Testament Monographs
NTS	*New Testament Studies*
NTT	New Testament Theology
OT	Old Testament
PNTC	Pillar New Testament Commentary
Pss Sol.	*Psalms of Solomon*
Rahlfs	A. Rahlfs and R. Hanhart (eds.), *Septuaginta*, rev. edn, Stuttgart: Deutsche Bibelgesellschaft, 2006
RNT	Regensburger Neues Testament
SBB	Stuttgarter biblische Beiträge
SBJT	*Southern Baptist Journal of Theology*
SBT	Studies in Biblical Theology
Schlachter	Schlachter, F. E. (2000), *Die Bibel*, Geneva: Genfer Bibelgesellschaft
Sib. Or.	*Sibylline Oracles*
SNTSMS	Society for New Testament Studies Monograph Series
SSEJC	Studies in Scripture in Early Judaism and Christianity
T. Ab.	*Testament of Abraham*
T. Jos.	*Testament of Joseph*
T. Levi	*Testament of Levi*
T. Reu.	*Testament of Reuben*
T. Sol.	*Testament of Solomon*

T. Zeb.	*Testament of Zebulun*
TDNT	*Theological Dictionary of the New Testament*, ed. G. Kittel and G. Friedrich, tr. G. W. Bromiley, 10 vols., Grand Rapids: Eerdmans, 1964–76
TENTS	Texts and Editions for New Testament Study
TH	Theodotion Recension of the Septuagint
Them	*Themelios*
TJ	*Trinity Journal*
TNTC	Tyndale New Testament Commentary
TOTC	Tyndale Old Testament Commentary
tr.	translated by
VTSup	Supplements to Vetus Testamentum
WBC	Word Biblical Commentary
WJE	Works of Jonathan Edwards
WTJ	*Westminster Theological Journal*
WUNT	Wissenschaftliche Untersuchungen zum Neuen Testament
WW	*Word and World*
ZNW	*Zeitschrift für die neutestamentliche Wissenschaft und die Kunde der älteren Kirche*

Chapter One

Introduction

Unravelling the riddle

For most Bible readers Revelation is a riddle that fascinates and frustrates. The last book of our Bibles has inspired innumerable commentaries, prophecy charts and dissertations but is rarely read aloud or preached in many modern churches. For example, the *Revised Common Lectionary* used by various Protestant denominations assigns only six brief passages from the Apocalypse for congregational reading every three years.[1] These chosen texts include scenes of heavenly worship and the promised new creation but conveniently avoid mention of the beast and the dragon, Babylon the great, the judgment cycles of seals, trumpets and bowls of divine wrath, and Christ's messages to the seven churches.[2] 'The result is a pleasant selection of texts that will not disturb or confuse anyone. The problem is that the omitted passages are precisely the ones that generate the most interest.'[3]

Scholars and teachers have proposed different keys to unlock this enigmatic book. A number of popular preachers and writers read the Apocalypse in the light of current world events. Best-selling books such as *The Late Great Planet Earth* by Hal Lindsey and the *Left Behind* novels by Tim LaHaye and Jerry Jenkins have popularized a dispensational futurist interpretation of Revelation.[4] This approach rightly stresses that Jesus will return and that God will fulfil his ancient promises. However, confident predictions and analyses by many so-called 'prophecy experts' often miss the mark and appear far removed from the late first-century context of John and his readers.

On the other hand, biblical scholars commonly emphasize that Revelation must be read strictly in the light of its historical context.

---

[1] In contrast, the *Revised Common Lectionary* (2009) assigns readings from 25 of Matthew's 28 chapters, 15 of the 16 chapters of Romans and every chapter of James.
[2] Rev. 1:4–8; 5:11–14; 7:9–17; 21:1–6; 21:10; 21:22–22:5; 22:12–14, 16–17, 20–21.
[3] Koester 2005: 271.
[4] For critical analysis, see ibid. 274–282; Gorman 2011: 70–73.

So, 'the beast' is not an antichrist figure that persecutes the saints in the distant future but the Roman Empire that presently promotes idolatrous emperor worship and economic oppression in the late first century. Scholars who adopt this historical-critical approach rightly relate Revelation to John and his first readers, but some stop short of reading the book as the capstone of Christian Scripture to be applied and lived out by believers today.

Neither the strictly futurist approach nor the historical-critical approach adequately demonstrates the ongoing vital relevance of the Apocalypse for the contemporary church.[5] The present volume stresses the vital importance of the *canonical* context of the book of Revelation. I argue that the Apocalypse presents itself as the climax of biblical prophecy that shows how various Old Testament prophecies and patterns find their consummation in the present and future reign of Jesus Christ, who decisively defeats his foes, saves his people and restores all things. As biblical prophecy, Revelation not only foretells the future but also calls for present obedience to God's revealed truth.[6] Additionally, the book's symbolic visions shape believers' world views around what is true, good and beautiful according to God's revealed standards and motivate them to live counterculturally in the world as faithful witnesses who 'follow the Lamb wherever he goes' (Rev. 14:4).[7] Revelation is not a riddle to be decoded by experts or marginalized by those in the pews. It is a book – indeed, the *final* book – of Christian Scripture meant to decode our reality, capture our imaginations and master our lives with the word of God and the testimony of Jesus.[8]

Revelation calls readers to hear and heed its message and so obtain a divine blessing. The following verses offer five important clues for discerning the book's message and aims:

> The revelation of Jesus Christ, which God gave him to show to his servants the things that must soon take place. He made it known by sending his angel to his servant John, who bore witness to the word of God and to the testimony of Jesus Christ, even to all that he saw. Blessed is the one who reads aloud the words of this

---

[5] 'Dispensational distraction and scholarly abstraction have conspired in their different ways to silence the canonical climax', according to Webster (2014: 11).

[6] Rightly stressed by Bandy and Merkle (2015: 33–35).

[7] Unless otherwise noted, Scripture citations are from the ESVUK.

[8] Bauckham (1993b: 159) writes that Revelation seeks 'to purge and to refurbish the Christian imagination'.

prophecy, and blessed are those who hear, and who keep what is written in it, for the time is near. (1:1–3)

These words are trustworthy and true. And the Lord, the God of the spirits of the prophets, has sent his angel to show his servants what must soon take place.

And behold, I am coming soon. Blessed is the one who keeps the words of the prophecy of this book. (22:6–7)

First, the opening phrase 'the revelation of Jesus Christ' introduces the book's central message (1:1). Some take this phrase to mean Jesus is the one revealed (revelation *about* Jesus), but most likely the stress is on Jesus as the one who reveals (revelation *from* Jesus).[9] This revelation originates with God, who gives it to Jesus, who sent his angel to John, who writes to God's people.

Second, this book is a 'prophecy' from the true God for the benefit of God's people (1:3; 22:7, 10, 18–19).[10] John writes as a Christian prophet who announces the imminent fulfilment of earlier biblical prophecies (10:7; 22:10).[11]

Third, it announces eschatological realities that 'must soon take place' (*ha dei genesthai en tachei* [1:1; cf. 22:6]). Significantly, this phrase alludes to Daniel 2:28 LXX: 'there is a Lord in heaven illumining mysteries who has disclosed to King Nabouchodonosor what must happen at the end of days [*ha dei genesthai ep' eschatōn tōn hēmerōn*]' (NETS).[12] Daniel writes about divine mysteries that concern the distant future, but the revelation John receives from the exalted

---

[9] Cf. NIV, NLT; Giesen 1997: 56; Osborne 2002: 52; Koester 2014: 222.

[10] Rev. 22:6 may echo Num. 27:16, 'Yahweh, the God of the spirits and of all flesh' (*kyrios ho theos tōn pneumatōn kai pasēs sarkos*), noted by Beale (2011a: 19).

[11] The author of Revelation introduces himself as John (1:4), God's 'servant' (1:1), who receives divine visions and writes as an authoritative prophet (1:10–11). John is not a pseudonym but the real name of a Jewish-Christian prophet who was well known to the seven Asian churches (1:4, 9). Critical scholarship typically argues against common authorship of Revelation and the Gospel of John because of perceived differences in the theological emphasis and literary style of the two works (first noted by Dionysius in the third century). Cf. Schüssler Fiorenza 1998: 85–113; Witherington 2003: 1–3; Koester 2014: 65–69. However, Maier (1981: 107) argues that Revelation has a stronger and earlier tradition affirming its apostolic authorship than any other NT book. Cf. Justin, *Dialogue with Trypho* 81.4; Irenaeus, *Against Heresies* 3.11.1; the Muratorian Fragment lines 57–60; Carson and Moo 2005: 700–706; Osborne 2002: 2–6; Beale 1999: 34–36. I hold that John refers to the apostle of Jesus who authored the fourth Gospel, but the approach to and analysis of Revelation in this book do not depend on this designation.

[12] On Revelation's allusion to Dan. 2, see Beale 1999: 50–52, 181–182.

Christ concerns the immediate future: the time is 'soon' and 'near' (Rev. 1:1, 3).[13]

Fourth, the words recorded in this book 'are trustworthy and true' (22:6). These same terms describe the risen Lord Jesus in Revelation 3:14 and 19:11, as well as God in Deuteronomy 32:4 LXX and God's promise to make all things new in Revelation 21:5 (cf. Isa. 65:16–17).[14] Beale explains, 'If absolute flawlessness be granted about God's character and spoken word, then the same should be granted about John's written word.'[15]

Finally, Revelation 1:3 and 22:7 promise blessing for those who read aloud, hear and respond rightly to the prophetic word. The seven beatitudes in Revelation comfort and challenge believers and stress that 'God's blessings will be experienced by those who persevere.'[16]

The following sections will consider how the book's prologue and epilogue establish *what* Revelation is (genre), *why* it is written (purpose), *how* it should be read (hermeneutics) and *where* it is situated in the Bible's storyline (biblical theology).

The genre(s) of Revelation

One reason many readers struggle to interpret Revelation is that they misunderstand its literary genre. The initial verses signal that this work belongs to three kinds of ancient literature: *apocalypse*, *prophecy* and *epistle*, each of which is important for considering what sort of book Revelation is and how we should interpret it.[17]

'The revelation of Jesus Christ' (*Apokalypsis Iēsou Christou*) serves as a title or shorthand summary for the book and also gives an initial clue concerning its genre. In the New Testament the Greek word *apokalypsis* (translated 'revelation') consistently refers to divine revelation or unveiling things hidden or unseen.[18] For example, Paul refers to 'the revelation [*apokalypsis*] of the mystery that was kept secret for long ages but has now been disclosed and through the prophetic writings has been made known to all nations' (Rom. 16:25–26). Daniel

---

[13] See ch. 10, pp. 213–215.
[14] Rev. 3:14 likely alludes to 'the God of truth' (Isa. 65:16), according to Beale (1999: 152–160).
[15] Beale 2011a: 19. Cf. ch. 10, pp. 220–223.
[16] Osborne 2002: 57. Cf. ch. 5, pp. 108–110.
[17] For similar assessments of the genre of Revelation, see Bauckham 1993b: 1–17; deSilva 2009b: 9–14; Gorman 2011: 13; Koester 2014: 104–112; Paul 2018: 25–30.
[18] Cf. *NIDNTTE*, 2: 616 (*kalyptō*).

stresses that God in heaven 'reveals mysteries' (*anakalyptōn mystēria*) and discloses things that must happen at the end of time (2:28–29 LXX). The first words of Revelation 1:1 recall Daniel 2 and emphasize that the exalted Christ now discloses unseen, divine realities 'which God gave him to show to his servants the things that must soon take place.'

The term *apokalypsis* also suggests that Revelation shares characteristics of biblical and extra-biblical writings commonly labelled *apocalypses*. John Collins defines apocalypse as

> a genre of revelatory literature with a narrative framework, in which a revelation is mediated by an otherworldly being to a human recipient, disclosing a transcendent reality which is both temporal, insofar as it envisages eschatological salvation, and spatial, insofar as it involves another, supernatural world.[19]

There is considerable variety within these writings, which include significant portions of the canonical book of Daniel as well as non-canonical texts such as *1 Enoch, 2 Enoch, 2 Baruch, 4 Ezra* and the *Apocalypse of Abraham*.[20] Apocalypses have two principal functions: (1) they encourage and comfort believers during severe trials or following disaster, and (2) they challenge readers to adopt a new perspective on reality in the light of coming judgment and to live accordingly.[21]

Revelation stands in this tradition of apocalyptic writings in at least four ways. First, like portions of Isaiah, Ezekiel and especially Daniel and unlike some extra-biblical Jewish apocalypses, John's apocalyptic visions disclose God's ultimate purposes in salvation and judgment. Second, John's apocalyptic visions present a transcendent, God-centred, heavenly perspective on reality. Third, Revelation like Jewish apocalypses employs symbolic imagery drawn from the Old Testament prophets. For example, the depictions of God's majestic throne and

---

[19] Collins 1979: 9.

[20] For further examples and analysis, see Collins 2010: 341–345. For introduction to these and other non-canonical Jewish texts, see Gurtner 2013b: 291–309.

[21] Collins 2010: 345; cf. deSilva 2009b: 9–10. Mazzaferri (1989: 257–258, 383) contends that Revelation 'cannot even be considered a proximate apocalypse', on the grounds that the book is not apocalyptic in form, lacks essential pseudonymity and has a different eschatological outlook and function than Jewish apocalypses. However, he unnecessarily drives a wedge between the OT prophetic tradition and later Jewish apocalypses and does not consider the possibility that Revelation combines multiple genres – the prevailing view among modern commentators. Cf. Mathewson 1992: 193–213; Osborne 2002: 12–15.

heavenly attendants in *1 Enoch*, *2 Enoch* and the Apocalypse allude to the foundational Old Testament visions in Ezekiel 1, Isaiah 6 and Daniel 7.[22] Likewise, Revelation 13 and *4 Ezra* 11 – 12 allude to the vision of terrible beasts arising from the sea in Daniel 7:3–8.[23] Fourth, though it seems like God's promises to establish his eternal kingdom and defeat his enemies go unfulfilled as the righteous suffer and the wicked prosper, nevertheless Revelation, like other apocalypses, maintains that God is sovereign and will ultimately triumph and achieve his purposes.

In Revelation 4 John receives a vision of God Almighty seated on his glorious throne receiving unending praise from the heavenly beings. This foundational vision alludes to the famous prophecies in Isaiah 6 and Ezekiel 1 and introduces the divine throne, one of the book's defining motifs.[24] Significantly, John's throne-room vision follows immediately after Jesus' messages to the seven churches in Revelation 2–3, where he summons them to repent of immorality, false teaching and worldliness and to persevere amidst persecution and pressure. This vision reorients believers' view of their present situation and challenges them to live by faith in the light of God's sovereign rule over all things, which is more real and lasting than the reality they see with their eyes.

Additionally, Revelation is *a book of prophecy* intended for public reading during corporate worship (1:3; 22:7, 10, 18–19). The designation 'book of prophecy' refers primarily 'to divine disclosure demanding an ethical response, in line with Old Testament "prophecy," which primarily addresses present situations and only secondarily foretells'.[25] John's prophecy brings the Scriptures to bear on his hearers' present circumstances and future hopes.[26]

John's commission to prophesy resembles Ezekiel's (Rev. 10:9–11; cf. Ezek. 2:8–3:3). Like the Old Testament prophets, John receives divine revelation 'in the Spirit' (Rev. 1:10; 4:2; 17:3; 21:10; Ezek. 3:12; 11:24),[27] and he also writes down what he sees and hears (Rev. 1:10, 19; Hab. 2:2; Jer. 30:2). Revelation contains 'the true words of God' (Rev. 19:9), and the concluding warning about adding to or taking

---

[22] Cf. *1 En.* 14.18–19 [Ezek. 1:20–22]; 47.3 and 60.2 [Dan. 7:9–10]; *2 En.* 21.1 [Isa. 6:2–3].

[23] See ch. 6, pp. 125–127.

[24] Cf. ch. 2, pp. 37–40, Gallusz 2014.

[25] Beale 1999: 185.

[26] Mathewson 2003b: 225.

[27] See ch. 4, pp. 71–74.

away from this book of prophecy (22:18–19) alludes to similar admonitions in Deuteronomy 4:2 and 29:19–20.[28]

Finally, Revelation presents its authoritative apocalyptic prophecy in the form of *a circular letter* that Jesus commands John to 'write' to seven Christian assemblies in Asia Minor (1:11).[29] Revelation 1:4–6 follows the usual form of New Testament letter openings: author ('John'), recipients ('to the seven churches') and Christian greeting ('Grace and peace'; cf. 1 Thess. 1:1). The book closes with a 'grace' benediction virtually identical to those concluding many New Testament letters (22:21; cf. Rom. 16:20).

These epistolary features signal first that the entire book, not merely chapters 2–3, is intended to communicate to the specific situation of the seven churches.[30] Second, by employing conventions very similar to those found in other New Testament letters, John situates his book within a wider Christian tradition of authoritative letters written to instruct and edify believers.[31] Third, like Elijah and Jeremiah before him, John writes letters to communicate his prophetic message of judgment and comfort.[32] Finally, Revelation's epistolary form signals that it 'is not an esoteric secret work' but one that should be regularly read aloud in the context of corporate worship.[33]

Thus Revelation presents itself as an apocalyptic prophecy in the form of a circular letter.[34] Webster aptly calls it 'John's prison epistle', written by a prophet, poet, pastor and political prisoner who was 'steeped in prophetic exile texts'.[35] The addresses to the seven churches in chapters 2–3 are commonly called 'letters'. However, the repeated invocation *Tade legei* (thus says the one . . .) recalls the refrain *Tade legei kyrios* (thus says the Lord) that regularly introduces prophetic oracles in the LXX and in Acts 21:11.[36] While specific to each church's situation, these oracles from the exalted Christ contain the Spirit's message to the *churches* (cf. 2:7 and parallels) and are included within

---

[28] Beale 1999: 1150–1154. Cf. *1 En.* 104.11; ch. 10, pp. 215–220.

[29] Schüssler Fiorenza 1998: 35. On the epistolary genre of the Apocalypse, see Gradl 2012: 413–433.

[30] Gradl 2012: 433.

[31] Koester 2014: 111–112.

[32] Cf. Jer. 29:1, 3, 25, 29; 2 Chr. 21:12; Aune 1997: lxxiv.

[33] Schüssler Fiorenza 1998: 35. Cf. Rev. 1:3.

[34] Bandy and Merkle (2015: 215) argue that Revelation is fundamentally a book of prophecy. DeSilva (2009b: 9–14) and Bauckham (1993a: xi–xii) argue for a mixed-genre classification with apocalyptic as primary.

[35] Webster 2014: 3.

[36] Rev. 2:1, 8, 12, 18; 3:1, 7, 14; Boxall 2006: 45.

one circular letter distributed to all. 'Through the interplay of the apocalyptic, prophetic, and epistolary genres, John brings a visionary message into the context of the readers.'[37]

The purpose of Revelation

Revelation's symbolic visions *challenge* readers to resist worldly compromise, spiritual complacency and false teaching. They also *encourage* embattled believers to persevere in faithful witness and hope in the present and future reign of God and the Lamb.[38] The visions offer a divine perspective on what is true, valuable and lasting. They expose the true nature of the world's ungodly political, cultural, economic and religious system destined for destruction, and they reorient believers' world views and values around God's eternal kingdom.[39]

The messages to the churches in Revelation 2 – 3 each conclude the same way: 'Whoever has an ear should hear what the Spirit is saying to the churches.'[40] This formula recalls Jesus' repeated summons to 'hear' his parables (cf. Matt. 13:9, 43), which conceal the mystery of the kingdom from the majority and reveal it to the faithful remnant with spiritual faculties to respond to the message (Matt. 13:13–17; cf. Isa. 6:9–10). Like Jesus and the Old Testament prophets, Revelation presents its message in symbolic, pictorial language to unveil true spiritual realities compellingly to those with ears to hear. Beale explains that John employs symbols so that faithful Christians 'should actually see and perceive spiritual reality . . . and, accordingly, be shocked concerning those sins about which we have become anesthetized'.[41] For example, the prophet John falls down like a dead man when he beholds the awesome glory of the exalted Son of Man (Rev. 1:17). Christ then highlights his presence among the lampstands (2:1), his sharp sword (2:12, 16), his flaming eyes and bronze feet (2:18) and the seven stars in his hand (2:1; 3:1) to stir compromising

---

[37] Koester 2014: 112.

[38] Bandy (2013: 398) offers a complementary summary: 'John's purpose, then, is to comfort the weary and oppressed, fortify fidelity and endurance, and cleanse the churches from heresy and compromise by depicting the heavenly reality of Jesus as the eschatological judge.'

[39] Revelation's visions 'create a symbolic world which readers can enter into so fully that it affects them and changes their perception of the world', according to Bauckham (1993b: 10).

[40] Rev. 2:7, 11, 17, 29; 3:6, 13, 22, my tr.

[41] Beale 2006: 65.

churches from their spiritual slumber and challenge them to repent. The Son of Man also comforts and emboldens the faithful, suffering churches of Smyrna and Philadelphia by reminding them that he is 'the first and the last, who died came to life' (2:8) and 'the holy one, the true one, who has the key of David' (3:7).[42]

David deSilva analyses John's purpose through the lens of ancient rhetoric and argues that 'John wants conquerors' who engage the world through prophetic witness while maintaining critical distance from its corrupt religious, economic and political systems.[43] Significantly, Revelation achieves this goal by depicting the idolatry of their cultural context and their identity as followers of the Lamb through the lens of the Old Testament Scriptures and the teaching of Jesus.[44]

Interpreting Revelation's symbolic visions

Thus far we have seen that Revelation is an apocalyptic prophecy in the form of a circular letter, written to comfort and challenge believers to hear and heed its prophetic message and so obtain a divine blessing. This section surveys several major approaches to interpreting the Apocalypse and argues that the Apocalypse communicates this message by recording highly symbolic apocalyptic visions which John skilfully and deliberately presents using images drawn primarily from the Old Testament and also conditioned by the Graeco-Roman context of John and his first readers.

Interpretations of the Apocalypse are often grouped into four basic categories: *futurist*, *preterist*, *historicist* and *idealist*. These approaches each have multiple variations, and many readers of Revelation argue for an *eclectic* approach that draws upon insights from multiple perspectives.[45]

Preterists hold that Revelation describes events that would 'soon take place' for John and his first-century readers.[46] For example, preterists typically interpret Babylon's destruction (14:8) to refer to judgment on apostate Israel when Rome destroyed Jerusalem (AD 70). Some 'partial preterists' allow for future fulfilment of some texts in

---

[42] For additional discussion of Christ's self-references in Rev. 2 – 3, see ch. 3, pp. 64–65.

[43] DeSilva 2009b: 70; cf. 90–91.

[44] Ibid. 71.

[45] See the survey by Menn (2013).

[46] See e.g. Gentry 1998: 35–92; Leithart 2018a: 27–43.

the second coming of Christ, the final judgment, the resurrection and the new heavens and new earth.

Futurists typically read Revelation 4 – 22 as referring to historical events in the distant future for John and the seven churches, though not all futurists agree as to how these future events will unfold. Dispensational futurists interpret chapters 6–19 as a prophecy of a literal seven-year tribulation after the church's rapture.[47] After the tribulation, God will fulfil his promises to bless Israel during a one-thousand-year period that does not directly pertain to the church (20:1–6), since the church is raptured before the great tribulation. Historical premillennialists espouse a modified futurist position and hold that the church will pass through the final tribulation and will share in Christ's future earthly rule during the millennium.[48] Many futurist interpreters affirm key elements of preterism or idealism.[49]

Historicists interpret 6:1 – 20:6 as a prophetic outline of the major historical developments from John's day (6:1) until Jesus' return (19:11), often focusing on Western church history.[50] There are many versions of historicism, though Protestant interpreters have sometimes connected the antichrist and Babylon to the Roman papacy. Few today follow a historicist interpretation of Revelation, though this approach has been very common at other points in church history.

For *idealists*, Revelation symbolically depicts the ongoing conflict between the forces of God and of Satan throughout the church age.[51] Idealists are reticent to identify John's symbols with particular past or future historical events, though many idealists affirm that Jesus will return to establish his eternal kingdom in the new creation.

This book adopts an *eclectic* or mixed approach, which may be called redemptive-historical idealism.[52] With *idealists*, I hold that Revelation has ongoing relevance to believers living throughout the church age and that most of John's symbolic visions may have multiple fulfilments. With *preterists*, I affirm that the entire Apocalypse – not

---

[47] For representative treatments of classical and progressive dispensationalism, see respectively Thomas 1998: 177–230; Pate 1998: 133–176.

[48] Blomberg and Chung 2009: 257–260; Bandy and Merkle 2015: 258 (Bandy's view).

[49] Osborne 2002: 21–22.

[50] This approach was common among Protestant reformers and Puritans, and early historicist interpreters include Joachim of Fiore (d. 1202) and Alexander Minorita (d. 1271). See the excellent surveys by Koester (2014: 29–65, esp. 44–53) and Maier (1981: 172–306).

[51] Cf. Hamstra 1998: 93–132.

[52] Similarly, Beale 1999: 48–49.

simply chapters 1–3 – is historically conditioned and addresses the circumstances and concerns of John's first-century audience. With *futurists* and *historicists*, I affirm that Revelation looks forward to the climactic return of Jesus, who will judge evil, deliver his people, establish God's everlasting kingdom and usher in the new creation. Put another way, the Apocalypse recounts how Jesus has *already* begun to fulfil biblical prophecy as the slain Lamb who conquered and sits enthroned in heaven. This book of prophecy encourages followers of the Lamb to hope in Jesus' *future* return, while also reorienting our perspective on *present* challenges and motivating us to conquer the dragon and his allies through the blood of the Lamb and the word of our testimony (Rev. 12:11).

Revelation 1:1 alludes to Daniel's interpretation of Nebuchadnezzar's dream. The opening verse of the Apocalypse includes three significant verbal parallels to Daniel 2:28–30, 45 LXX:

(1) 'what must happen' (*ha dei genesthai* [Rev. 1:1; Dan. 2:28, 29])
(2) 'made known' (*sēmainō* [Rev. 1:1; Dan. 2:30, 45])
(3) 'revelation' (*apokalypsis* [Rev. 1:1]) and 'reveals' (*anakalyptō* [Dan. 2:28, 29; cf. 2:22]).[53]

Jesus Christ 'made known' or 'signified' (*sēmainō*) the revelation to John by sending an angel (Rev. 1:1). Similarly, Daniel 2:30, 45 LXX says that the mystery of the king's dream 'was shown' (*sēmainō*) to Daniel and 'the great God has shown [*sēmainō*] the king what will be at the end of the days' (NETS). In Daniel, 'the revelation is not abstract but pictorial', communicated through a symbolic dream vision of a massive image and a stone cut without hands.[54] In some contexts *sēmainō* may mean simply 'make known, report, communicate',[55] but the term frequently occurs in the context of prophecy and indicates some sort of symbolic communication.[56] The term *sēmainō* in Revelation 1:1 signals that the book's revelatory contents come in the form of symbolic visions, a reading cue that is reinforced by the summary term *apokalypsis*, the prominent role of angels beginning in 1:1 and John's initial vision of the Son of Man in 1:12–20.

[53] Cf. Beale and McDonough 2007: 1088–1089.
[54] Beale 1999: 51.
[55] Cf. BDAG 920 (*sēmainō*); Acts 25:27.
[56] Cf. Dan. 2:23; John 11:28; 12:33; 18:32; 21:19; *1 En.* 107.2; Beale 1999: 50–52; Johnson 2001: Bandy 2010a: 48–49.

Thus 'a proper hermeneutic for interpreting the Apocalypse must give primacy to the symbolic nature of the text'.[57] Interpreting the book's symbolic visions in their literary, historical and theological contexts includes at least three key considerations.[58]

First, *interpreters must determine if a symbol alludes to the Old Testament.* Beale writes, 'The OT and Judaism are the primary background against which to understand the images and ideas of the Apocalypse.'[59] Indeed, scholars generally acknowledge that Revelation includes more Old Testament references than any other New Testament book, though John's scriptural appeals are not explicit, direct citations but more subtle allusions to biblical words, phrases, events, figures and themes.[60] For example, the identification of Christ's two witnesses as olive trees and lampstands standing before the Lord in Revelation 11:4 alludes to Zechariah 4:2–14,[61] while the terrifying ten-horned beast from the sea in Revelation 13:1 recalls Daniel 7:3–8.[62]

Second, *interpreters must note how John employs and explains elsewhere in Revelation.* Frequently the seer introduces a symbol with Old Testament background, records an interpretation of that symbol for the readers and then reintroduces that symbol later in the book (see Table 1.1 on p. 13).[63]

Third, *interpreters must consider how a given symbol pictures reality and what sort of response it calls for.* Many of the symbols in Revelation resonate with the late first-century cultural-historical context of John and the churches to whom he writes, featuring ubiquitous images of Roman imperial power and pagan religion on coins, murals, statues and temples.[64] John's symbolic visions sometimes recall and recast these popular Roman images.

For example, in Revelation 17:3–6 John sees a shocking vision of a woman 'arrayed in purple and scarlet, and adorned with gold and jewels and pearls', riding on a seven-headed scarlet beast. The woman's name 'Babylon the great' recalls the angelic declaration in 14:8, 'Fallen, fallen is Babylon the great, she who made all nations

---

[57] Bandy 2010a: 46. So also Beale 2006: 54–56. For careful discussion of image, symbol and metaphor in the Apocalypse, see Paul 2001: 131–148.

[58] On the 'hermeneutical triad' of history, literature and theology, see Köstenberger and Patterson 2011.

[59] Beale 1999: 56. Similarly, Keener 2000: 33.

[60] Cf. Paul 2000: 256. See section below, 'The use of the Old Testament in Revelation', pp. 15–17.

[61] See ch. 5, pp. 99–100.

[62] See ch. 6, p. 121.

[63] Table adapted from Tabb 2015: 2583.

[64] Hopkins (2000: 7) aptly calls it 'a world full of gods'.

Table 1.1: Symbols interpreted in Revelation

Reference	Symbol	Revelation's interpretation
1:20	seven stars	the angels of the seven churches
1:20	seven lampstands	the seven churches
4:5	seven torches of fire	the seven spirits of God
5:6	Lamb's seven horns and eyes	the seven spirits of God
5:8	golden bowls full of incense	the prayers of the saints
7:9–14	a great white-robed multitude	the ones coming out of the great tribulation
11:4	the two olive trees and lampstands	the two witnesses who prophesy
14:3–4	the 144,000	those who follow the Lamb
17:9–10	the beast's seven heads	seven mountains and kings
19:8	fine linen	the righteous deeds of the saints
20:5	thousand-year reign with Christ	the first resurrection
20:14	the lake of fire	the second death

drink the wine of the passion of her sexual immorality', which begins with a clear allusion to Isaiah 21:9 ('Fallen, fallen is Babylon').[65] In the remainder of Revelation 17 the angel explains 'the mystery of the woman, and of the beast with seven heads and ten horns that carries her' (v. 7). The woman John saw is 'the great city' (v. 18); the beast 'was, and is not, and is about to rise from the bottomless pit and go to destruction' (v. 8); the beast's heads correspond to seven mountains and seven kings (vv. 9–10); the ten horns refer to kings who cede their power to the beast and then war against the Lamb (vv. 12–14).

John's vision of the woman in Revelation 17 shares affinities with first-century depictions of the goddess Roma, who personified Rome's vast power and was sometimes portrayed as a virtuous woman clothed in battle attire, reclining on Rome's seven hills (cf. v. 9).[66] However, John's vision recasts the dignified Roma as a debauched, bloodthirsty prostitute. Further, the name 'Babylon the great' (17:5) associates Rome with Babylon in the Old Testament – the violent, idolatrous nation that persecuted God's people, destroyed the temple and finally received God's judgment (14:8; 16:19; 18:2; cf. Isa. 13; Jer. 50–51).[67]

[65] Cf. Jer. 51:8; Rev. 18:2.

[66] Cf. Pliny, *Natural History* 3.66–67; Virgil, *Aeneid* 6.781–783; Aune 1998b: 920–923, 944–945; Keener 2000: 405; Koester 2014: 684–686.

[67] Other first-century Jewish and Christian texts depict Rome as Babylon; e.g. 1 Peter 5:13; *4 Ezra* 3.1; 15.46 – 16.2; *2 Bar.* 11.1; *Sib. Or.* 5.143, 159.

Further, Genesis 11:1–9 presents Babylon (MT, *bābel*) as the archetypal pagan city, the site of ancient humanity's proud idolatry that led to confusing languages and scattering peoples. This vision not only presents the recipients' reality as it truly is from God's perspective, it also prepares them to heed the exhortation

> Come out of her, my people,
> lest you take part in her sins.
> (18:4)

John's satirical presentation moves his audience to resist the temptation to compromise loyalty to Jesus for the pleasure and peace that the world offers.

The Apocalypse employs numbers in a symbolic, figurative way.[68] For example, the number seven and its multiples signifies fullness or perfection (see Table 1.2 below).[69] In the Old Testament God completes his creation of the heavens and the earth in seven days (Gen. 1:1 – 2:3), and people of the ancient world recognized seven days in a week, seven seas and seven planets.[70] John writes to *seven* churches in Asia that represent the fullness of 'the churches', who must hear the Spirit's

Table 1.2: The number seven in Revelation

blessings	1:3; 14:13; 16:15; 19:9; 20:6; 22:7, 14
angels	8:2, 6; 15:1, 6; 16:1; 17:1; 21:9
churches	1:4, 11, 20
spirits of God	1:4; 3:1; 4:5; 5:6
golden lampstands	1:12, 20; 2:1
stars	1:16, 20; 2:1; 3:1
torches of fire	4:5
seals	5:1, 5; 6:1
horns, eyes	5:6
trumpets	8:2, 6
thunders	10:3–4
heads	12:3; 13:1; 17:3, 7, 9
plagues	15:1, 6, 8; 21:9
bowls of God's wrath	15:7; 16:1; 17:1; 21:9
mountains, kings	17:9

[68] See the detailed discussions in Bauckham 1993a: 7–15, 30; Beale 1999: 58–64.
[69] Table adapted from Tabb 2015: 2582.
[70] Paul 2018: 35.

message (1:4; 2:7).[71] The seven golden lampstands John sees in his opening vision represent these churches, while the seven stars represent the angels of these churches (1:20). In 1:14–16 the seer describes the Son of Man's hair, eyes, feet, voice, right hand, mouth and face, offering a sevenfold complete portrait of the risen Christ. The Lamb has seven horns and eyes (5:6), and both God and the Lamb receive sevenfold comprehensive praise from the heavenly assembly (5:12; 7:12).[72] The cycles of seven seals, trumpets and bowls disclose God's consummate plans for judgment and salvation. The book also presents seven beatitudes that promise divine favour for the faithful who hear and heed the words of prophecy.[73]

Additionally, the number four in Revelation signifies the complete cosmos, as there are four corners of the earth (Rev. 7:1; 20:8), four winds (7:1) and four divisions of creation into heaven, earth, sea and fresh waters (14:7).[74] Likewise, four living creatures resemble a lion, an ox, a man and an eagle – the strongest, swiftest and most dignified of God's created beings – and reflect the design of all creatures to worship the Creator (4:6–8).[75]

The number twelve is associated with the people of God. John hears that 12,000 are sealed from each of Israel's twelve tribes (7:4–8) and sees a woman with a crown of twelve stars (12:1), alluding to Joseph's dream in Genesis 37:9.[76] The glorious city of God has twelve pearl gates inscribed with the names of Israel's sons, as well as twelve foundations with the names of the apostles (21:12, 14, 21). Finally, the tree of life bears twelve varieties of fruit for God's people to eat (22:2; cf. 2:7).

The use of the Old Testament in Revelation

Thus far we have seen that Revelation's symbolic visions draw extensively upon the Old Testament Scriptures. These visions put the audience's present circumstances in their proper, God-centred perspective, motivating them to resist idolatrous compromise and complacency and persevere in faithful witness and confident hope.

---

[71] The Muratorian Fragment (c. AD 170) asserts, 'John . . . though he writes to seven churches, nevertheless speaks to all' (lines 57–60).
[72] Similarly, Webster 2014: 24.
[73] Cf. ch. 10, pp. 223–225.
[74] Bauckham 1993a: 29–37.
[75] Koester 2014: 369.
[76] See ch. 5, pp. 105–107.

This section will further probe Revelation's use of the Old Testament and its place in the biblical story.

Leithart aptly writes that John 'writes *with* Scripture rather than *about* it. John paints an apocalypse, and the OT is his pallet'.[77] Revelation alludes to the Old Testament in various ways.[78] First, the Apocalypse develops important scriptural *themes* such as creation versus new creation, plagues of judgment and new-exodus redemption of God's people. Second, the content of John's visions frequently suggests an *analogy* or comparative relationship with Old Testament persons, places and events. For example, the names Balaam and Jezebel in Revelation 2:14, 20 recall Old Testament characters infamous for promoting idolatry within Israel (Num. 31:16; 2 Kgs 9:22). Revelation 11:8 associates 'the great city' (Babylon) with Sodom, Egypt and Jerusalem, notorious places of immorality, oppression and persecution. Third, Revelation includes not infrequent examples of *typology*, which are characterized by redemptive-historical continuity and escalation of biblical patterns.[79] Examples include 'the key of David' in Revelation 3:7 (cf. Isa. 22:22),[80] the designation of the church as 'kingdom' and 'priests' (Rev. 1:6; cf. Exod. 19:6),[81] and the trumpet and bowl judgments that correspond to and intensify the plagues on Egypt (Rev. 8:7 – 9:21; 11:15–19; 16:1–21; cf. Exod. 7:14 – 11:10).[82] Fourth, Revelation announces the *direct fulfilment of Old Testament prophecies* (cf. Rev. 10:7). For example, John sees 'one like a son of man' (1:12) and declares that he 'is coming with the clouds' (1:7), signalling the inaugurated and future fulfilment of Daniel 7:13.[83] Fifth, John may employ segments of Old Testament prophecy as *blueprints* or literary prototypes for his own prophetic composition (e.g. Dan. 7 in Rev. 13; Ezek. 26 – 27 in Rev. 18).[84] Sixth, the Apocalypse reflects *stylistic* usage of Old Testament language. For example, in the greeting in 1:4 John writes the objects of the preposition *apo* in the nominative case (*ho ōn kai ho ēn kai ho*

---

[77] Leithart 2018a: 5, emphasis original.

[78] For a similar overview with numerous examples, see Beale 1999: 86–96.

[79] Cf. Tabb 2011: 495–505. Beale (2012: 14) defines typology as 'the study of analogical correspondences among revealed truths about persons, events, institutions, and other things within the historical framework of God's special revelation, which, from a retrospective view, are of a prophetic nature and are escalated in their meaning.'

[80] Beale 2012: 133–147. Cf. Fekkes 1994: 130–132, though he resists the label 'typology' to avoid compartmentalization (15–16).

[81] See ch. 5, pp. 90–91.

[82] See ch. 7, pp. 148–158.

[83] See ch. 3, pp. 48–53.

[84] Cf. Beale 1999: 86–88; Bandy 2009: 481–487, 490–491.

erchomenos). Commentators generally recognize this breaks the normal conventions of Greek language here to recall the divine name *egō eimi ho ōn* deliberately in Exodus 3:14 LXX.[85] Additionally, Revelation frequently *conflates* multiple Old Testament texts and expands upon specific Old Testament texts by employing *universal terminology*.[86] In Revelation 1:7, for example, John combines Daniel 7:13 and Zechariah 12:10 and also applies Zechariah's prophecy concerning 'the inhabitants of Jerusalem' to 'every eye' and 'all tribes of the earth'.[87]

Scholars have proposed various criteria for assessing and validating scriptural allusions in the New Testament, particularly with reference to Paul's letters.[88] Revelation's use of the Old Testament presents particular challenges since the book includes no citation formulae like 'as it is written' or 'Scripture says' and frequently combines words and imagery from multiple Old Testament sources. The most reliable measures for determining Old Testament allusions in the Apocalypse are clear *verbal coherence* and *thematic coherence* between the two texts.[89] While these criteria for identifying and validating Old Testament allusions are important, 'such data cannot be separated from discussion of the significance of each case'.[90]

Revelation and biblical theology

How does John situate his 'book of prophecy' in the light of the larger biblical story? Royalty provocatively charges that 'Revelation swallows the biblical subtext' and 'subversively reinscribes the Hebrew Scriptures to effectively eliminate the prophets as authoritative texts' in order to control John's readers and condemn his opponents.[91] However, Royalty's view that John *replaces* the Scriptures with his

---

[85] McDonough 1999: 199–202. For discussion of Revelation's 'solecisms', see Beale 1999: 100–105. On Rev. 1:4, see ch. 2, pp. 30–34.

[86] On Revelation's 'universal terminology', see esp. Bauckham 1993a: 239–243.

[87] See ch. 6, pp. 114–116.

[88] See e.g. the well-known seven criteria proposed by Hays (1989: 29–32). Cf. Litwak 1998: 260–288; Beale 2012: 32–35; Shaw 2013: 234–245. For criticisms of Hays's criteria and terminology, see Porter 2008: 29–40.

[89] 'The telltale key to discerning an allusion is that of recognizing an incomparable or unique parallel in wording, syntax, concept, or cluster of motifs in the same order or structure', according to Beale (2012: 31). Similarly, Porter (1997: 95) urges focus on 'formal correspondence with actual words found in antecedent texts'.

[90] Paul 2000: 261.

[91] Royalty 2004: 293, 298–299.

own revelation is unfounded.[92] Rather, as Bauckham explains, the Apocalypse

> is a book designed to be read in constant intertextual relationship with the Old Testament. John was writing what he understood to be a work of prophetic Scripture, the climax of prophetic revelation, which gathered up the prophetic meaning of the Old Testament scriptures and disclosed the way in which it was being and was to be fulfilled in the last days.[93]

Revelation 10 offers particular insight into the book's relationship to the Old Testament Scriptures. First, these verses depict John as a genuine prophet. Like the prophet Ezekiel, John takes and eats the scroll to signify 'his identification with its message'.[94] He then receives the heavenly commission 'You must again prophesy about many peoples and nations and languages and kings' (v. 11). Second, in verse 7 an angel announces the imminent fulfilment or completion (*teleō*) of 'the mystery of God . . . just as he announced to his servants the prophets'.[95] John thus stands in *continuity* with God's servants who formerly prophesied about this divine mystery, who are called 'your brothers' in 22:9. At the same time, John uniquely receives a 'revelation from Jesus Christ' (1:1) and is commanded not to 'seal up the words of the prophecy of this book' (22:10), indicating the reversal of the command to Daniel (Dan. 8:26; 12:4, 9). Thus the Apocalypse presents the *culmination* of biblical prophecy. Bauckham writes:

> It seems that John not only writes in the tradition of the Old Testament prophets, but understands himself to be writing at the climax of the tradition, when all the eschatological oracles of the prophets are about to be finally fulfilled, and so he interprets and gathers them up into his own prophetic revelation. What makes him a Christian prophet is that he does so in the light of the fulfilment already of Old Testament prophetic expectation in the victory of the Lamb, the Messiah Jesus.[96]

[92] Rightly deSilva 2009b: 154–155.
[93] Bauckham 1993a: xi.
[94] Beale and McDonough 2007: 1118. Cf. Ezek. 2:8 – 3:3.
[95] For discussion of the content of the 'mystery' in Rev. 10:7, see Beale and Gladd 2014: 271–279.
[96] Bauckham 1993b: 5.

Thus Revelation is both the climax of prophecy and the unsealed scroll.[97] It announces the fulfilment or goal of previous prophecy (10:7) and also discloses or unveils that which was previously hidden from the prophets before Christ.[98]

The structure of Revelation

Osborne notes, 'Outlines of Revelation vary perhaps more than with any other book of the Bible.'[99] Many interpreters view 1:19 as an interpretive key to the book's content and structure.[100] Some discern in this verse a threefold outline for the Apocalypse: 'what you have seen' (ch. 1), 'what is now' (chs. 2–3) and 'what will take place later' (chs. 4–22).[101]

Others propose that this verse indicates a twofold division between things present and future.[102] Alternatively, Beale argues that 1:19 alludes to Daniel 2:28–29, 45 and 'highlights not so much the chronological order of either the visions or the events that the visions represent, but focuses on those events in order to describe the climactic end of the ages'.[103]

Readers of Revelation have often observed the presence of recapitulation or progressive parallelism.[104] Beale writes, 'The strongest argument for the recapitulation view is the observation of repeated combined scenes of consummative judgment and salvation found at the conclusions of various sections throughout the book.'[105] Hendriksen discerns seven parallel sections, each spanning the period from Christ's ascension to his return: (1) chapters 1–3; (2) chapters 4–7; (3) chapters 8–11; (4) chapters 12–14; (5) chapters 15–16; (6) chapters 17–19; (7) chapters 20–22.[106] Alternatively,

---

[97] Cf. ch. 10, pp. 213–215.

[98] Thus Revelation reflects the two pairs of polarities ('promise [however construed] and fulfilment' and 'hiddenness and revelation') described by Carson (2004: 397).

[99] Osborne 2002: 29. Cf. Dow 2012: 435. A number of major structural proposals are summarized in Köstenberger et al. 2016: 956–964.

[100] For analysis and critique, see Schüssler Fiorenza 1977: 362; Beale 1992: 360–387.

[101] Thomas 1992: 115; Blomberg 2006: 516.

[102] Mounce 1997: 62.

[103] Beale 1999: 152.

[104] See e.g. Wilcock 1975: 88–89; Collins 1976: 32–56; Giblin 1994: 81–95; Beale 1999: 121–126.

[105] Beale 1999: 121. Thomas (1993: 45–66) acknowledges a limited place for recapitulation in the Apocalypse but argues for 'a telescopic form of progression' in which the final seal contains the seven trumpets and the seventh trumpet includes the bowl judgments.

[106] Hendriksen 1998: 28.

Elizabeth Schüssler Fiorenza proposes a chiastic structure for the Apocalypse:

A   1:1–8
B   1:9 – 3:22
C   4:1 – 9:21; 11:15–19
D   10:1 – 15:4
C' 15:1, 5 – 19:10
B' 19:11 – 22:9
A' 22:10–21[107]

While there is little agreement about an overall outline to the book, there is emerging consensus about at least four key structural features. First, Revelation begins with an epistolary prologue (1:1–8) and concludes with an epilogue (22:6–21).[108] Revelation 1:4 includes the key features of New Testament letter openings: (1) author (John), (2) recipients (the seven churches in Asia) and (3) blessing (grace to you and peace). Likewise, the book closes with a standard benediction: 'The grace of the Lord Jesus be with all' (22:21; cf. Eph. 6:24; 2 Thess. 3:18; Titus 3:15; Heb. 13:25). Further, the opening verses of the epilogue include several notable parallels with the prologue, as indicated in Table 1.3 below.[109]

Table 1.3: Parallels between Revelation's prologue and epilogue

Revelation 1:1–8	Revelation 22:6–8
God sent his angel (v. 1)	The Lord sent his angel (v. 6)
'show to his servants the things that must soon take place' (v. 1)	'show his servants what must soon take place' (v. 6)
John 'bore witness . . . to all that he saw' (v. 2)	John 'heard and saw these things' (v. 8)
'Blessed is the one who reads aloud the words of this prophecy, and blessed are those . . . who keep what is written in it' (v. 3)	'Blessed is the one who keeps the words of the prophecy of this book' (v. 7)
'Behold, he is coming with the clouds' (v. 7)	'And behold, I am coming soon' (v. 7)

---

[107] Schüssler Fiorenza 1977: 364. Alternative chiastic structures are proposed by Lee (1998: 164–194) and Heil (2014: 1–10).

[108] Cf. Aune 1997: c; Bandy 2009: 472; Koester 2014: 112; Heil 2014: 12–14; Karrer 2017: 106–107. For Bauckham (2001b: 1305), 22:6–9 concludes the previous vision and begins the Epilogue.

[109] Table adapted from Tabb 2015: 2585.

Second, the book includes at least four series of sevens: (1) edicts to the seven churches (Rev. 2:1 – 3:22), (2) the seven seals opened (6:1 – 8:1), (3) seven trumpets blown (8:2 – 11:19) and (4) seven bowls of God's wrath poured out (15:1 – 16:21).[110] In the Apocalypse the number seven frequently signifies perfection or completion, so the sevenfold cycles indicate the totality and completeness of God's true and just judgments (cf. 16:7).[111] Some interpreters discern additional septets. For example, Gentry identifies seven visions of warfare (chs. 12–14), seven visions of victory (chs. 17–19) and seven visions of the end of the age and the new creation (20:1 – 22:5).[112]

Third, the visionary sections deliberately overlap with each other, a technique sometimes labelled 'interlocking' or 'interweaving'.[113] For example, 4:5 says, 'From the throne came flashes of lightning, and rumblings and peals of thunder' (*astrapai kai phōnai kai brontai*), and John repeats and expands upon this formula to conclude the cycles of seals, trumpets and bowls (8:5; 11:19; 16:18–21).[114] Revelation 5:1 introduces the scroll with seven seals, which the Lamb opens in 6:1 – 8:1. Further, this interlocking technique signals a subtle yet profound link between the prayers of God's people and the cycles of divine judgment.[115] The golden bowls of incense representing the prayers of the saints (5:8) are offered on the heavenly altar following the seal judgments (8:3–4), anticipating the golden bowls full of wrath in 15:7 and the response of the altar to the bowl judgments in 16:7. Likewise, the casting of fire on the earth in 8:5 foreshadows the role of fire in each of the first four trumpets (8:6–12).[116]

Fourth, 'in the Spirit' (*en pneumati*) occurs four times at key transition points within the book (1:10; 4:2; 17:3; 21:10) and is the 'most plausible phrase for marking major structural divisions of the Apocalypse'.[117] In 1:10 the phrase introduces John's foundational Son of Man vision and the edicts to the seven churches. In 4:2 the phrase begins John's vision of the heavenly throne room (chs. 4–5) and the

---

[110] Cf. Bauckham 1993a: 7–15; Bandy 2009: 472–473, 475–476.

[111] See ch. 1, p. 14.

[112] Gentry 2017: 125–132. He asserts that the division of the book into seven large sections each with seven subunits 'is fairly obvious from the text' but does not offer detailed defense of this proposal (128).

[113] See respectively Collins 1976: 16–19; Bauckham 1993a: 5–9.

[114] Bauckham 1993a: 8.

[115] See ch. 7, pp. 140–143.

[116] Collins 1976: 17.

[117] Bandy 2009: 475. Cf. Rusten 1977: 106–111; Bauckham 1993a: 3–4; Waddell 2006: 138; Heil 2014: 2. The phrase's structural significance is downplayed by Osborne (2002: 82–83).

sequence of judgments through chapter 16. The final two occurrences in 17:3 and 21:10 initiate the contrasting visions of Babylon the harlot and Jerusalem the bride.[118] In addition to serving as a structural marker, *en pneumati* indicates that John is a true prophet whose revelatory visions come by the Holy Spirit and thus carry the divine authority as the Old Testament prophets.[119]

Several interpreters argue that the Old Testament influences not only John's thought and symbolic visions but also serves as an 'intertextual layer' or 'literary prototype'.[120] Bandy writes, 'The allusions to the Old Testament and the apparent modeling evident in both the macro and micro structural levels of the Apocalypse suggests that the Old Testament functions like a basic framework for the presentation of his vision.'[121] A number of recent studies have proposed structural parallels between Revelation and Ezekiel, Daniel and Isaiah.[122] In the following chapters I argue that Old Testament segments serve as patterns for significant sections of the Apocalypse. For example, the heavenly throne room in chapters 4–5 is modelled after Ezekiel 1, Isaiah 6 and Daniel 7.[123] Likewise, John's prophetic commissioning closely parallels Ezekiel's (Rev. 10:8–11; Ezek. 2:8 – 3:3).[124] The judgment cycles of trumpets and bowls are typologically patterned after the plagues against Egypt in Exodus 7 – 10, while the lament over Babylon's fall follows the blueprint of Ezekiel 26 – 28.[125] Finally, Revelation's grand vision of the glorious temple city alludes extensively to restoration prophecies of Isaiah, Ezekiel and Zechariah.[126]

In summary, Revelation exhibits epistolary structure with an introduction (1:1–8), conclusion (22:6–21) and body (1:9 – 22:5).[127] In the first major section of the body (1:9 – 3:22), John's initial vision

[118] See Table 8.3 on p. 183.
[119] John's use of *en pneumati* particularly recalls Ezekiel's experience of the Spirit, as noted by Beale (1999: 203). See further ch. 4, pp. 71–74.
[120] Respectively Bandy 2009: 481–483 and Beale and McDonough 2007: 1086.
[121] Bandy 2009: 490–491; cf. 481–487. Cf. Beale 1984a; Vanhoye 1962: 440; Moyise 1995: 115.
[122] Representative studies include Kowalski 2004; Beale 1984b; Fekkes 1994. For a measured assessment of Zechariah's alleged function as a literary prototype, see Jauhiainen 2005: 151–153.
[123] See ch. 2, pp. 37–40.
[124] See ch. 10, pp. 212–213.
[125] See Table 7.2 on p. 154 and Table 8.1 on p. 172.
[126] See ch. 8, pp. 174–180.
[127] Similarly, Koester (2014: 112) reads Revelation as 'a series of six vision cycles, which are framed by an introduction and conclusion'.

'in the Spirit' of the glorious Son of Man (1:9–20) is the foundation for Christ's edicts to the seven churches (chs. 2–3). Likewise, John's vision 'in the Spirit' of the heavenly throne room (chs. 4–5) initiates the major cycles of judgment: seven seals (6:1 – 8:1; cf. 5:5), trumpets (8:6 – 11:19; cf. 8:2) and bowls (15:1 – 16:21; cf. 5:8). Revelation 12 – 14 depicts the cosmic conflict between the dragon and the beast on the one hand and the Lamb and his followers on the other.

There is no scholarly consensus regarding the outline of Revelation 17 – 22, though there are clear structural markers that signal new major visionary sections beginning at 17:1 and 21:9, as noted in Table 1.4 below.[128]

Table 1.4: Parallels between John's final visions in the Spirit

Revelation 17:1–3	Revelation 21:9–10
Then one of the seven angels who had the seven bowls came and said to me	**Then came one of the seven angels who had the seven bowls . . . and spoke to me**, saying
'Come, I will show you the judgement of the great prostitute . . .'	**'Come, I will show you** *the Bride, the wife of the Lamb.'*
And he carried me away in the Spirit *into a wilderness . . .*	**And he carried me away in the Spirit** *to a great, high mountain . . .*

John's penultimate vision 'in the Spirit' concerns the destruction of the great prostitute, Babylon (17:1 – 19:10), expanding upon proleptic proclamations of the great city's fall in 14:8 and 16:19. The visionary material in 19:11 – 20:15 offers resolution to the conflict between Christ and his adversaries the dragon, the beast and the false prophet (cf. 12:1 – 13:8). The flight of earth and heaven and the death of death itself (20:11–15) prepares for 'a new heaven and a new earth' and 'the holy city' where God dwells with his people (21:1–8). The book's concluding vision 'in the Spirit' in 21:9 – 22:5 elaborates on the description of the glorious city of God and new creation introduced in 21:1–8.[129]

---

[128] Bauckham 1993a: 4 writes, 'These structural markers delimiting two parallel sections – 17:1–19:10 and 21:9–22:9 – are so clear that it is astonishing that so many attempts to discern the structure of Revelation have ignored them.' While I follow Bauckham in affirming the close parallel between 17:1–3 and 21:9–10, the conclusion of the former section at 19:10 is less clear.

[129] This outline is similar to that proposed by Leithart (2018a: 44–45), who discerns an epistolary introduction (1:1–8) and conclusion (22:6–21) and outlines the body following the four visions *en pneumati*: (1) 'In Spirit on Patmos, 1:9–3:21'; (2) 'In Spirit

Thus I propose the following outline of the Apocalypse:

1 Introduction (1:1–8)
2 Body (1:9 – 22:5)
    (a) Christ in the midst of the lampstands (1:9 – 3:22)
    (b) The throne room of God and the Lamb (4:1 – 5:14)
    (c) The wrath of the Lamb: seven seals and trumpets
        (6:1 – 11:19)
    (d) Christ, the dragon and the beast in conflict (12:1 – 14:20)
    (e) The wrath of the Lamb: seven bowls (15:1 – 16:21)
    (f) The destruction of Babylon and Christ's cosmic victory
        (17:1 – 20:15)
    (g) The denouement of Jerusalem the bride and new creation
        (21:1 – 22:5)
3 Epilogue: invitation and warning (22:6–21)

The plan of this book

Bauckham aptly refers to the Apocalypse as 'the climax of prophetic revelation'.[130] This book seeks to show how Revelation brings the scriptural narrative concerning God, his people and his world to its grand conclusion in the already-not-yet reign of Christ and the glorious new creation.

The following chapters will consider key themes in the Apocalypse in their redemptive-historical, canonical context. The chapters are organized in four groupings: (1) the triune God, (2) the worship and witness of Christ's followers and foes, (3) God's plan for judgment, salvation and restoration, and finally (4) the word of God.

Part 1 offers a careful biblical-theological investigation of the triune God in the Apocalypse. Chapter 2 considers Revelation's biblically saturated portrayal of the almighty God on his throne, the eternal Creator, Sustainer and Judge of all. Chapter 3 focuses on Jesus as the conquering Lamb, faithful witness and the resurrected, reigning, returning messianic king. Chapter 4 explores Revelation's presentation of the Holy Spirit as the creative and revelatory presence of God, who speaks to the churches through this authoritative book of prophecy.

(note 129 *cont.*) in heaven, 4:1–16:21'; (3) 'In Spirit in the wilderness, 17:1–21:8' and (4) 'In Spirit on the mountain, 21:8–22:5'. I have chosen to include the transitional unit 21:1–8 as the introduction of the final unit of the body, since 21:9 – 22:5 elaborates on the holy city prepared as a bride (21:2) and the dwelling of God with humanity (21:3).
[130] Bauckham 1993a: xi.

Part 2 explores the Apocalypse's biblical-theological depiction of the people of God and the nations and enemies of God, highlighting in particular the themes of worship and witness. Chapter 5 analyses the suffering, witnessing, reigning and conquering people of God. Chapter 6 addresses the cosmic conflict between the beast and the Lamb for the nations' adoration and allegiance.

Part 3 attends to the book's sweeping account of God's plan to judge his enemies, save his people and restore all things. Chapter 7 unpacks the interrelated themes of the plagues of judgment and the new-exodus deliverance. Chapter 8 compares and contrasts Revelation's presentation of the harlot city, Babylon, and the New Jerusalem, the bride of the Lamb. Chapter 9 argues that John's vision of the new creation represents a new and greater Eden where God's people will serve him for ever.

Part 4 closes this biblical-theological study by considering the book's multifaceted self-presentation as genuine prophecy and authoritative Scripture revealed by the risen Lord Jesus for the benefit of his people (chapter 10). The conclusion (chapter 11) briefly summarizes key biblical-theological themes in the Apocalypse and calls readers to hear and heed the book's urgent message.

Part I:
The triune God

Chapter Two

The Sovereign on the throne: God at the centre

Grace to you and peace from him who is and who was and who is to come. (Rev. 1:4)

And the four living creatures, each of them with six wings, are full of eyes all round and within, and day and night they never cease to say,

> 'Holy, holy, holy, is the Lord God Almighty,
> who was and is and is to come!'

And whenever the living creatures give glory and honour and thanks to him who is seated on the throne, who lives for ever and ever, the twenty-four elders fall down before him who is seated on the throne and worship him who lives for ever and ever. (Rev. 4:8–10)

God is utterly supreme and central in the Apocalypse. He is the beginning and end of all reality, 'the Alpha and the Omega' (Rev. 1:8). Angelic worshippers in his heavenly throne room never cease declaring that God Almighty is thrice holy (4:8). He is unrivalled and pre-eminent, ruling the universe that he created as the sovereign King and Judge (4:11). God 'lives for ever and ever' (4:9). God simply *is*, as he declared to Moses, 'I AM WHO I AM' (Exod. 3:14; cf. Rev. 1:4). Only God is absolute and self-determining. Everything else is contingent, created by God and sustained by the divine will.

And yet there are opponents who dare to challenge the divine sovereign and defy their maker. John writes that the beast '*was given* [*edothē*] a mouth uttering haughty and blasphemous words, and it *was allowed* [*edothē*] to exercise authority for forty-two months' (Rev. 13:5).[1] The ancient nemesis, the diabolical dragon, authorizes the beast's rule and

---

[1] 'The beast' receives further discussion in ch. 6, pp. 121–124.

invests it with his own authority (13:2). However, 'God is the ultimate source of the beast's authority'.[2] The beast's mouth and authority are derivative, given by God for the time he allows – a brief three-and-a-half years (cf. Dan. 7:25). Similarly, the false prophet 'is allowed' [*edothē*] by God to work signs that deceive earth dwellers (Rev. 13:14). For a while the Almighty permits the nations to fawn after falsehood. Their chorus 'Who is like the beast, and who can fight against it?' (13:4) offers an irreverent remix of the splendid Song of the Sea 'Who is like you, O Yahweh, among the gods?' (Exod. 15:11). Believers must not be deceived. The Almighty is still seated on his glorious throne, and all rival sovereigns must follow the example of the heavenly elders, who cast their crowns before his throne (Rev. 4:10), or face the prospect of fiery judgment (19:20).

This chapter considers the rich Old Testament roots of John's theology and shows how the Apocalypse offers the consummate biblical depiction of God as Creator, Sovereign Lord and Judge. The one true God has begun to establish his kingdom and execute his end-time purposes to save his people and judge evil through the Messiah Jesus, and he will surely fulfil his ancient promises and make all things new (21:5). This chapter focuses on five important divine titles and attributes that summarize Revelation's remarkable presentation of God as (1) the one who is, who was and who is coming (1:4, 8), (2) the Alpha and the Omega (1:8), (3) the Lord Almighty (1:8), (4) the holy one on the throne (4:2) and (5) the sovereign Creator (4:11).

The One who is, who was and who is coming

Ian Paul asserts that Revelation has 'the most developed Trinitarian theology of any New Testament book'.[3] The salutation in Revelation 1:4–5 is one of the most succinct and profound trinitarian declarations in the Scriptures:

> Grace to you and peace from him who is and who was and who is to come, and from the seven spirits who are before his throne, and from Jesus Christ the faithful witness, the firstborn of the dead, and the ruler of kings on earth.

---

[2] Beale 1999: 695. The passive verb *edothē* occurs twenty-one times in Revelation and six times in the parallel passage Dan. 7 LXX, always with God as the implied agent. Cf. Schreiner 2013: 620; Wallace 1996: 436–437.

[3] Paul 2018: 4. Similarly, Gladd 2016: 157.

The collocation 'grace and peace' (*charis kai eirēnē*) reflects the standard early Christian adaptation of the traditional Hellenistic 'greetings' (*charein*) and the Jewish expression 'peace' (*šālôm*), which the apostle Paul characteristically extends 'from God our Father and the Lord Jesus Christ'.[4] However, Revelation elaborates significantly on the divine source of the grace and peace offered to the recipients. The distinctive titles for the triune God in verses 4–5 are rich with biblical-theological significance and prepare readers for the absolute centrality of God in the symbolic universe of the Apocalypse.[5]

The phrase 'from him who is and who was and who is to come' (*apo ho ōn kai ho ēn kai ho erchomenos*) is one of many 'solecisms' or grammatical irregularities in the Apocalypse, since the preposition *apo* consistently takes a genitive object but Revelation 1:4 uses the nominative case.[6] Since John 'correctly' uses the genitive twice in 1:4b–5 (*apo tōn hepta pneumatō . . . apo Iēsou Christou*) and elsewhere in Revelation, his poor grammar in verse 4a likely signals a deliberate allusion to Exodus 3:14 LXX.[7]

In Exodus 3 Moses encounters the God of Abraham, Isaac and Jacob at the burning bush. God has heard the cries of his oppressed people, so he commissions Moses to lead Israel out of Egypt and promises in verse 12, 'I will be with you' (LXX, *esomai meta sou*). Moses then asks what he should tell Israel about the name of their God, and God replies:

> I AM WHO I AM . . . Say this to the people of Israel, 'I AM has sent me to you.' . . . Say this to the people of Israel, 'Yahweh, the God of your fathers, the God of Abraham, the God of Isaac, and the God of Jacob, has sent me to you.' This is my name for ever, and thus I am to be remembered throughout all generations. (vv. 14–15)[8]

In this famous exchange God expresses not only what his name is (Yahweh) but also what that name's significance is for his people

---

[4] Rom. 1:7; 1 Cor. 1:3; 2 Cor. 1:2; Gal. 1:3; Eph. 1:2; Phil. 1:2; 2 Thess. 1:2; Titus 1:4; Phlm. 1:3.

[5] Chs. 3 and 4 will offer extended discussion of 'the seven spirits' and the seminal description of Jesus in Rev. 1:4–5.

[6] Beale 1999: 188. BDAG 106 (*apo*) calls Rev. 1:4 'quite extraordinary'.

[7] McDonough 1999: 199–202; Beale 1999: 188; Giesen 1997: 74; Karrer 2017: 214–215.

[8] This translation modifies the ESV by substituting the personal name 'Yahweh' for 'The LORD'.

enslaved in Egypt.[9] The Greek translators render the opening Hebrew phrase *'ehyeh 'ăšer 'ehyeh* (I AM WHO I AM) with the expression *egō eimi ho ōn* ('I am The One Who Is', NETS).[10] In verse 15 the Greek translators render the personal name Yahweh as *kyrios* (Lord), which denotes the God of Israel's legal authority as the legitimate sovereign over all.[11] Yahweh calls Israel his firstborn son and promises to redeem his enslaved people and be their God (Exod. 4:22; 6:6–8). God's mighty actions of salvation and judgment reveal to Israel and the Egyptians that he alone is *kyrios* (Exod. 6:7; 7:5; 8:18; 14:4, 18; 29:46).

The expression *ho ōn kyrie* appears three times in LXX Jeremiah.[12] The usage at Jeremiah 1:6 (NETS, 'You That Are, Sovereign Lord!') strengthens the link between the call of Jeremiah and Moses (Exod. 3 – 4).[13] Additionally, Philo frequently refers to God by using the full phrase *egō eimi ho ōn* or the abbreviated *ho ōn*.[14] Reflecting on Exodus 3:14, Philo says that God is 'the only being to whom existence [*to einai*] belongs'.[15] This suggests early acceptance by Greek-speaking Jews of *ho ōn* from Exodus 3:14 as a divine epithet.[16]

Revelation's distinctive divine title *ho ōn kai ho ēn kai ho erchomenos* (1:4) recalls Yahweh's foundational self-disclosure 'I AM WHO I AM' at the burning bush, but it also has notable extrabiblical parallels. For example, the first-century Roman Stoic Seneca writes, 'Life is divided into three periods – that which has been, that which is, that which will be.'[17] Elsewhere Seneca notes the difficulty of translating the Greek term *ōn* into Latin and discusses Plato's six modes of being.[18] Seneca interprets Plato's second category (being par excellence) to denote not a form but *God*, 'this pre-eminent Being . . . one who is greater and more powerful than anyone else'.[19] According to Pausanias, the prophetesses at the oracle at Dodona sang, 'Zeus was [*ēn*], Zeus is

---

[9] Kaiser 2008: 370.

[10] The Greek recensions Aquila and TH render the Hebrew more formally *esomai hos esomai*. Cf. Gurtner 2013a: 206.

[11] *NIDNTTE*, 2: 773.

[12] Jer. 1:6; 14:13; 39:17 [MT 32:17], according to Göttingen LXX. In each instance, Rahlfs reads *ō kyrie*.

[13] McDonough 1999: 137.

[14] Examples include *Abraham* 121; *Worse* 160; *Unchangeable* 110; *Names* 7–12, 14, 17; *Dreams* 1.231.

[15] Philo, *Moses* 1.75. For discussion of Philo, see McDonough 1999: 79–84.

[16] McDonough 1999: 137.

[17] Seneca, *On the Happy Life* 10.2.

[18] Seneca, *Epistle* 58.7–8, 16. For extended discussion, see McDonough 1999: 34–41.

[19] Seneca, *Epistle* 58.17. Cf. Inwood 2007: 125.

[*esti*], Zeus shall be [*essetai*]. O mighty Zeus!'[20] This formula combines the common tripart division of time with the notion of deity as being par excellence. Thus John's presentation of God as *ho ōn kai ho ēn kai ho erchomenos* suggests awareness of and engagement with contemporary Graeco-Roman theological claims. The God of Israel whose definitive revelation comes in and through Jesus Christ (Rev. 1:1) is the only true claimant to be 'the one who is and who was and who is coming'.[21]

McDonough explains that the threefold expression 'him who is and who was and who is to come' (1:4) not only recalls Exodus 3:14 but also presents 'a sophisticated "unpacking" of the name which reveals its universal significance'.[22] John employs a form of this divine title five times in the Apocalypse:

ho ōn kai ho ēn kai ho erchomenos (1:4)
ho ōn kai ho ēn kai ho erchomenos (1:8)
ho ēn kai ho ōn kai ho erchomenos (4:8)
ho ōn kai ho ēn (11:17)
ho ōn kai ho ēn (16:5).[23]

The variations in order are noteworthy. The formula in 4:8 moves from past ('who was') to present ('who is') to future ('who is to come'). However, elsewhere John begins with the present tense *ho ōn*, which stresses above all that God *now is*.[24] The recipients receive grace and peace from *ho ōn*, which implies that God is present with his people.[25] Further, *ho ōn* may emphasize that God is real and true, in contrast to lifeless idols 'which cannot see or hear or walk' (9:20) or the beast who 'was, *and is not*' (17:8).[26]

The second divine title in 1:4, *ho ēn*, implies that God has always existed as God and 'created all things' (4:11).[27] The third title is the most surprising adaptation of the divine name, as *ho erchomenos* denotes not simply 'God's future existence, but his coming to the world to consummate his kingdom'.[28] Significantly, the thematic

---

[20] Pausanias, *Description of Greece* 10.12.10. Cf. McDonough 1999: 49.
[21] McDonough 1999: 233.
[22] Ibid. 204.
[23] Noted by Bauckham 1993b: 28.
[24] McDonough 1999: 206.
[25] Ibid. 207, n. 37.
[26] Michaels 1991: 604–620; McDonough 1999: 206, 227–228.
[27] McDonough 1999: 212.
[28] Ibid. 214.

summary statement in 1:7–8 refers to Jesus '*coming* [*erchetai*] with the clouds' (cf. Dan. 7:13) and then to the Lord God 'who is and who was and *who is to come* [*ho erchomenos*], the Almighty'. Isaiah 40:10 asserts that Yahweh 'comes [LXX, *erchetai*] with might, and his arm rules for him; behold, his reward is with him, and his recompense before him'.[29] In Revelation 22:12 the Lord Jesus declares, '*I am coming soon* [*erchomai tachy*], bringing *my* recompense with me, to repay everyone for what he has done'. Thus Revelation like other New Testament documents applies Old Testament descriptions of the 'coming' of God to Christ's parousia.[30] Said another way, Jesus will bring to pass the promised eschatological coming of Yahweh.

The Old Testament prophets anticipate Yahweh's future coming, but the abbreviated divine title *ho ōn kai ho ēn* in 11:17 and 16:5 signals that the eschatological 'coming' of Yahweh has become a present reality. The Lord God Almighty has 'begun to reign' (11:17), as the eternal kingdom of 'his Christ' is established and the nations cease to rage (11:15, 18; cf. Ps. 2:1–2). The Holy One acts to avenge the blood of his saints and prophets and punish their bloodthirsty oppressors (Rev. 16:5–7; cf. Isa. 49:26). The declaration that the Almighty's judgments are 'true and just' comes from 'the altar', where the cries of the slain are heard and the prayers of the saints are offered as incense (Rev. 6:9; 8:3). Thus the Apocalypse presents this establishment of God's reign as his faithful and just response to the petitions of his persecuted people.[31] Bauckham writes, 'This is the biblical God who chooses, as his own future, his coming to his creation, and whose creation will find its own future in him (cf. 21:3).'[32]

The Alpha and the Omega

The Apocalypse includes two occasions when the one seated on the throne speaks directly.[33] In 1:8 God identifies himself by using four important titles: (1) the Alpha and the Omega, (2) the Lord God, (3) who is and who was and who is to come and (4) the Almighty. The second divine declaration begins in similar fashion: 'I am the Alpha and the Omega, the Beginning and the End' (21:6).

---

[29] Cf. Pss 96:13; 98:9; Isa. 66:15; Zech. 14:5, 9; Bauckham 1993b: 29; Adams 2006: 3–8.
[30] Adams 2006: 19.
[31] See ch. 7, pp. 140–146.
[32] Bauckham 1993b: 30.
[33] Ibid. 25.

In Isaiah 44:6 (cf. 41:4; 48:12) Yahweh declares:

I am the first and I am the last [*'ănî ri'šôn wa'ănî 'aḥărôn*];
besides me there is no god.

He alone is Israel's Creator, Redeemer, King and Rock; by comparison idols made with human hands are merely blocks of wood, suitable for stoking a fire but utterly incapable of saving their worshippers (Isa. 44:6–20). The divine epithet 'the Alpha and the Omega' employs the first and last letters of the Greek alphabet and is equivalent in meaning to 'the first and the last' and 'the beginning and the end' (Rev. 21:6; 22:13). The expression 'the beginning and the end' is broadly attested in Greek philosophy, and some Jewish writers 'apply it to the Jewish God for apologetic reasons'.[34] For example, Josephus writes that Israel's God is not made with human hands but is 'the beginning and end of all things' (*archē kai telos tōn hapantōn*).[35]

'The Alpha and the Omega' is 'a rhetorical merism' that expresses totality.[36] The God who controls the beginning and the end is by implication supreme over all things. He is before all rival sovereigns – including the dragon and the beast – and will outlast them all. He alone is the divine Creator who rules over his created realm and will bring it to its appointed *telos*, when he announces 'it is done' and makes all things new (21:5–6).

In 22:12–13 Jesus climactically declares, 'Behold, I am coming soon. . . . I am the Alpha and the Omega, the first and the last, the beginning and the end' (cf. 1:17). By ascribing to himself titles reserved only for Yahweh, Jesus thus profoundly and unmistakably identifies himself with the sovereign Creator God, not as a second God but included 'in the eternal being of the one God of Israel who is the only source and goal of all things'.[37] Aurelius Prudentius Clemens's hymn *Corde natus* captures this profound theological point well:

> Of the Father's love begotten,
> ere the worlds began to be,
> he is Alpha and Omega,
> he the source, the ending he,
> of the things that are, that have been,

---

[34] Fekkes 1994: 123.
[35] Josephus, *Jewish Antiquities* 8.280; cf. *Against Apion* 2.190; Philo, *Planting* 77.
[36] Heil 2014: 25.
[37] Bauckham 1993b: 58.

and that future years shall see,
evermore and evermore.[38]

The Lord God Almighty

The prologue concludes with the Lord God's declaration that he is
'the Almighty' (*ho pantokratōr*, 1:8). The Apocalypse refers to God
as 'Almighty' nine times, seven times using the full phrase 'the Lord
God, the Almighty' (*kyrie ho theos ho pantokratōr*). *Pantokratōr* is a
common title in the LXX prophetic books that usually translates the
Hebrew phrase *yhwh 'ĕlōhê-ṣĕbā'ôt* (The Lord GOD of hosts).[39] The
Almighty 'makes all things' and shakes the earth (Amos 5:8; 9:5); he
is with his people and establishes them securely (2 Sam. 5:10; Amos
5:14; 9:15), but he is against his enemies and draws near in judgment
(Nah. 2:14; Mal. 3:5). This title conveys God's omnipotence and
universal sovereignty over his creation, underscoring 'his actual
control over all things'.[40] The Almighty is 'King of the nations' (Rev.
15:3), who reigns in power (11:17; 19:6) and executes 'true and just'
judgments (16:7).

If God is *pantokratōr*, then *ipso facto* the beast is not. John sees 'a
beast rising out of the sea' (Rev. 13:1), which incorporates the
ferocious features of the four beasts in Daniel 7:3–8.[41] The dragon
invests this beast with its own power, throne and authority (Rev. 13:2),
and the whole earth marvels, 'Who is like the beast, and who can fight
against it?' (13:4). The nations' blasphemous praise of the beast apes
the biblical acclaim 'Who is like you, O Yahweh, among the gods?'
(Exod. 15:11; cf. Ps. 113:5).[42] This haughty beast exerts its satanic
power to war against and conquer God's holy people (Rev. 13:7;
cf. Dan. 7:21). Under the beast's seductive influence, the kings of
the whole world will assemble for battle 'on the great day of God the
Almighty' (Rev. 16:14). However, one day the beast will be thrown
into the lake of fire (19:20; cf. Dan. 7:11), and all rulers and other
great and powerful humans who oppose God Almighty and the Lamb
will flee in fear on 'the great day of their wrath' (Rev. 6:15–17). In
contrast, the multitude of the redeemed will triumphantly celebrate

---

[38] Cited in Koester 2014: 36.
[39] Cf. Hos. 12:6 [12:5 ET]; Amos 3:13; 4:13; 5:8; 9:5; Nah. 3:5; Zech. 10:3. For
discussion, see Glenny 2009: 186–189.
[40] Bauckham 1993b: 30.
[41] Beale and McDonough 2007: 1127–1128. See ch. 6, pp. 121–124.
[42] Bauckham 1993a: 305.

the reign of the Almighty (19:6), whose glorious, enduring presence will illumine the New Jerusalem for ever (21:22–23). In the city of God, only the true throne remains to the unending joy and benefit of God's people (22:1–5).

The Holy One on the throne

Revelation refers to God's throne nearly forty times, including twelve times in chapter 4 and five times in chapter 5. The Apocalypse presents God's throne 'as the centre of the universe'; all creation 'finds its significance in orientation toward the throne' and its almighty occupant.[43] The throne 'indicates how decisive for the theological perspective of Revelation is faith in God's sovereignty over all things'.[44] Beginning in 4:2, God Almighty is referred to as the 'one seated on the throne' (*epi ton thronon kathēmenos*). The throne is the dominant feature of John's heavenly vision: everything else is introduced in relation to this throne. The seven Spirits (4:5; cf. 1:4), the sea of glass (4:6) and the golden altar (8:3) are *before* (*enōpion*) the throne. A rainbow, twenty-four thrones and the elders are positioned *around* (*kyklothen*) the throne (4:3–4). The four living creatures are *in the midst of* (*en mesō*) and *around* (*kyklō*) the throne (4:6). *From* (*ek*) the divine throne come forth flashes of lightning, rumblings and peals of thunder (4:5). This imagery recalls Ezekiel's heavenly vision in Ezekiel 1:13 and the awesome presence of Yahweh at Sinai in Exodus 19:16 and 20:18, which prompts the people to tremble. Additionally, the phrase 'flashes of lightning, and rumblings and peals of thunder' recurs at strategic junctures of the Apocalypse, after the seventh seal (8:5), the seventh trumpet (11:19) and the seventh bowl (16:18).[45] According to 4:5, these judgments proceed from the heavenly throne of God, which offers readers assurance that the sovereign God will judge evil and vindicate his suffering people.[46]

John's vision in chapter 4 recalls the Old Testament prophets' depictions of God seated on his heavenly throne, surrounded by his heavenly attendants (cf. 1 Kgs 22:19; Isa. 6:1–4; Ezek. 1:26–28; 10:1; Dan. 7:9). Ezekiel 1 is the most dominant Old Testament influence on Revelation's presentation of the heavenly throne room.[47] John sees

---

[43] Gallusz 2014: 331.
[44] Bauckham 1993b: 31.
[45] See ch. 7, pp. 143–146.
[46] Beale 1999: 326.
[47] See Vogelgesang 1985: 169–182.

'a door standing open in heaven' (Rev. 4:1), which is similar to Ezekiel 1:1, 'the heavens were opened'. John and Ezekiel each describe a rainbow (Rev. 4:3; Ezek. 1:28), flashes of lightning and fiery torches (Rev. 4:5; Ezek. 1:13; 1:27) and a crystal expanse (Rev. 4:6; Ezek. 1:22), which combine to stress the transcendent glory of God (Rev. 4:11; Ezek. 1:28).[48] John's reference to 'four living creatures' (*tessara zōa*) in Revelation 4:6b–8 clearly alludes to Ezekiel 1:5, 15 LXX. Ezekiel alone in the Old Testament refers to these heavenly beings as 'living creatures'. He sees four living creatures emerging out of the fiery storm cloud (1:4–5). Each creature has four faces (1:6), four wings (1:6, 11) and eyes all around (1:18). Ezekiel later identifies the living creatures as 'cherubim' (10:15), which are frequently associated with the presence of God throughout the Old Testament and later Jewish writings.[49] Revelation 4 fuses together the image of Ezekiel's four living creatures with the seraphim in Isaiah, who have *six wings* (Isa. 6:2) and who call out, 'Holy, holy, holy' (Isa. 6:3; cf. *1 En.* 39.12).

Additionally, G. K. Beale argues that Revelation 4 – 5 corresponds closely to the order and structure of Daniel 7.[50] As in Ezekiel 1 and Revelation 4, Daniel 7 depicts the Ancient of Days seated on a heavenly throne resplendent in glory and power (v. 9), with fire before the throne (vv. 9–10) and angelic servants standing before him (v. 10). Revelation 5 continues to follow the basic script of Daniel 7. Both passages feature the opening of the heavenly scroll(s) (*biblion* [Rev. 5:1–5; Dan. 7:10]), as well as a divine figure who approaches God's throne (Rev. 5:6–7; Dan. 7:13) and receives glory and dominion over 'all peoples, nations, and languages'. It is remarkable that Jesus the slain and conquering Lamb receives the same exclusive praise and accolades due to the one seated on the throne (5:11–13; 7:10) and then sits down on God's own throne (3:21; cf. 22:1, 3). Beale observes, 'It

---

[48] *1 En.* 14.18–19 similarly draws upon details of Ezekiel's heavenly vision: 'And I observed and saw inside it a lofty throne – its appearance was like crystal and its wheels like the shining sun; and (I heard?) the voice of the cherubim; and from beneath the throne were issuing streams of flaming fire.' Citations of the OT Pseudepigrapha follow the translations in Charlesworth 1983–5.

[49] God sits 'enthroned above the cherubim' (1 Chr. 13:6; Pss 80:1; 99:1) and rides on a cherub (Ps. 18:10). Cherubim overshadow the mercy seat in the tabernacle and Solomon's temple (Exod. 25:20; 1 Kgs 8:6; Heb. 9:5), and also feature in Ezekiel's restored temple (41:18, 20, 25). The cherubim guard the tree of life (Gen. 3:24) and the divine throne (*1 En.* 71.7; cf. 14.18).

[50] Beale 2010: 181–182. *1 Enoch* refers to the Ancient of Days on his glorious throne (47.3; 60.2), reflecting the language of Dan. 7.

is the picture of Christ in 3:21 presently sitting on His Father's throne which leads into the vision of chaps. 4–5.'[51]

Revelation also refers to 'Satan's throne' (2:13) and 'the throne of the beast', given him by the dragon (16:10; cf. 13:2). Koester notes, 'The way the beast shares the throne of Satan is a demonic imitation of the way the Lamb shares the throne and authority of God.'[52] The Apocalypse thus presents a fundamental cosmic struggle over who is the true sovereign authority to which allegiance is due: God or the beast. In its late first-century context, this vision of the awesome heavenly throne of God calls into question Rome's claims of absolute power and demands for worship of the emperors.[53]

The term 'holy' (*hagios*) occurs twenty-five times in Revelation but is applied to God only in 4:8 and 6:10.[54] The Apocalypse presents the sovereign Lord as 'holy' in that he is completely devoted and committed to his own standards of righteousness and justice.[55] God's holiness inspires unceasing praise in heaven (4:8) that recalls the chorus of the seraphim in Isaiah 6:3. Moreover, the martyrs invoke God's character as 'holy and true' when crying out for divine justice and vindication (6:10).

In heaven, the Holy One seated on the throne rules perfectly and receives unending praise from his creatures (4:9–11).

> The worship scenes of Revelation 4 and 5 articulate a model *of* a well-ordered cosmos in which all created beings in every region of the map turn toward this one centre – the throne of God and of the Lamb – to offer their grateful adoration. In so doing, they also articulate a model *for* the orientation of the congregations in the seven churches.[56]

Revelation 20:11–12 portrays the dead standing before the great white throne to be judged according to their deeds. Unbelieving humanity will hide in terror before the wrath of the one seated on the throne and the Lamb (6:16). Conversely, suffering faithful believers long for God to execute his righteous judgment (6:10) and offer them shelter, comfort and an enduring place before the throne (7:15–17; 22:3–5).

---

[51] Beale 2010: 180. On the Lamb and God sharing a singular throne without rivalry, see Gallusz 2014: 142–175.

[52] Koester 2014: 570. Cf. Gallusz 2014: 222.

[53] Bauckham 1993b: 34.

[54] In Rev. 3:7 Jesus introduces himself as 'the holy one, the true one'.

[55] Cf. Gentry 2013: 413.

[56] DeSilva 2009b: 98, emphases original.

In the culminating vision of the new creation, 'God's presence decisively shifts from heaven to earth.'[57] The singular throne of God and of the Lamb is the source (*ek*) of the river of the water of life in the new creation (22:1). All rivals will be for ever displaced, and the throne of God and the Lamb – the central reference point of heaven – will be the defining feature of the new creation that will give light and life to his people, who will worship him and reign for ever (22:3–5).[58]

John receives this vision of the heavenly sovereign on his throne while relegated to the island of Patmos 'on account of the word of God and the testimony of Jesus' (1:9).[59] Likewise, the Old Testament's three principal throne-room visions – Isaiah 6, Ezekiel 1 and Daniel 7 – all come amidst displacement, uncertainty and spiritual crisis for God's people. In times of trouble the biblical prophets perceive clearly the enduring throne of the Ancient of Days, and they remind the faithful that 'the powers that be' – whether Assyria, Babylon or Rome – are accountable to the absolute authority of the one seated on the throne.

The sovereign Creator

'In the beginning God created the heavens and the earth' (Gen. 1:1). Biblical writers consistently stress that the God of Israel created all things, which demonstrates his consummate power and lordship over the world and everything in it, including human beings. Yahweh's creative work demonstrates that 'he is Yahweh . . . there is no other' and exposes the utter futility of calling upon 'wooden idols . . . that cannot save' (Isa. 45:18, 20; cf. Ps. 115:4–8). Yahweh is

> the everlasting God,
> the Creator of the ends of the earth.
> (Isa. 40:28)

The one who alone made all things also redeems and sustains his people, who belong to him (Isa. 43:1; 44:24).

---

[57] Middleton 2014: 169.

[58] See further ch. 9, p. 197.

[59] On John's specific sentence, see Koester 2014: 242–243. For an alternative explanation that John was not exiled to Patmos, see Dixon 2017: 73–79.

Creation theology 'virtually dominates the Bible . . . and is a key theme throughout the Apocalypse'.[60] The seminal throne-room vision in Revelation 4 emphasizes God as supreme Creator in at least three ways. First, the rainbow around the divine throne in Revelation 4:3 alludes to Ezekiel 1:28 and may also recall the sign of God's covenant in Genesis 9:13–16.[61] John's term *iris* does not occur in LXX Genesis but is found in Josephus' description of the rainbow after the flood (*Jewish Antiquities* 1.103). The rainbow in Revelation 4:3 and Ezekiel 1:28 thus conveys the Creator's faithfulness and commitment to his creation, which he will demonstrate by 'destroying the destroyers of the earth' (Rev. 11:18; cf. Gen. 6:11–13) and ushering in the new creation free from the threat of evil (Rev. 21:1, 8).[62]

Second, the enigmatic 'living creatures' (*zōa*) introduced in verse 6 are likely angelic beings who worship the Creator, who alone 'lives' (*zaō*) for ever. The four living creatures bear the likenesses of the strongest wild and domestic animals (lion and ox), the swiftest bird of the heavens (eagle), and the most dignified creature of all, a human being made in God's image (4:7; cf. Ezek. 1:10). 'The four creatures show that in the proper order of things, all creation glorifies the Creator.'[63]

Third, in Revelation 4:10–11 the twenty-four elders lay their golden crowns before the throne in submission to the Creator's supreme authority and declare:

> Worthy are you, our Lord and God,
>   to receive glory and honour and power,
> for you created all things,
>   and by your will they existed and were created.

This song brings the heavenly throne-room scene of chapter 4 to a fitting climax: all things owe their existence to the Creator God, who alone is worthy to receive glory, honour and power.

This scene of heavenly praise contrasts sharply with acclamations of the Roman emperors. According to Josephus, Vespasian was hailed as benefactor and saviour, the only 'worthy' (*axion*) ruler of Rome.[64] Further, the titles 'lord' and 'god' were used to flatter or praise

---

[60] Osborne 2002: 241.
[61] Bauckham 1993b: 51–53; Giesen 1997: 149; Beale 1999: 321.
[62] Bauckham 1993b: 52–53.
[63] Koester 2014: 369.
[64] Josephus, *Jewish War* 7.71.

Domitian and other sitting emperors before him.[65] In Revelation 14:7–10 one angel commands, 'worship him who made heaven and earth, the sea and the springs of water', while another warns that all who worship the beast and its image 'will drink the wine of God's wrath'. The crucial choice facing humanity is whether to worship and glorify the supreme Creator God or the beast.[66] The true God 'lives for ever and ever' and created every sphere of life: heaven, earth and the sea, and he will fulfil his purposes without delay (10:6). Revelation 5:13 presents every creature in these spheres declaring unending praise to God and the Lamb for their work of creation and redemption.

This confession of Yahweh as Creator has direct implications not only for protology but also for eschatology. Revelation is clear that the sovereign God who brought the world into existence is also responsible for its future.[67] God declares in Isaiah 65:17:

> For behold, I create new heavens
>   and a new earth,
> and the former things shall not be remembered
>   or come into mind.

And John sees this prophetic hope realized in Revelation 21:1: 'Then I saw a new heaven and a new earth, for the first heaven and the first earth had passed away, and the sea was no more.' The beast arises from the abyss and the sea (11:7; 13:1; cf. Dan. 7:2–3). The sea symbolizes the forces of evil, chaos and hostility towards God and his people, and these forces have no part of the new creation.[68] Further, God's eradication of the sea may also relate to the prophetic hope of the new exodus for God's people.[69] The God who made (*poieō*) the heaven, the earth and the sea and everything in them (Rev. 14:7) announces that he is making all things new (*idou kaina poiō panta*, 21:5). This declaration alludes to Isaiah 43:19 LXX, which depicts the hope of a new-exodus deliverance in terms of new creation: 'Look, I am doing new things [*idou poiō kaina*] that will now spring forth, and you will know them, and I will make a way in the wilderness and rivers in the dry land' (NETS).

---

[65] Suetonius, *Domitian* 13.2; Dio Cassius, *Roman History* 67.5.7; Josephus, *Jewish War* 2.184. Cf. Aune 1997: 311–312; Koester 2014: 365–366.
[66] See further ch. 6, pp. 113–135.
[67] Nicklas 2012: 148.
[68] Middleton 2014: 169. Cf. Beale 1999: 1043.
[69] Mathewson 2003a: 243–258. Cf. Isa. 51:9–11; ch. 7, pp. 158–160.

In Revelation 3:14 the risen Christ introduces his message to the church at Laodicea as follows: 'The words of the Amen, the faithful and true witness, the beginning of God's creation.'[70] Jesus' poignant self-description contributes in two important ways to Revelation's divine Creator motif. First, Jesus is 'the Amen', which recalls the divine title for 'the God of truth' (MT, *bē'lōhê 'āmēn*) in Isaiah 65:16.[71] It is noteworthy that in the next verse the God of truth declares:

> For behold, I create new heavens
> and a new earth.

This new creation promise finds fulfilment in Revelation 21:1. As the 'Amen', Jesus is the embodiment of divine truthfulness; he not only testifies truly to God's activity in the world (cf. 1:5; Isa. 43:10–12) but also faithfully brings God's divine promises to their appointed *telos* in the new creation. Second, Jesus is the *archē*, the 'beginning' or 'ruler'. This designation prepares for Jesus' climactic self-designation as 'the first and the last' (22:13) and thus presents Jesus as the *originator* of God's creation. He existed *before* God's work of creation and is thus, as the 'ruler [*archōn*] of kings on earth' (1:5), sovereign *over* all that is created.[72]

Conclusion

Revelation's glorious and sweeping depiction of God draws repeatedly on God's self-disclosure throughout Israel's Scriptures. John's book of prophecy also announces the climactic revelation of the triune God, who gives grace and peace to his redeemed people (1:4–5). Revelation contributes to the canonical presentation of God in three crucial ways.

First, Revelation 4 presents God as the supreme sovereign who created all things (Gen. 1:1) and rules over his creation. The four living creatures and twenty-four elders model the intended vocation of all creatures: unceasing worship of the all-powerful, holy God who lives for ever and ever. This scene of the Creator God on his heavenly throne draws upon the Old Testament theophanies in Isaiah 6 and Ezekiel 1. Revelation 5 moves beyond the Old Testament and Jewish theology of chapter 4 to articulate a profound Jewish *Christian*

---

[70] Cf. ch. 3, pp. 53–55.
[71] Beale 1996: 137–144.
[72] For further discussion, see ch. 3, pp. 61–63.

theological vision of Jesus the Lamb, who is worthy to open the sealed scroll and is worshipped together with one God.[73]

Second, the Maker of heaven and earth is also the God of the exodus. He is Yahweh, the covenant God of Israel who revealed himself to Moses as *ho ōn*, 'I AM' (Exod. 3:14), who sent plagues on Egypt, dried up the sea and saved his people with an outstretched arm. The prophets expected the God of the exodus to act definitively one day to rescue his people after exile and judge their oppressors. Revelation presents the ultimate fulfilment of this biblical hope, as God redeems his people from bondage and makes them a kingdom and priests through Jesus, the slain and conquering Lamb (Rev. 5:9–10; cf. Exod. 19:4–6). In response God's redeemed people 'sing the song of Moses . . . and the song of the Lamb' (15:3; cf. Exod. 15:1), bringing together the two great saving events in redemptive history: the exodus from Egypt and the cross of Christ.[74]

Third, God is 'the Alpha and the Omega', the Creator of all things in the beginning who will bring all things to their appointed goal in the new creation, a new and greater Eden. Revelation 21:1 announces the glorious redemption and transformation of the cosmos, where the present order will give way to 'the new heavens and the new earth' prophesied in Isaiah 65:17 and 66:22. The prophets wrote that God would dwell among his people for ever in the temple (Ezek. 37:27; 43:4), and the Apocalypse shows this hope fulfilled and exceeded as God Almighty and the Lamb will *be* the temple of the New Jerusalem, illumining the new creation with their glorious, enduring presence (Rev. 21:22–23).[75]

This God is the very centre of all reality. The Almighty has defeated all rivals in heaven (12:7–8), where angelic beings worship and serve him day and night (4:6–11) and his slain martyrs enjoy rest in his presence as they await the denouement of his dominion (6:10–11). What is true in heaven now will be true on earth as well. God will reassert himself as 'King of the nations' and will execute judgments on the beast and all rival sovereigns who usurp his praise and oppress his people (15:3; 16:5–7). Therefore, readers must heed the angel's repeated exhortation to John: 'Worship God' (19:10; 22:9).

Revelation's consummate vision of God should profoundly shape the world view and lifestyle of its readers. First, the Apocalypse *clarifies* for readers that the Creator God – not Caesar – has ultimate

[73] Bauckham 1993b: 32, 60.
[74] See ch. 7, pp. 158–160.
[75] See ch. 8, pp. 174–180.

authority and thus deserves ultimate allegiance. Second, John's prophecy *challenges* readers to resist and repent of spiritual complacency, worldly compromise and false teaching, while holding fast to the sure promises of God. Third, Revelation *comforts* afflicted believers with assurances that the supreme Judge will hold their oppressors accountable, will vindicate his people and will secure a glorious future for those who conquer 'by the blood of the Lamb and by the word of their testimony' (12:11; cf. 6:9–11).

Chapter Three

The Lion and the Lamb: Jesus the reigning, returning king

Grace to you and peace . . . from Jesus Christ the faithful witness, the firstborn of the dead, and the ruler of kings on earth. (Rev. 1:4–5)

And between the throne and the four living creatures and among the elders I saw a Lamb standing, as though it had been slain, with seven horns and with seven eyes, which are the seven spirits of God sent out into all the earth. (Rev. 5:6)

Christ is the Lion, the Lamb and the Lord of lords. He is both the supreme victor and sacrificial victim. The Apocalypse truly discloses 'an admirable conjunction of diverse excellencies in Jesus Christ', as Edwards says.[1]

The prologue sets the stage for Revelation's kaleidoscopic portrait of the Lord Jesus, the supreme sovereign who saves his people by his own shed blood and returns to execute divine vengeance on his foes. Jesus reveals and communicates to God's people the things that must soon take place (Rev. 1:1). John extends grace and peace to the Asian believers 'from Jesus Christ' and identifies him as 'the faithful witness, the firstborn of the dead, and the ruler of kings on earth' (1:5). The prophet then erupts in doxology to Jesus, 'who loves us and has freed us from our sins by his blood', and announces that 'he is coming with the clouds, and every eye will see him' (1:5, 7).

Revelation 1:5–7, 1:10–20 and 5:5–14 serve as foundational distillations of the book's Christology. Jesus discloses and consummates God's purposes in judgment and redemption (1:1; 5:7). He fulfils and transforms Old Testament promises of kingship

---

[1] Edwards 1723: 441.

(Gen. 49:9; Isa. 11:1; Pss 2:7–9; 89:27) by triumphing as the slain Lamb, faithful witness and firstborn from the dead, who has sat down on the throne of God (Rev. 1:5; 3:21). The Lamb saves, forgives and redeems God's people (1:5; 5:9; 7:10) and will return as the conquering King (19:11–16). Jesus the glorious Son of Man bears the attributes of the Ancient of Days (Dan. 7:9–14), shares fully in the divine identity (Rev. 22:13) and receives worship appropriate for God alone (5:13). This chapter focuses on five Christological titles in the Apocalypse that are rich in biblical theological significance and together highlight Jesus' divine identity, prerogatives and activity: (1) the Son of Man (1:7, 13), (2) the faithful witness (1:5), (3) the messianic ruler (1:5), (4) the slain Lamb (5:6) and (5) the first and the last (1:17).

The Son of Man

Jesus refers to himself as 'the Son of Man' more than eighty times in the Gospels, with at least three connotations. First, he stresses his unique authority as the Son of Man, who is 'Lord of the Sabbath' (Matt. 12:8). Second, he also repeatedly predicts that the Son of Man will soon be betrayed, suffer many things and die before rising again (e.g. Mark 8:31; 9:12, 31; 10:33–34; John 3:14; 8:28). Third, Jesus warns that the Son of Man will come with power and glory, most notably before his transfiguration and at his trial before the Sanhedrin (Luke 9:26; 21:27).[2] While scholars continue to debate the background and significance of Jesus' most frequent and elusive self-reference, most discern that Daniel 7:13 stands behind the dominical designation 'Son of Man'.[3]

The opening chapter of the Apocalypse presents Christ's 'coming with the clouds' as the 'son of man' figure from Daniel 7:13. Revelation's prologue concludes with this dramatic confession:

---

[2] Commenting on the thirteen Son of Man references in the Fourth Gospel, Carson (1991: 165) explains that 'John fuses the themes' of suffering, revelation and eschatological glory to stress that 'the climactic glorification of the Son of Man is achieved *through* his cross, resurrection and exaltation. It is the *combination* of associated themes that is characteristic of Jesus' use of the title' (emphases original).

[3] France 1998: 135–148. For recent scholarship on 'the Son of Man', see Hurtado and Owen 2011; Bock 2012. The designation 'Son of Man' occurs frequently in the apocalypse *1 Enoch*, beginning in 46.3–4. For discussion, see Hannah 2011: 130–158. The clear allusions to Dan. 7:9, 13 in *1 En.* 46 make clear that the author refers to the Danielic Son of Man.

Behold, he is coming with the clouds, and every eye will see him, even those who pierced him, and all tribes of the earth will wail on account of him. Even so. Amen.

'I am the Alpha and the Omega,' says the Lord God, 'who is and who was and who is to come, the Almighty.' (1:7–8)

These verses announce 'the basic perspective of the book',[4] and serve as a bridge from the doxology in 1:5–6 to the Son of Man vision and edicts to the churches in 1:9 – 3:21.[5] The opening words of 1:7, 'Behold, he is coming with the clouds', clearly recall Daniel 7:13:

I saw in the night visions,

> and behold, with the clouds of heaven
> there came one like a son of man,
> and he came to the Ancient of Days
> and was presented before him.[6]

In Revelation 1:13 John sees 'in the midst of the lampstands one like a son of man'. The evocative depiction of Jesus in verses 13–16 is laden with Old Testament symbolism. Jesus' clothing with a long robe suggests a king's authority (cf. Isa. 22:21), a high priest's purity (Exod. 28:4; 29:5–9) or both. His presence amidst the lampstands also suggests a priestly role.[7] The sword from his mouth recalls Isaiah 11:4 and 49:2 and signals that Christ will execute judgment on the nations (Rev. 19:15) and on false teaching and immorality within the church (2:12, 16). John writes further, 'The hairs of his head were white, like white wool, like snow,' ascribing to the Son of Man a defining attribute of the all-wise Ancient of Days described as follows in Daniel 7:9:

As I looked,

> thrones were placed,
> and the Ancient of Days took his seat;

---

[4] Osborne 2002: 50.

[5] Johnson 2001: 51.

[6] Rev. 1:7 (*Idou erchetai meta tōn nephelōn*) more closely follows the MT and TH recension of Dan. 7:13 than the Old Greek (*idou epi tōn nephelōn tou ouranou hōs huios anthrōpou ērcheto*).

[7] Leithart (2018a: 9) writes, 'The "one like a Son of Man" stands among golden lampstands, which makes him an Aaronic priest, trimming the lamps of the churches to keep them burning as lights in a dark world.'

his clothing was white as snow,
    and the hair of his head like pure wool;
his throne was fiery flames;
    its wheels were burning fire.

John likens the Son of Man's voice to the sound of rushing waters. This comparison likely alludes to Ezekiel 1:24 or 43:2, where the prophet likens the deafening sound of the living creatures' wings and the coming of the divine glory to many waters. Thus this description of Jesus' voice signals that he speaks with awesome, divine authority. The Son of Man's other remarkable features recall the vision of the heavenly man in Daniel 10:5–6 (see Table 3.1 below).

Table 3.1: The use of Daniel 10 in Revelation 1

The Son of Man in Revelation 1:13–16	The heavenly Man in Daniel 10:5–6
a golden sash round his chest (*periezōsmenon . . . chrysan*)	a belt of fine gold . . . round his waist (*periezōsmenē en chrysiō*)
his eyes were like a flame of fire (*hoi ophthalmoi autou hōs phlox pyros*)	his eyes like flaming torches (*hoi ophthalmoi autou hōsei lampades pyros*)
his feet were like burnished bronze (*chalkolibanō*)	his arms and legs like the gleam of burnished bronze (*chalkou*)
his voice [*phōnē*] was like the roar of many waters	the sound [*phōnē*] of his words like the sound of a multitude
his face [*hē opsis autou*] was like the sun shining in full strength	his face [*to prosōpon autou*] like the appearance of lightning

Daniel sees 'one like a son of man' (*hyios anthrōpou*, LXX), who approaches the glorious divine Judge, the Ancient of Days (cf. 7:9–10) and receives 'dominion and glory and a kingdom' (Dan 7:13–14). Daniel 7:14 clearly recalls previous descriptions of the Most High's indestructible, everlasting kingdom, in contrast to human dynasties that rise and fall:

And in the days of those kings the God of heaven will set up a kingdom that shall never be destroyed, nor shall the kingdom be left to another people. It shall break in pieces all these kingdoms and bring them to an end, and it shall stand for ever. (2:44)

For his dominion is an everlasting dominion,
and his kingdom endures from generation to generation.
(4:34)

he is the living God,
enduring for ever;
his kingdom shall never be destroyed,
and his dominion shall be to the end.
(6:26)

his dominion is an everlasting dominion,
which shall not pass away,
and his kingdom one
that shall not be destroyed.
(7:14)

Further, according to 7:18, '*the saints* of the Most High shall receive the kingdom and possess the kingdom for ever, for ever and ever' (cf. 7:22, 27). Thus Daniel 'oscillates between a singular unity with traces of an individual ("the one like a human being") and a collective unity ("the holy ones") and revolves around the "Kingdom of God"'.[8] Revelation offers the definitive biblical-theological resolution to this tension. When the seventh trumpet is blown, heavenly voices declare, 'The kingdom of the world has become the kingdom of our Lord and of his Christ, and he shall reign [*basileusei*] for ever and ever' (11:15; cf. 12:10). The twenty-four elders then praise the Lord God Almighty who reigns (11:17).[9] Thus the Apocalypse encapsulates 'all these kingdoms' envisioned by Daniel 2:44 as a singular reality – 'the world's kingdom' – which comes to an end as God consummates his enduring kingdom. Further, God's eternal kingdom is inextricably bound to 'his Christ', who returns as 'King of kings' (Rev. 11:15; 19:16).[10] Moreover, on multiple occasions the Apocalypse notes that the saints 'reign' or 'rule', as envisioned by Daniel 7:18. Jesus' blood has made his people 'a kingdom' and 'priests' (Rev. 1:5–6; 5:9–10; cf. Exod. 19:6), who will reign with him

[8] Hieke 2012: 59.
[9] Many commentators explain the aorist *ebasileusas* in 11:17 as ingressive ('begun to reign'); however, the verb's perfective aspect presents God's reign externally, as a completed whole, and 'refers to the simple act of reigning', according to Mathewson (2010: 56).
[10] On this title see Beale 1985: 618–620; Slater 1985: 159–160.

(*basileusousin met' autou*) for a thousand years (20:6) and for ever in the new creation (22:5).[11]

The Danielic expression 'one like a son of man' recurs in Revelation 14:14: 'Then I looked, and behold, a white cloud, and seated on the cloud one like a son of man [*homoion huion anthrōpou*], with a golden crown on his head, and a sharp sickle in his hand.' Aune argues that the immediate context and a parallel with Daniel 10:16 suggest that the Son of Man in Revelation 14:14 refers 'to an angelic being'.[12] This is unlikely for several reasons.[13] First, the book's opening chapter unambiguously applies the language of Daniel 7:13 to the exalted Jesus, who 'is coming with the clouds' and is 'one like a son of man' (Rev. 1:7, 13). Second, Aune overlooks the significance of the Son of Man's position 'seated on the cloud' (*epi tēn nephelēn kathēmenon*). The Scriptures present Yahweh himself *seated* in heaven on his throne with the multitudes of heaven standing around him (1 Kgs 22:19; Isa. 6:1–2; Ps. 99:1 [98:1 LXX]). Commentators typically overlook a verbal parallel between Revelation 14:14 and Isaiah 19:1 LXX: 'Behold, the Lord is seated on a swift cloud' (*kathētai epi nephelēs kouphēs*). In Revelation 14:14 the Son of Man's seated posture suggests his divine authority to rule and recalls his declaration in 3:21 that he conquered and 'sat down' with his Father on his heavenly throne. The golden crown symbolizes Jesus' regal authority as 'the ruler of kings on earth' who 'shall reign for ever' (1:5; 11:15).

Jesus' 'coming' is a major theme in the Apocalypse that is introduced in 1:7 with the allusion to Daniel 7:13, 'Behold, he is coming [*erchetai*] with the clouds'. Most commentators interpret Christ's 'coming with the clouds' as a reference to the parousia at the end of history,[14] but Paul reasons that here and elsewhere in the New Testament Jesus' 'coming' as Son of Man depicts Christ's 'victorious ascent to the right hand of the Father'.[15] In 16:15 Jesus interrupts the presentation of the sixth bowl judgment to exhort faithful readers, 'Behold, I am coming [*erchemai*] like a thief!' He also declares three times in the epilogue, 'I am coming soon' (*erchomai tachy* [22:7, 12, 20]).

The Apocalypse teaches that the exalted Son of Man has approached the Ancient of Days and is crowned on the cloud, sitting on the throne

---

[11] See further ch. 5, pp. 90–95.
[12] Aune 1998a: 841.
[13] For additional discussion and defence of the Christological reading of Rev. 14:14, see Holtz 1962: 128–134; Koester 2014: 622–623, 627–628; Smith 2016: 77.
[14] E.g. Mounce 1997: 50–51; Osborne 2002: 69–70; Koester 2014: 229.
[15] Paul 2018: 63.

of heaven (3:21; 5:7; 14:14). Christ will also return at the end of history as 'King of kings' to execute righteous judgment and divine wrath on the forces of evil and establish his unending kingdom (19:11–16; cf. 11:15). This expectation inspires faithful endurance and hope for suffering believers who join with John in declaring, 'Amen. Come [*erchou*], Lord Jesus!' (22:20). The repeated stress on Jesus' coming also serves as a sober warning for all who are complacent in faith, calloused towards God or compromising with the world. The risen Christ warns the churches at Ephesus and Pergamum that he is coming (*erchemai*) to them in judgment unless they repent (2:5, 16),[16] and he tells Sardis that he 'will come [*hēxō*] like a thief' if they do not wake up (3:3). This recalls the earlier warning to Sardis as well as Jesus' teaching in Matthew 24:42–44 and anticipates his promise in Revelation 16:15. Christ warns the churches that if they do not repent, he will 'come' and deal severely with them ahead of his return at the end of history. Beale explains that Christ's pending, historical visitations to the churches are 'connected to the final coming in that both are part of the same inaugurated end-time process'.[17] As the drama of Revelation 5 makes clear, the crucified, risen and exalted Lord Jesus has inaugurated God's end-time plans for salvation and judgment, which he will consummate at the end of history.

The faithful witness

The opening salutation in 1:4–5 extends grace and peace to readers 'from Jesus Christ the faithful witness, the firstborn of the dead, and the ruler of kings on earth'. This remarkable Christological summary likely alludes to Psalm 89:27, 37 (88:28, 38 LXX).[18] Verse 37 compares the enduring reign of David's offspring to the moon's faithful witness in the sky (*ho martys en ouranō pistos*). John goes further than Psalm 89 by identifying the risen King Jesus *himself* as the faithful witness. This designation may reflect the influence of the witness motif in Isaiah 40 – 55 and especially John's Gospel.[19] Yahweh calls Israel as 'my witnesses' to testify among the nations that he alone is God, in contrast to the nations' lifeless idols that cannot save (Isa. 43:10, 12;

---

[16] The present tense *erchetai* is 'future referring', according to Mathewson (2016: 21).

[17] Beale 1999: 275.

[18] Beale and McDonough 2007: 1089; Karrer 2017: 217–218.

[19] For discussion of Isaiah's influence on the Fourth Gospel's lawsuit motif, see Lincoln 2000: 36–56.

44:8).[20] In Isaiah 55:4 Yahweh designates David 'a witness' (MT, *'ēd*) or 'testimony' (LXX, *martyrion*) to the peoples. During his trial Jesus testified before Pilate, 'You say that I am a king. For this purpose I was born and for this purpose I have come into the world – to bear witness [*martyrēsō*] to the truth' (John 18:37).[21]

The Apocalypse prominently features the interrelated themes of 'witness' and 'testimony'. In the prologue John states that he *testified* (*emartyrēsen*) to the Word of God and the *testimony of Jesus Christ* (*tēn martyrian Iēsou Christou* [1:2]), and returns three times to this emphasis in the book's closing:

I, Jesus, have sent my angel *to testify* [*martyrēsai*] to you about these things for the churches. (22:16)

I *testify* [*martyrō*] to all who hear the words of the prophecy of this scroll. (22:18)

He who *testifies* [*ho martyrōn*] to these things says, 'Yes, I am coming soon.' (22:20)[22]

Key terms such as *martys* (witness), *martyria* (testimony) and *martyreō* (testify) are all drawn from the law court. According to Trites, in the Apocalypse *martyria* 'retains its juridical sense, and means the open confession of the truth'.[23] Bauckham explains, 'The world is a kind of court-room in which the issue of who is the true God is being decided. In this judicial contest Jesus and his followers bear witness to the truth.'[24]

Jesus is 'the faithful witness' (*ho martys, ho pistos*), who verbally declared God's truth and embodied that truth in his death (1:5).[25] However, the designation 'faithful witness' goes further and includes the reliable testimony of the risen, reigning and returning Lord to his servant John (1:2; 22:20).[26] In 3:14 Jesus identifies himself to the

---

[20] Bauckham 1993b: 73.

[21] For discussion of Jesus' testimony before Pilate, see Lincoln 2000: 123–138.

[22] See further ch. 10, pp. 208–210.

[23] Trites 1977: 159. Cf. Rev. 1:9; 6:9; 11:7; 12:11, 17; 17:6; 20:4; Dehandschutter 1980: 283–288; Bandy 2010b: 135–139.

[24] Bauckham 1993b: 73. Bandy (2011: 178–205) plausibly argues that the addresses to the seven churches in Rev. 2 – 3 are prophetic oracles closely patterned after OT covenant lawsuit speeches.

[25] Trites 1977: 158.

[26] Dixon 2017: 137.

Laodicean church as 'the Amen, the faithful and true witness' (*ho martys ho pistos kai alēthinos*). 'The Amen' probably identifies Jesus with 'the God of truth' (Isa. 65:16) and underscores the authenticity of his testimony, over against the church's unfaithful witness.[27] He testifies to their true spiritual condition and summons them to repent. Thus Jesus 'the faithful witness' communicates the truth and also provides a model for his suffering followers to emulate as they conquer 'by the blood of the Lamb and by the word of their testimony' (Rev. 12:11).[28]

Jesus not only bears witness to the truth; he also establishes truth and justice. The sharp sword from his mouth signifies that 'the actual weapon of judgment is Christ's word of truth' (1:16; 2:16; 19:15, 21).[29] Jesus the faithful witness is also seated on God's throne as the supreme King and Judge (3:21). He shares the divine prerogative to render to all people according to their deeds (2:23; 20:12; 22:12; cf. Matt. 16:27; Jer. 17:10), and executes God's righteous and terrifying judgment in the great day of their wrath (Rev. 6:16–17; cf. 19:11).

The messianic ruler

The Apocalypse repeatedly emphasizes that Jesus is the messianic King who establishes God's kingdom and executes justice and right-eousness. Revelation presents Jesus' sovereign reign by invoking a cluster of five Old Testament motifs: (1) Messiah and Son of God (2:18; 11:15), (2) firstborn and ruler (1:5), (3) the Lion of Judah (5:5), (4) the Root of David (5:5) and (5) King of kings (17:14; 19:16).

Revelation employs the common term *christos* only seven times: 'Jesus Christ' (1:1, 2, 5), 'his Christ' (11:15; 12:10) and 'the Christ' (20:4, 6). Revelation 11:15 clearly illustrates the rich biblical-theological significance of this title: 'The kingdom of the world has become the kingdom of our Lord and of his *Christos*.' This verse likely draws upon Psalm 2:2 LXX, where the earth's kings and rulers gather 'against the Lord and against his anointed [*christos*]'.[30] Psalm 2 is according to Witetschek 'the favourite psalm of the seer'.[31] In

[27] Cf. ch. 2, pp. 40–43; Rissi 1972: 21; Fekkes 1994: 138–139; Beale 1996: 133–152; Osborne 2002: 204.

[28] See ch. 5, pp. 97–101.

[29] Beale 1999: 949.

[30] Boxall 2006: 169.

[31] Translating the German title 'Der Lieblingspsalm des Sehers' of Witetschek (2006: 407–502). He suggests (490–491) allusions to Ps. 2 in Rev. 2:26–27; 11:18; 12:5, 10; 19:15.

Revelation the raging nations face God's rage (11:18; cf. Ps. 2:2, 5), and Jesus returns to rule over the nations with a rod of iron (Rev. 12:5; 19:15; cf. Ps. 2:9 LXX; *Pss Sol.* 17.24).[32] In Revelation 2:18 Jesus presents himself to Thyatira as 'the Son of God', which may also recall the reference to divine sonship in Psalm 2:7 ('You are my Son; today I have begotten you.').[33]

The Christological titles 'firstborn' and 'ruler of kings on earth' in Revelation 1:5 allude to Psalm 89:27 (88:28 LXX): 'I will make him the firstborn [*prōtotokon*], the highest of the kings of the earth' (*tois basileusin tēs gēs*). This psalm recalls Yahweh's loyalty to his covenant with David (vv. 3–4; cf. 2 Sam. 7:12–16) in a time when God has seemingly renounced his covenant and rejected his anointed (vv. 38–46) and when enemies mock God's people and his king (vv. 50–51). The psalmist asks, 'Who is the person who shall live and not see death, shall rescue his soul from the power of Hades?' (88:49 NETS [89:48 MT]). According to Revelation 1:18, Jesus is 'the living one' who 'has the keys of death and Hades'. His resurrection decisively answers the psalmist's longing question and fulfils Yahweh's promise to make David 'the firstborn' (Ps. 89:27). The designation 'firstborn of the dead' in Revelation 1:5 conveys Jesus' superior rank and supreme status as the first to overcome death and experience eschatological resurrection life (cf. Col. 1:18) – a life that he promises to share with his people who overcome (Rev. 2:10–11).

The throne-room vision in Revelation 4 is programmatic for the book's depiction of God as the holy, omnipotent, sovereign Creator and Judge of all; similarly, the heavenly drama of Revelation 5 is foundational for John's depiction of Jesus as Israel's promised king, who triumphs as the slain Lamb and receives universal worship. Chapter 5 opens with the sealed scroll, modelled after Ezekiel 2:9–10, which no one is found worthy to open (Rev. 5:1, 4).[34] Then one of the heavenly elders announces that 'the Lion of the tribe of Judah, the Root of David, has conquered, so that he can open the scroll and its seven seals' (5:5).

'The Lion of the tribe of Judah' alludes to Jacob's blessing of Judah in Genesis 49:8–12. Genesis 49:1 LXX highlights the prophetic nature of this patriarchal blessing, as Jacob tells his sons what would happen 'in the last days' (*eschatōn tōn hēmerōn*). In verse 8, Jacob prays that

---

[32] Rev. 2:26–27 presents a corporate application of Ps. 2:9 to those who conquer. See ch. 5, pp. 90–95; Quek 2009: 175–187.

[33] Koester 2014: 297, 514.

[34] For discussion of the seven-sealed scroll in Rev. 5:1, see ch. 10, pp. 213–215.

Judah's brothers may praise and bow down to him as he triumphs over his enemies. Then in Genesis 49:9 LXX he declares, 'Judah is a lion's cub [*skymnos leontos Iouda*]; from the prey, my son, you have gone up. He stooped down; he crouched as a lion [*leōn*] and as a cub; who shall rouse him?'[35] Genesis 49:10 LXX explains that Judah will not lack a 'ruler' and 'a leader'.[36] The lion thus symbolizes the power and kingship that Jacob's blessing ascribes to Judah. Elsewhere in the Old Testament, 'the lion suggests ferocity, destructiveness and irresistible strength'.[37]

Victor Hamilton asserts, 'The NT does not appropriate any part of this messianic oracle',[38] but this minimizes the unmistakable allusion to Genesis 49:9 in Revelation 5:5 and the plausible link between Genesis 49:11 and Jesus' entry on a donkey's colt in John 12:15.[39] Additionally, Genesis 49:11 LXX says that the ruler from Judah 'shall wash his robe in wine and his garment in the blood of a bunch of grapes' (NETS). Revelation 7:14 refers to the redeemed who have washed their robes in the blood of the Lamb, which may reflect the influence of Genesis 49:11 and may suggest that John presents the saints 'as corporately participating in the ironic victory that the Messiah has inaugurated at the cross'.[40]

In Revelation 5:5 the heavenly elder further identifies the lion of the tribe of Judah as 'the root of David' (cf. 22:16). This title alludes to Isaiah 11:1, 10 LXX:

> And a rod shall come out of the root of Jesse [*ek tēs rhizēs Iessai*], and a flower shall go up out of his root . . .
>
> And it shall be on that day that the root of Jesse [*hē rhiza tou Iessai*], even the one who arises to rule nations – in him shall nations hope, and his rest shall be honor.[41]

Isaiah 11:1–9 recalls the promise of a coming king in David's line in 9:6–7 (9:5–6 LXX) and emphasizes his endowment with the divine

---

[35] My tr. 'A messianic interpretation of the Gen. 49:9 lion occurs in the targumic literature and in other later Jewish writings', according to Beale (1999: 349).

[36] The LXX reads 'ruler' (*archōn*) in place of 'scepter' (*šebeṭ*) in the MT. On this and other textual matters in Gen. 49:10, see Wenham 1993: 476–478.

[37] Bauckham 1993a: 182.

[38] Hamilton 1995: 662.

[39] Cf. Köstenberger 2007: 472.

[40] Beale 1999: 438.

[41] The formulation 'root of David' may also reflect Sir. 47:22: 'the Lord . . . gave a remnant to Jacob, and to David a root [*tō Dauid ex autou rhizan*] from him'.

spirit and his perfect justice and righteousness in ruling God's people and striking the wicked.[42] Bauckham observes that Isaiah 11 and Genesis 49 'were *loci classici* of Jewish Messianic hopes in John's time'.[43] Notably, the Dead Sea Scrolls link Genesis 49:9–11 and Isaiah 11:1–9 and interpret these texts messianically:

> A ruler shall [no]t depart from the tribe of Judah while Israel has dominion. [And] the one who sits on the throne of David [shall never] be cut off, because the 'ruler's staff' is the covenant of the kingdom, [and the thous]ands of Israel are 'the feet,' until the Righteous Messiah, the Branch of David, has come. (4Q252 5.1–3)[44]

Thus the elder's announcement in Revelation 5:5 invokes the biblical promise of the ideal king descended from Judah and David who would execute perfect justice and slay the wicked 'with the word of his mouth' (Isa. 11:4 LXX; cf. *Pss Sol.* 17.24). Later, the vision of the woman and the dragon dramatically presents Jesus' cosmic significance as the 'male child' who would shepherd the nations with an iron rod (Ps. 2:9 LXX) and who receives divine protection from the dragon's assault (Rev. 12:5).

The vision of Jesus' coming on a white horse in Revelation 19:11–16 brings the book's stress on his messianic kingship to a glorious climax. Once again, John's description of Christ alludes to Psalm 2:9 and Isaiah 11:4, signalling that he fulfils his messianic destiny as Ruler and Judge of the nations at his regal return (Rev. 19:15). The 'blood' on his robe (v. 13) most likely does not refer to his own blood that redeems and cleanses his people (1:5; 5:9; 7:14).[45] Rather, his garment is crimson because he 'will tread the winepress of the fury of the wrath of God the Almighty' (v. 15), recalling the bloody scene of judgment in 14:19–20.[46] Christ's attire and activity in 19:13, 15 allude to Isaiah 63:1–6, which presents Yahweh as the divine warrior wearing bloodstained garments as he tramples the nations in his anger.

In Revelation 17:12–14 the angel reveals that the Lamb will triumph over the ten kings that war against him in the beast's service 'because

---

[42] Isa. 11:2 LXX is the likely source for 'the seven spirits' in Rev. 1:4; 3:1; 4:5; 5:6. See further ch. 4, pp. 68–71.

[43] Bauckham 1993a: 180–181.

[44] Tr. Wise et al. 1996. Cf. 1Q28b 5.24–26, 28–29; Koester 2014: 375–376.

[45] Contra Wall 2006: 231; Phillips 2017: 544.

[46] Thomas 1995: 386–387; Mounce 1997: 353–534; Beale and McDonough 2007: 1143.

he is Lord of lords and King of kings' (*kyrios kyriōn estin kai basileus basileōn*).[47] This Christological title likely alludes to Daniel 4:37 LXX, where the king of Babylon acknowledges and praises the Most High 'because he is God of gods and Lord of lords and King of kings' (*theos tōn theōn kai kyrios tōn kyriōn kai basileus tōn basileōn*). In Revelation 19:16 the name written on Christ's robe and thigh – 'King of kings and Lord of lords' – reiterates 17:14 and identifies the messianic ruler with Yahweh, the divine sovereign. Thus Jesus the 'King of kings' shares Yahweh's title, wears his robes and executes his righteous judgment.

The slain Lamb

Revelation's favourite and most distinctive Christological title is 'the Lamb'. After John hears the triumphant heavenly announcement that 'the Lion of the tribe of Judah, the Root of David, has conquered', he sees 'a Lamb standing, as though it had been slain, with seven horns and with seven eyes, which are the seven spirits of God sent out into all the earth' (Rev. 5:6). Bauckham writes, 'The key to John's vision of the slaughtered Lamb . . . is to recognize the contrast between what he hears (5:5) and what he sees (5:6).'[48] The titles Lion of Judah and Root of David evoke images of a powerful Davidic king who would establish Israel and judge the ungodly nations (e.g. 1QS 5.21–29; *Pss Sol.* 17.21–29), while a slain Lamb connotes innocence, vulnerability and sacrifice.[49] John's vision of the slain Lamb (5:6) reinterprets the messianic hopes of 5:5: Jesus conquers (*enikēsen*) in his first coming not by military might but by sacrificial death.[50] Thus Jesus fulfils Old Testament prophecies of messianic kingship in an ironic and surprising way.

Other New Testament writings refer to Jesus as *amnos*, 'lamb' (John 1:29, 36; Acts 8:32; 1 Peter 1:19) or *pascha*, 'Passover sacrifice' (1 Cor 5:7). However, the Apocalypse uniquely refers to Jesus as *arnion* twenty-eight times.[51] The LXX employs *arnion* metaphorically and not in sacrificial contexts. However, Josephus uses *arnion* and the cognate *arēn* to refer to lambs offered as sacrifices (e.g. *Jewish Antiquities*

---

[47] For additional explanation and support of this reading, see Beale 1985: 618–620.
[48] Bauckham 1993b: 74.
[49] Similarly, Koester 2014: 376–377.
[50] Bauckham 1993b: 74; Osborne 2002: 256.
[51] Rev. 5:6, 8, 12–13; 6:1, 16; 7:9–10, 14, 17; 12:11; 13:8; 14:1, 4, 10; 15:3; 17:14; 19:7, 9; 21:9, 14, 22–23, 27; 22:1; 22:3.

3.221–222, 226, 228), suggesting that these terms have a similar connotation to *amnos* around the time Revelation was written.

Scholars have proposed various interpretations and backgrounds for Revelation's lamb image, including (1) the Passover lamb (Exod. 12:3–6; cf. John 1:29), (2) the lamblike servant (Isa. 53:7; cf. Acts 8:32), (3) the suffering prophet (Jer. 11:19; cf. Luke 11:50) and (4) the warrior ram (*1 En.* 90.9–12; *T. Jos.* 19.8).[52] The Apocalypse's dramatic presentation of Jesus as the slain Lamb fuses elements from multiple biblical and Jewish apocalyptic traditions.

The seer describes the Lamb as having 'seven horns' and 'seven eyes', which are identified as the seven spirits of God (Rev. 5:6). 'Horns' in prophetic and apocalyptic literature regularly signify sovereign strength (Dan. 7:24; 8:21–22; *1 En.* 90.9; Rev. 17:12). Thus the Lamb's seven horns convey his complete power, by which he executes wrathful judgment (6:16) and leads the army of the redeemed (14:1, 4; 17:14). 'Seven eyes' alludes to Zechariah 4:10 and represents Jesus' perfect understanding as one endowed with the fullness of God's Spirit (Isa. 11:2 LXX; cf. Rev. 1:4).[53] Thus the exalted Jesus 'searches mind and heart' and renders to each person according to their works (2:23), with the comprehensive knowledge and penetrating insight characteristic of Yahweh alone, who declares in Jeremiah 17:10:

> I Yahweh search the heart
>   and test the mind,
> to give every man according to his ways,
>   according to the fruit of his deeds.

However, the foundational vision in Revelation 5 emphasizes the Lamb's sacrificial death that achieves redemption and prompts heavenly worship. John sees the Lamb standing as though slain (*esphagmenon*), and the worshippers extol the Lamb as worthy because (*hoti*) he was slain and ransomed people for God by his blood (5:6, 9, 13; cf. 1:5) and made them a kingdom and priests (5:10; cf. 1:6; Exod. 19:6).[54] The verb *sphazō* denotes violent killing of human beings (Rev. 6:4, 9; 18:24; cf. 1 John 3:12; Jer. 52:10) or the slaughter

---

[52] For an overview, see Osborne 2002: 255–256; Johns 2003: 108–149; Huber 2012: 460–461; Rutledge 2017: 255–258.

[53] See ch. 4, pp. 68–71.

[54] Rev. 13:1–4 presents the beast as a parody of the slain Lamb. See ch. 6, pp. 121–124.

of animals, including the Passover lamb (Exod. 12:6; 34:25). Jesus is not merely slaughtered as a victim of violence; he is also sacrificed as the Passover Lamb.[55]

Paradoxically, Jesus is the messianic ruler descended from David and Judah who conquers *as* the slaughtered Lamb. Through his death and vindication, Jesus also achieves a new-exodus deliverance for the people of God. According to Revelation 1:5, Jesus 'has freed us from our sins' (*lysanti hēmas ek tōn hamartiōn hēmōn*), which likely alludes to Isaiah 40:2 LXX, 'her sin has been loosed' (*lelytai autēs hē hamartia*). He also achieves 'salvation' (*sōtēria*) for a multi-ethnic multitude (Rev. 7:9–10). 'Salvation' is exodus language (Exod. 14:13; 15:2), and the reference to the palm branches in the worshippers' hands recalls the feast of booths, which memorialized Israel's exodus from Egypt and anticipated their ultimate redemption after exile (Lev. 23:40–43; Zech. 14:16; cf. John 12:13).

According to Revelation 7:17, the Lamb will shepherd (*poimanei*) and lead (*hodēgēsei*) his people to springs of living water. In the LXX Israel's God leads (*hodēgeō*) his people out of Egypt and through the wilderness by the pillar of fire and cloud.[56] Yahweh also shepherds (*poimainō*) his people.[57] Further, he appoints David as Israel's shepherd-ruler (2 Sam. 5:2; 7:7), and promised that he would shepherd (*poimaneis*) the nations with an iron rod (Ps. 2:9 LXX).[58] Jesus the slain Lamb fulfils this Old Testament hope as the messianic shepherd (Rev. 12:5; 19:15) and embodies God's own shepherd-care for his people. Moreover, the victorious Lamb-Shepherd promises that those who conquer will share in his regal authority (2:26–27; 3:21).[59]

The first and the last

Following his dramatic self-disclosure in Revelation 1:12–16, the resplendent Son of Man addresses John with words of comfort: 'Fear not, I am the first and the last, and the living one' (1:17–18). 'The first

---

[55] Bauckham 1993a: 184; deSilva 2009b: 102, n. 20; Estelle 2017: 304. Alternatively, Johns (2003: 38–39, 130–133) denies a connection to the Passover Lamb and argues that *arnion* in Revelation designates a 'nonsacrificial lamb'.

[56] See Exod. 13:17; 15:13; 32:34; Num. 24:8; Deut. 1:33; 2 Sam. 7:23; Neh. 9:12, 19; Isa. 63:15; Pss 77:14, 53; 105:9 LXX [78:14, 53; 106:9 ET].

[57] Pss 22:1; 27:9; 47:15; 48:15; 77:71–72; 79:2 LXX [23:1; 28:9; 48:14; 49:14; 78:71–72; 80:1 ET]; Isa. 40:11.

[58] Ps. 2:9 MT reads 'smash' (*rʿʿ*); cf. *Pss Sol.* 17.24.

[59] For further discussion, see ch. 5, pp. 90–95; Quek 2009: 175–187.

and the last' invokes a title used in Isaiah to underscore that Yahweh is the only true God, in contrast to the lifeless, useless idols fashioned by human hands (Isa. 44:6; 48:12; cf. 41:4). In Revelation Jesus' self-description as 'the first and the last' in 1:17 parallels the Almighty's declaration 'I am the Alpha and the Omega' in 1:8.[60] Similarly, God declares in 21:6, 'I am the Alpha and the Omega, the beginning and the end', and Jesus says in the epilogue, 'I am the Alpha and the Omega, the first and the last, the beginning and the end' (22:13). Bauckham rightly notes that this pattern reveals 'the remarkable extent to which Revelation identifies Jesus Christ with God', the Almighty Creator who is the beginning and end of all things.[61]

Jesus is also 'the living one' (*ho zōn*), and he explains this title in 1:18: 'I died, and behold I am alive for evermore, and I have the keys of Death and Hades.' In Revelation 4:9–10 the living creatures and elders praise God 'who lives for ever', and in John 5:26 Jesus explains that the Son, like the Father, 'has life in himself'. Bauckham reasons that according to Revelation 1:17–18, Jesus' 'eternal livingness was interrupted by the experience of a human death, and he shares the eternal life of God through triumph over death'.[62]

In Revelation 3:14 Jesus presents himself as *hē archē tēs ktiseōs tou theou*. We have seen that God and Jesus self-identify as 'the first and the last' (*hē archē kai to telos*), emphasizing their absolute sovereignty over all creation (21:6; 22:13). There are at least three plausible interpretations of *archē* in 3:14.

First, many interpret *archē* as 'beginning' (ESV, NASB), 'originator' (NET, HCSB) or 'origin' (NRSV).[63] In this reading, *archē* conveys not that Jesus is the first created being but that he is the divine source or originator of creation (*ktisis*).[64] The term *ktisis* occurs only here in the Apocalypse, though the verbal cognate *ktizō* refers to God's creating all things (4:11; 5:13).[65]

---

[60] See ch. 2, pp. 34–35.

[61] Bauckham 1993b: 55, 58.

[62] Ibid. 56. Wellum (2016: 438) appeals to the traditional doctrine of 'communication of attributes' to clarify the relationship and union of God the Son's divine and human natures: 'The person of Christ experienced death through his human nature, including physical pain and the separation of his human body and soul. The divine person of the Son did not cease to exist in the death of Christ but continued subsisting in his divine nature and in his human soul.'

[63] German Bibles translate *archē* with 'Ursprung' (Schlachter) or 'Anfang' (Luther); cf. Giesen 1997: 137, 139; Karrer 2017: 358, 363.

[64] Bauckham 1993b: 56; Aune 1997: 256.

[65] Koester 2014: 336. Paul twice employs the phrase *kainē ktisis* (2 Cor. 5:17; Gal. 6:15).

Second, Beale suggests that this title in 3:14 presents Christ as 'the beginning of the new creation of God' by virtue of his resurrection.[66] Beale argues that the other two titles used by Christ in Revelation 3:14, 'the Amen' and 'the faithful and true witness', derive from Isaiah 65:16 and Isaiah 43:10–12, respectively.[67] Each of these Isaianic texts immediately precedes an announcement that God will do a 'new' (MT, *ḥādāš*) work of salvation and re-creation that contrasts with the 'former things' (MT, *ri'šōnôt*) of trouble and distress (Isa. 43:16–21; 65:16–19). This interpretation receives further support from Colossians 1:18, 'He is the beginning [*archē*], the firstborn from the dead, that in everything he might be preeminent.'

The NIV offers a third possible interpretation of the title *hē archē tēs ktiseōs tou theou*: 'the ruler of God's creation'. The translation 'ruler' fits well with the earlier depiction of Jesus as the 'ruler [*archōn*] of kings on earth' (1:5) and also with Christ's declaration in 3:21: 'I also conquered and sat down with my Father on his throne.'[68] However, elsewhere in Revelation *archē* clearly means 'beginning' (contrasted with *telos*), while other terms such as *archōn* (1:5) and *basileus* (19:16) indicate Jesus' kingship.

Bauckham argues that *archē* in 3:14 carries the same sense in the address to Laodicea that it has in 21:6 and 22:13: 'Christ preceded all things as their source.'[69] He rightly insists that 3:14 does not imply an adoptionist Christology, as Jesus' divine titles 'indicate that he shared the eternal being of God from before creation'.[70] However, Bauckham dismisses the possible reference to Jesus as *archē* of God's new creation.[71] Yet in 1:17–18, and again in 2:8, Jesus refers to himself as 'the first and the last' who died and came to life. The resurrection thus confirms Jesus' divine identity as well as his regal status.

Most likely, Revelation 3:14 presents Jesus as the beginning of God's new creation through his resurrection from the dead. The risen Christ is the 'Amen', who embodies divine truthfulness (cf. Isa. 65:16), and he is 'the faithful and true witness', who testifies truly to God's activity in the world (cf. Rev. 1:5; Isa. 43:10–12). He is also the *archē*, who inaugurates the fulfilment of God's new-creation promises and will bring them to their appointed *telos*.

---

[66] Beale 1996: 152.
[67] Ibid. 137–152.
[68] Koester 2014: 336; Paul 2018: 112.
[69] Bauckham 1993b: 56.
[70] Ibid. 58.
[71] Ibid. 56.

Conclusion

It is impossible to overstate the importance and centrality of Jesus in this book of prophecy that describes itself as 'the revelation of Jesus Christ' and concludes with the prayer 'Amen, come Lord Jesus!' (1:1; 22:20). Jesus rises from death victorious, reveals the eschatological divine plan, rebukes and reassures struggling churches, returns to judge evil and save his people, and reigns eternally on the divine throne. The disclosure of Jesus' divine identity and activity in Revelation brings together seemingly divergent and contradictory categories. Christ is the Son of Man, yet shares the attributes and the authority of the Ancient of Days. He is the faithful witness and the righteous Judge, the strong Lion and the slaughtered Lamb, the Shepherd-Lamb, the eternally existing Alpha and Omega, who died and lives for evermore. This revelation of Jesus Christ bursts the wineskins as he brings a panoply of biblical prophecies and patterns to their appointed apogee.

In six of the edicts to the churches in Revelation 2 – 3, the exalted Christ highlights features of his earlier self-revelation in 1:12–20 that apply particularly to each church's situation.[72] He reminds Ephesus and later Sardis that he 'holds the seven stars' and 'walks among the seven golden lampstands' (2:1; 3:1; cf. 1:20), stressing his supreme power over and awesome presence in the churches.[73] The Son of Man reminds the beleaguered church of Smyrna that he is 'the first and the last, who died and came to life' (2:8; cf. 1:17–18), stressing his divine identity and resurrection life. He addresses Pergamum as the one 'who has the sharp two-edged sword' (2:12; cf. 1:16), signifying his ultimate authority to execute judgment. The risen Christ speaks to the church of Thyatira as 'the Son of God, who has eyes like a flame of fire, and whose feet are like burnished bronze' (2:18; cf. 1:14–15). He, not the popular deity Apollo, is the true divine Son worthy of their allegiance and trust, and possesses penetrating, divine insight as the glorious heavenly Judge.[74] The Son of Man addresses Philadelphia as 'the holy one, the true one, who has the key of David, who opens and no one will shut, who shuts and no one opens' (3:7). This self-disclosure invokes Jesus' victory over the cosmic forces of death and Hades

---

[72] Only the self-disclosure to Laodicea in Rev. 3:14 does not explicitly invoke the Son of Man vision in 1:12–20. For discussion of 3:14, see ch. 2, pp. 40–43.

[73] For further discussion, see ch. 5, pp. 95–97.

[74] For discussion of the Apollo background, see Hemer 1986: 106–123.

(1:17; cf. 20:13–14) and his sovereign right to give or deny people access to God's kingdom (cf. Isa. 22:22; Matt. 16:19). These references to his authority, life, knowledge and control make clear that the Son of Man who bears the exalted features of the Ancient of Days in Revelation 1:12–16 possesses 'divine power and prerogative . . . Jesus knows and does what only God can know and do'.[75] Christ concludes his messages to the seven churches by declaring that he sits on his Father's throne (3:21), which sets the stage for John's remarkable vision of the heavenly throne in chapter 4 and the drama of the conquering Lamb in chapter 5.[76]

We have seen that Jesus shares God's appellations, attributes and activities. He is the messianic ruler, who is 'worthy' to take the sealed scroll from the Almighty, and has conquered not by shedding enemy blood but by offering his own (Rev. 5:5–6, 9; cf. 1:5). The Lamb was slain to redeem his people (5:9), stands victorious over death (5:6) and sits down with his Father on the divine throne (3:21). Thus the Lamb is 'worthy' to receive power, wealth, wisdom, might, honour, glory and blessing (5:13) – accolades elsewhere reserved for the Creator God (4:9, 11; 7:12).[77] However, the Apocalypse does not present the Lamb as a rival to God but as a sharer in God's glory and identity and as the executor of God's previously inscrutable plan. Thus 'the worship of Jesus must be understood as indicating the inclusion of Jesus in the being of the one God defined by monotheistic worship'.[78] Indeed, the only proper response to the Apocalypse's dramatic presentation of Jesus is joyous worship and steadfast loyalty fuelled by confident hope in his regal return.

---

[75] Hays 2012: 71.
[76] Beale 1999: 321.
[77] Smith 2016: 81.
[78] Bauckham 1993b: 60. On the worship of Jesus, see also Wellum 2016: 195–196.

Chapter Four

The Spirit of prophecy: the empowering presence of God's sevenfold Spirit

Grace to you and peace from him who is and who was and who is to come, and from the seven Spirits who are before his throne. (Rev. 1:4)

For the testimony of Jesus is the Spirit of prophecy. (Rev. 19:10)

The one seated on the throne and the Lamb take centre stage in the Apocalypse's drama of eschatological judgment and salvation, while the Spirit seems relegated to the supporting cast. God and the Lamb receive heavenly worship (Rev. 7:10) and reign for ever on the divine throne (3:21; 11:15; 22:3), while references to 'the Spirit' or 'the seven Spirits' are comparatively few. Nevertheless, the book's trinitarian salutation communicates grace and peace not only from God and Christ but also from 'the seven Spirits who are before his throne' (1:4). Further, the pivotal vision of the divine throne room in Revelation 4 – 5 depicts the divine Spirits as seven burning torches before the divine throne (4:5) and seven eyes on the Lamb (5:6), images that draw especially on Zechariah 4. Further, the sevenfold Spirit of God is not confined to the heavenly courts but ranges 'through the whole earth' (Rev. 5:6; cf. Zech. 4:10). As Bauckham asserts, 'The Spirit plays an essential role in the divine activity of establishing God's kingdom in the world.'[1]

This chapter explores various ways that the Apocalypse describes the nature and activity of the divine Spirit in biblical-theological perspective. The distinctive reference to 'the seven spirits who are before his throne' (Rev. 1:4; cf. 4:5) likely draws upon Zechariah 4 and Isaiah 11:2 LXX and depicts the fullness of the divine Spirit. The subtle mention of 'the Spirit of life' (*pneuma zōēs*) in Revelation 11:11 recalls

---

[1] Bauckham 1993b: 109.

67

God's vivifying work in creation (Gen. 2:7) and especially the hope of resurrection by the Spirit (Ezek. 37). Above all, the Apocalypse stresses that the Spirit is the divine agent of prophecy. John's four references to being 'in the Spirit' (Rev. 1:10; 4:2; 17:3; 21:10) serve as major literary markers for the book and establish that he is a true prophet who, like Ezekiel, receives divine visions by the Holy Spirit. Moreover, at several points the Spirit speaks distinctly (14:13; 22:17), and readers are urged to 'hear what the Spirit says to the churches' (2:7, 11, 17, 29; 3:6, 13, 22). Jesus discloses divine revelation to his servant John for the benefit of his servants when the prophet is 'in the Spirit on the Lord's day' (1:1, 10). Likewise, the risen Christ addresses each of the seven churches in Revelation 2 – 3, yet his authoritative messages are also the very words of the Spirit. De Smidt asserts that 'the whole Apocalypse could . . . be regarded as a "speaking of the Spirit" (14:13). Indeed, the whole book is called a prophecy (22:18), which again implies the inspiration of the Spirit.'[2] Revelation urges readers to discern between false prophecy that deceives and destroys (2:14, 20; 13:11–18; 16:13–14) and genuine prophecy from the divine Spirit that amounts to 'the testimony of Jesus' and leads people to 'worship of God' (19:10).

The sevenfold Spirit of God

The Apocalypse's initial reference to the divine Spirit comes in the opening salutation, where John wishes grace and peace 'from him who is and who was and who is to come, and from the seven Spirits who are before his throne, and from Jesus Christ . . .' (Rev. 1:4–5). Revelation's use of 'the seven Spirits' is distinctive and has been interpreted in two primary ways: (1) seven angels or (2) the sevenfold Holy Spirit.[3]

In support of the first option, Koester suggests that the seven spirits 'are probably angelic spirits'.[4] He observes that seven spirits (1:4; 3:1; 4:5; 5:6) and seven angels (8:2) both appear before the divine throne and notes that Christ refers to the seven stars in his hand as both angels and spirits (1:20; 3:1).[5] Aune similarly identifies Revelation's seven spirits 'as the seven principal angels of

---

[2] De Smidt 1994: 242.
[3] Waddell 2006: 9–21. Osborne (2002: 74) outlines four views of the 'seven Spirits'.
[4] Koester 2014: 226.
[5] Ibid. 216.

God'.[6] Tobit 12.15 refers to 'the seven angels who stand ready and enter before the glory of the Lord' (NRSV; cf. *1 En.* 20.1–8). Further, Koester reasons that John's depiction of the seven spirits as flaming torches in Revelation 4:5 may recall Psalm 104:4, 'he makes his angels spirits and his servants a flaming fire' (cf. Heb. 1:7).[7] Additionally, 'angels' and 'spirits' are used interchangeably in the Dead Sea Scrolls (1QM 12.8–9; 4Q405 f23i.8–10),[8] though references to seven 'spirits' in the Gospels and early Jewish writings typically refer to evil spirits (Matt. 12:45; Luke 8:2; 11:26; *T. Sol.* 8.1–2; *T. Reu.* 2.1). While some object that it would be improper to mention angelic spirits alongside God and Christ as the source of grace and peace,[9] Mounce suggests that Luke 9:26 and 1 Timothy 5:21 offer precedent for this.[10]

Alternatively, others identify 'the seven Spirits who are before his throne' as a reference to the Holy Spirit for several reasons. First, the seven Spirits as the divine spirit rather than angels presents a trinitarian source of divine grace and peace for the churches (cf. 1 Peter 1:2; 2 Cor. 13:13). Second, Revelation refers to 'the seven angels' standing before God with trumpets in 8:2 in quite different terms from 'the seven Spirits' in 1:4.[11] Third, it makes more sense to identify the divine eyes of the Lamb as the sevenfold Spirit of God rather than as seven angels.[12] Third, interpreters since Victorinus have commonly cited Isaiah 11:2 LXX as a likely source for the Apocalypse's imagery of the 'seven spirits'.[13] Elsewhere John, using imagery drawn from Isaiah 11:1, 4, presents Jesus as the 'root of David' (Rev. 5:5) who will strike the nations with the sword of his mouth (19:15; cf. 1:16; 2:12, 16). Isaiah 11:2 states that the Messiah will be endowed with the fullness of the divine Spirit: 'And the spirit of God shall rest on him, the spirit of wisdom and understanding, the spirit of counsel and might, the spirit of knowledge and godliness' (NETS). Fekkes argues that 'the relevance of Isaiah 11:2 is problematic' because the Hebrew text lists only six qualities, while the LXX and later interpreters

---

[6] Aune 1997: 34.

[7] Koester 2014: 216; Aune (1997: 33) claims that the plural 'spirits' (*rûḥôt*) 'is never used of *angels* in the OT' (emphasis original), yet he curiously overlooks Ps. 104:4.

[8] Koester 2014: 216.

[9] Thomas 1992: 67.

[10] Mounce 1997: 47. A similar defence for identifying the seven Spirits as angels is offered by sixth-century commentator Oecumenius (*Commentary on the Apocalypse* 1.4).

[11] Bauckham 1993a: 162.

[12] Jauhiainen 2005: 87.

[13] Victorinus writes, 'These seven gifts are of one Spirit, that is, they are gifts of the Holy Spirit' (*Commentary on the Apocalypse* 1.1).

list seven.[14] However, it seems plausible that John has access to the Greek translation of the Old Testament, and the images of Christ 'who has the seven Spirits of God' (Rev. 3:1) strengthens the link with Isaiah 11:2 LXX.

Fourth, Beale argues that 'the wording "seven spirits" is part of a paraphrased allusion to Zech. 4:2–7'.[15] The prophet Zechariah sees a golden lampstand with seven lamps, which the angel explains as 'the eyes of Yahweh, which range through the whole earth' (4:2, 10). This vision reassures the exiles that Zerubbabel will complete the work begun on the temple by God's Spirit (4:6). John's identification of the two witnesses as 'olive trees' and 'lampstands' in Revelation 11:4 clearly alludes to Zechariah 4:2–3,[16] and the seer makes explicit what is implicit in Zechariah's vision by identifying the sevenfold Spirit with 'seven torches of fire' (Rev. 4:5; cf. Zech. 4:2, 6) and with 'seven eyes' (Rev. 5:6; cf. Zech. 4:6, 10).[17] Bauckham observes, 'In Revelation the eyes of Yahweh are also the eyes of the Lamb', and the Lamb's seven horns and seven eyes signify his divine ability 'to see what happens throughout the world' and also 'to act powerfully wherever he chooses'.[18] Furthermore, in Revelation 1:4 John prays that his readers may receive 'grace . . . from the seven Spirits', which may allude to Zechariah's progression from the assurance of the Spirit's power to the promised shouts of 'Grace, grace' when the temple is rebuilt (Zech. 4:6–7).[19]

The weight of evidence suggests that 'the seven Spirits' in Revelation 1:4 and elsewhere is John's distinctive idiom for the divine Spirit. Zechariah 4 is the primary Old Testament background for Revelation's phrase in 1:4 and 5:6, but a secondary allusion to Isaiah 11:2 LXX also seems likely in Revelation 5:6, where the 'seven Spirits of God' endow the Lamb who is in the previous verse identified as 'the root of David' that Isaiah promised (Rev. 5:5; Isa. 11:1). Beale writes, 'Isa. 11:2ff. (LXX) shows that God's sevenfold Spirit is what equips the Messiah to establish his end-time reign.'[20]

---

[14] Fekkes 1994: 108.

[15] Beale 1999: 189. Similarly, Bauckham (1993a: 162) reasons that John employs this distinctive phrase for God's Spirit 'on the basis of his exegesis of Zechariah 4:1–14'.

[16] See ch. 5, pp. 97–101.

[17] Bauckham 1993a: 163. Jauhiainen (2005: 88–89) writes, 'What in Zech 4 is at best implicit, John's two "X is Y" statements in 4:5 and 5:6 make explicit: the seven eyes and lamps are God's seven spirits.'

[18] Bauckham 1993a: 164. Cf. Jauhiainen 2005: 84–85.

[19] Beale 1999: 189.

[20] Ibid. 189–190. 'Elsewhere the seven spirits appear as attributes or accessories of the risen Christ,' according to Bruce (1973: 334).

John's reference to 'the seven Spirits' (1:4) should be understood in the light of the book's highly symbolic use of numbers. The number seven and its multiples signifies fullness or completion.[21] In keeping with this pattern, Revelation's unique expression 'the seven Spirits before his throne' stresses the fullness or totality of God's Spirit. Mangina explains, 'The sevenfoldness of the Spirit binds his identity to God and to Christ and symbolizes both the diversity of his gifts and their unrestricted scope.'[22]

John further develops the reference to seven Spirits before the divine throne in Revelation 4:5: 'From the throne came flashes of lightning, and rumblings and peals of thunder, and before the throne were burning seven torches of fire [*hepta lampades pyros*], which are the seven spirits of God.' Zechariah sees seven lamps [*lychnoi*] on the golden lampstand (4:2), which recalls the golden lampstands before the inner sanctuary of the temple (1 Kgs 7:49). The lampstands' continually burning lamps 'were a symbol of Yahweh's presence with his people', and Zechariah's vision 'suggests a resplendent new temple, not to be built by worldly power but by God's Spirit'.[23] The imagery of the Apocalypse suggests that these 'lamps' (the sevenfold Spirit) burn on the seven lampstands (the churches; cf. Rev. 1:20).[24]

Additionally, *lampades* in Revelation 4:5 may denote 'lamps' as a synonym for *lychnoi*, but it also recalls the presence of 'flaming torches' in Old Testament theophany scenes (Gen. 15:17; 20:18) and in Ezekiel's heavenly vision (Ezek. 1:13). The reference to 'lightning' and 'thunder' in John's throne-room vision (Rev. 4:5) further links this scene with Old Testament depictions of God's awesome presence (cf. Exod. 19:16; 20:18). In Revelation 4:5 this same imagery recurs at the conclusion of seal, trumpet and bowl judgments (8:5; 11:19; 16:18), which signals that the sovereign on the heavenly throne will definitively judge his enemies.[25]

The Spirit of vision

On four occasions, the seer recounts that he receives divine visions or is carried away 'in the Spirit' (*en pneumati*). As discussed in the introduction, this phrase serves as a major structural marker at

---

[21] Cf. ch. 1, pp. 19–24.
[22] Mangina 2010: 44.
[23] Jauhiainen 2005: 46–47.
[24] Beale 1999: 189. Cf. Bauckham 1993a: 165–166.
[25] See further ch. 7, pp. 143–146.

important transition points in the Apocalypse (Rev. 1:10; 4:2; 17:3; 21:10).[26] Interpreters differ over the precise connotation of John's visions *en pneumati* and over the literary and theological significance of this phrase.

John introduces his foundational vision of the risen Christ by writing, 'I was in the Spirit [*egenomēn en pneumati*] on the Lord's day, and I heard behind me a loud voice like a trumpet' (1:10). Interpreters have understood the phrase *en pneumati* in the Apocalypse in various ways.[27] Morris suggests that *en pneumati* denotes 'something like a trance . . . a state in which the Seer is specially open to the Holy Spirit and ready to see visions'.[28] Alternatively, Osborne asserts that the phrase 'refers not to ecstatic experience but to "participation in the community of the Holy Spirit"'.[29] Bauckham reasons that 'John is much less interested than many other apocalyptists in describing psychologically his visionary experience. His purpose was not so much to describe how he received the revelation as to communicate it to his readers.'[30]

Most likely, 'I was in the Spirit' in 1:10 emphasizes that John is a true prophet who receives visions from the divine Spirit. John's language recalls the experience of the prophet Ezekiel, who writes that 'the Spirit lifted me up and brought me in the vision by the Spirit of God [*en horasei en pneumati theou*]' (Ezek. 11:24) and recounts that Yahweh 'brought me out in the Spirit [*en pneumati*]' (37:1). Additionally, the Spirit 'came upon' (2:2; 3:24), 'fell upon' (11:5) and 'lifted' up the prophet (3:12, 14; 8:3; 11:1; 43:5). Further, in Micah 3:8 LXX the prophet stresses that he will be filled with strength 'in the Spirit of the LORD' (*en pneumati kyriou*), in contrast to the false prophets who lead the people astray by their dreams and divinations (3:5–7). Jeske suggests that in Micah and in Revelation *en pneumati* stresses not an ecstatic experience but that the prophet has received a true message from God.[31] According to Revelation 1:1–2, Jesus communicated his revelation to John by sending his angel, and the prophet testifies 'to all that he saw'. John 'sees' heavenly visions and receives this revelation from the risen Christ 'in the Spirit' (1:10).

[26] See ch. 1, pp. 19–24.
[27] De Smidt (1994: 239–241) surveys six major interpretive perspectives: (1) psychological and phenomenological, (2) literary, (3) rhetorical, (4) theological, (5) liturgical and (6) eschatological.
[28] Morris 1987: 57. Similarly, Aune 1997: 83; Boxall 2006: 39.
[29] Osborne 2002: 83.
[30] Bauckham 1993a: 158.
[31] Jeske 1985: 454–455.

Furthermore, through written testimony to all that he saw the Spirit imparts grace and peace (1:4) and 'speaks' to the churches (2:7).[32] Thus 'As God's Spirit brings the word of the risen Jesus to John, the Spirit speaks through him.'[33]

The use of *en pneumati* in 4:2 signals a structural transition from Christ's messages to the churches to the heavenly throne room and the unfolding drama of the sealed scroll, which the Lamb alone is worthy to open (chs. 4–5). In 4:1 John sees a 'door standing open in heaven', which he begins to describe in detail in verse 2. Ezekiel 1:1 offers the nearest biblical parallel as the prophet recounts how 'the heavens were opened, and I saw visions of God'.[34] In Revelation 19:11 'I saw heaven opened' recalls 4:1 and similarly introduces a new major literary unit.

Bauckham reasons that since 4:1 includes the language of vision (*meta tauta eidon*), '4:2 cannot be the beginning of a second trance', as John is already 'in the Spirit'. He concludes that while 1:10 indicates that the seer 'fell into a trance', 4:2 refers to 'John's rapture to heaven'.[35] While this is possible, it is noteworthy that 4:1–2 includes at least three clear parallels to John's initial commissioning in chapter 1. First, 'the first voice, which I had heard speaking to me like a trumpet' refers back to the 'loud voice like a trumpet' (1:10). Second, the promise 'I will show you what must take place after this [*deixai soi ha dei genesthai meta tauta*]' echoes the Danielic language in 1:1 and 1:19 (cf. Dan. 2:28–29, 45 LXX). Third, the precise phrase *egenomēn en pneumati* ('I was in the Spirit') occurs only in 1:10 and 4:2. These links suggest that *egenomēn en pneumati* in 4:2 introduces a new vision closely related to the book's initial vision in 1:10 – 3:21.[36] John continues to carry out his prophetic commissioning to record his visions to send to the churches.[37]

The final two uses of *en pneumati* in 17:3 and 21:10 introduce contrasting visions of Babylon the harlot and Jerusalem the bride.[38] While John states that he 'was in the Spirit' in 1:10 and 4:2, the phrase *en pneumati* functions instrumentally in 17:3 and 21:10 as he is 'carried

---

[32] See ch. 4, pp. 80–84.
[33] Koester 2014: 243.
[34] Other examples of the heavens being opened in visionary contexts include Matt. 3:16; Acts 10:11; *T. Levi* 2.6; *Apoc. Ab.* 7.3; Herm., *Vis.* 1.1.4. *1 En.* 14.15 refers to an 'open door'.
[35] Bauckham 1993a: 153–154.
[36] Similarly, Bandy and Merkle 2015: 221.
[37] Beale 1999: 316–317.
[38] See further ch. 8, pp. 168–174.

. . . away in the Spirit' to a wilderness and then to a high mountain.[39] Again this recalls how Ezekiel was 'lifted up' and taken in visions to Jerusalem (8:3), to the temple (11:1) and to 'a very high mountain' (40:2),[40] and also famously led out 'in the Spirit of Yahweh' and set down in a valley of dry bones (37:1). The deliberate parallels with Ezekiel further reinforce that John is a genuine prophet who receives divine revelation by the Holy Spirit and writes with the authority of the biblical prophets.[41]

The Spirit of resurrection life

John's vision of the two witnesses in Revelation 11:3–13 includes a subtle yet significant reference to the divine Spirit. The reference to these witnesses as 'lampstands' in 11:4 signals that they represent the church.[42] The witnesses prophesy for a symbolic three-and-a-half-year period of tribulation (11:3–6; cf. Dan. 7:25) before the beast wars against and conquers them (11:7; cf. Dan. 7:21). Their bodies lie unburied in the street of 'the great city', while their opponents rejoice and revel at their apparent demise (11:8–10).[43] Then verse 11 records the surprising reversal: 'But after the three and a half days a breath of life from God entered them, and they stood up on their feet, and great fear fell on those who saw them.' Many interpreters recognize that this verse is 'a direct allusion to the valley of dry bones in Ezek. 37'.[44]

The phrase 'a breath/Spirit of life' (*pneuma zōēs*) recalls Ezekiel 37:5 LXX (*pneuma zōēs*), and the remainder of the verse alludes to Ezekiel 37:10 LXX: 'And the Spirit came into them, and they lived and stood upon their feet' (*eisēlthen eis autous to pneuma, kai ezēsan kai estēsan epi tōn podōn autōn*). The Greek version of verse 5 ('Behold I am bringing into you a Spirit of life') abbreviates the Hebrew text ('Behold, I will cause breath to enter you, and you shall live') and interprets this promise in the light of Genesis 2:7, where the Lord

---

[39] Bauckham 1993a: 157.
[40] Bauckham (1993a: 156–157) lists a number of Jewish and early Christian parallels and notes that most 'copy the language of Ezekiel'.
[41] Cf. Beale 1999: 203.
[42] For further discussion of Rev. 11, see ch. 5, pp. 97–101.
[43] See ch. 8, pp. 164–168.
[44] Osborne 2002: 429; Giesen 1997: 256–257; Smalley 2005: 284; Moyise 1995: 105; Waddell 2006; Beale and McDonough 2007: 1121. Unfortunately, the seminal study of Revelation's use of Ezekiel by Vogelgesang (1985) does not discuss this allusion to Ezek. 37:5, 10.

God breathed into the man's nostrils 'the breath of life' (*pnoēn zōēs*).[45]

Ezekiel 37 is one of the clearest and most vivid Old Testament prophecies of Israel's restoration from Babylonian exile. Israel has 'defiled' their land with evil deeds and idolatry and so Yahweh pours out his wrath upon them (Ezek. 36:17–18). The people resemble a valley of dry bones – spiritually dead, without hope and 'cut off' (37:1–3, 11). Then Yahweh commands the prophet to prophesy to these bones that they may live (vv. 4–6), which vividly unfolds in verses 7–10. According to Ezekiel's vision, Israel will return to their land (37:14, 21), be cleansed from their impurity (37:23) and experience restored covenant fellowship with Yahweh (37:23, 27–28).[46] Though Ezekiel 37 is obviously metaphorical, verses 12–13 suggest that Israel's hopes extend further to life after death, as Yahweh promises to open their tombs and graves. Thus Samson Levey calls Ezekiel 37 the '*locus classicus* of the resurrection in the Hebrew Scriptures'.[47]

The Spirit features prominently in the restoration prophecies of Ezekiel 36 – 37. Three times Yahweh promises, 'I will put my Spirit into you.'[48] This divine action brings new life, knowledge of God and restoration from exile (37:6, 14), as well as new obedience to Yahweh's statutes and judgments (36:27). In 37:7–10 Ezekiel prophesies to the dry bones and sees the dramatic transformation as the bones rattle and grow sinews, flesh and skin. Then in a great act of new creation the breath or Spirit (*pneuma*) enters the corpses and gives life.

The dramatic resurrection of the two witnesses in Revelation 11:11 recalls Ezekiel's vision of Israel's 'resurrection' after exile. The time marker 'after three days and a half' (*meta tas treis hēmeras kai hēmisy*) also resembles references to Jesus' resurrection 'after three days' (*meta treis hēmeras*; Matt. 27:63; Mark 8:31; 9:31; 10:34).[49] The variation 'after three days and a half' rather than 'after three days' as in the Gospels may signal that 'John's mind is still running on the mysterious

---

[45] Cf. Allen 1990: 185. 'The writer clearly intends us to hear echoes of Genesis 2:7 and Ezekiel 37:5–14', according to Wright (2003: 471).

[46] This summary adapts Tabb 2017: 117.

[47] Levey 1987: 13. Cf. Block 1992: 113–141.

[48] Ezek. 36:27 LXX (*to pneuma mou dōsō en hymin*); 37:6 LXX (*dōsō pneuma mou eis hymas*); 37:14 LXX (*dōsō to pneuma mou eis hymas*).

[49] Wright (2003: 472) says that John's description of the witnesses' resurrection 'is based, of course, on Jesus himself, and his own achievement in death and resurrection'. Similarly, Waddell 2006: 185.

half-week of Daniel's prophecy.'[50] Some interpreters take John's allusion to Ezekiel 37 as a prediction that Israel's conversion 'is to be accomplished by a miracle of resurrection'.[51] However, if the two witnesses represent the church, which is likely given their designation as 'lampstands' in 11:4, then John here describes the vindication of the church as the true people of God (cf. Ezek. 37:12–13) and anticipates the day when believers will be 'finally released from their earthly pilgrimage of captivity and suffering'.[52]

Thus 'the Spirit of life' in Revelation 11:11 echoes God's creative act of breathing life into the man of dust (Gen. 2:7) and invokes his promise to restore and revivify his people after exile (Ezek. 37:1–14). John's vision of the two witnesses stresses that life, not the suffering and death, is the final word for followers of the Lamb. After a period of difficulty and seeming defeat, the living God will decisively vindicate believers and raise them from the dead by his life-giving Spirit, following the pattern of their resurrected Lord who now holds the keys of Death and Hades (1:18).

The Spirit of prophetic testimony

In Revelation 19:9 the revealing angel instructs John to 'write' and affirms the veracity of what he has heard by declaring, 'These are the true words of God.'[53] In verse 10 the seer falls down before the angel and is rebuked, 'You must not do that! I am a fellow servant with you and your brothers who hold to the testimony of Jesus. Worship God.' The phrase that follows – 'For the testimony of Jesus is the spirit of prophecy' (*hē gar martyria Iēsou estin to pneuma tēs prophēteias*) – likely continues the angel's words to John and explains the meaning of 'the testimony of Jesus' earlier in the verse.[54] This enigmatic statement has been understood in a number of ways.

First, interpreters are divided on whether the phrase *hē martyria Iēsou* refers to the testimony borne *by* Jesus (subjective genitive) or the testimony *about* Jesus (objective genitive) in its two occurrences

[50] Caird 1984: 138.
[51] Ladd 1972: 158.
[52] Beale 1999: 597. For defence of a corporate interpretation of the two witnesses in Rev. 11, see ch. 5, pp. 95–97.
[53] For discussion of 19:10 and related statements in Rev. 21:6 and 22:6, see ch. 10, pp. 220–223.
[54] Dixon 2017: 105.

in 19:10 and elsewhere in the Apocalypse.[55] Three times 'the testimony of Jesus' occurs alongside the parallel expression 'the Word of God' as the content of John's own prophetic witness (1:2), the reason why he was relegated to the island of Patmos (1:9) and why the martyrs were beheaded (20:4). Similarly, 12:17 refers to the dragon's hostility towards those 'who keep the commandments of God and the testimony of Jesus'. 'The Word of God' and 'the commands of God' do not present God as the one that the words and commands are about (objective genitive) but the one who speaks and gives commands; the parallel genitive phrase 'the testimony of Jesus' is best taken in the same way as a subjective genitive construction.[56] This interpretation fits well with Revelation's description of Jesus as 'the faithful witness' (1:5; 3:14; cf. 22:20), and with the book's opening words *Apokalypsis Iēsou Christou*, which present Jesus as the one who discloses God's revelation (1:1). Recently, Dixon has argued plausibly that *hē martyria Iēsou* 'is best understood as a reference to the message of the book of Revelation', the *Apokalypsis Iēsou Christou* (1:1–2).[57]

There is a similar divergence of views on how to interpret the phrase *pneuma tēs prophēteias* in 19:10.[58] Some scholars understand *to pneuma* to mean 'the essence' or 'the true spirit' of prophecy.[59] Alternatively, Beale explains *to pneuma* as a collective singular and *tēs prophēteias* as a descriptive genitive, and he renders the phrase '"prophetic spirit[s]" or "prophetic soul[s]," that is, prophets'.[60] Most likely, *to pneuma* refers to the Holy Spirit, who inspires prophecy.[61] In the Apocalypse *to pneuma* in the singular consistently refers to the divine Spirit unless modified by descriptors such as 'unclean' (18:2). Beale rightly notes that Revelation 22:6 and 1 Corinthians 14:32 refer to 'the spirits of the prophets'; however, these texts refer to 'spirits' plural, while *to pneuma* in Revelation 19:10 is singular. Further, in Revelation and throughout Scripture the divine Spirit comes upon

---

[55] In favour of the objective genitive, see Bruce 1973: 338; Aune 1998b: 1039; Osborne 2002: 677. For the subjective genitive, see Trites 1977: 155–159; Giesen 1997: 414–415; Mounce 1997: 349; Karrer 2017: 186. Beale (1999: 947) proposes a mediating position, 'the witness by and to Jesus'.

[56] *Tou theou* functions as a genitive of source or subjective genitive in 1:2 and 12:17, according to Mathewson (2016: 3, 168).

[57] Dixon 2017: 163. For a review of Dixon's study, see Tabb 2018. Cf. ch. 10, pp. 208–210.

[58] See the recent survey of scholarship in Dixon 2017: 106, n. 30.

[59] Respectively Wilson 1994: 196; Morris 1987: 217.

[60] Beale 1999: 947.

[61] De Smidt 1994: 243; Osborne 2002: 678; Koester 2014: 732; Dixon 2017: 106–108.

and fills prophets to enable them to prophesy; never in these contexts does *pneuma* refer to the 'essence' of prophecy.[62]

In Numbers 11:25–26 the seventy elders prophesy when Yahweh places on them the Spirit that was upon Moses. In verse 29 Moses not only approves of their prophecy but states his hope 'that all Yahweh's people might be prophets, when Yahweh puts his Spirit upon them' (my tr.). In 1 Samuel the Spirit of God rushes upon King Saul and then upon his messengers and they prophesy (10:6, 10; 19:20, 23). Yahweh commands his servants by his Spirit (Zech. 1:6 LXX) and repeatedly warns and instructs Israel by his Spirit by the hands of the prophets (Neh. 9:30; Zech. 7:12). Echoing Moses' hope in Numbers 11:29, Joel 2:28 (3:1 LXX) declares that God will one day pour out his Spirit on all flesh and they will prophesy. Acts stresses that Jesus has poured out the divine Spirit in the last days as he promised (1:5; 2:17, 33). In contrast, Yahweh sends 'a lying spirit' (MT, *rûaḥ šeqer*; LXX, *pneuma pseudes*) into the mouth of Ahab's prophets to entice the wicked king (1 Kgs 22:22), and pours out 'a spirit of deep sleep' on the people's prophets and seers (Isa. 29:10).

As in the Old Testament, Revelation contrasts true prophets like John who speak by the divine Spirit with false prophets who speak by unclean, demonic spirits. In 2:14 the risen Christ chides some in Pergamum for holding 'the teaching of Balaam', the Gentile prophet who could not curse Israel but advised the Moabite king Balak to seduce the people into sexual immorality and idolatry (Num. 22 – 24; 25:1–2; 31:16; cf. *LAB* 18.13–14). Later biblical writers present Balaam as a prototypical false prophet motivated by profit (2 Peter 2:15–16; Jude 11). In 2:20 Jesus rebukes the churches for tolerating the prophetess Jezebel. The moniker Jezebel alludes to Ahab's notorious wife who promoted unprecedented Baal worship, sorcery and evil in Israel (1 Kgs 16:31–32; 21:25–26; cf. *2 Bar.* 62.3; Philo, *On the Migration of Abraham* 113–115). Balaam and Jezebel are 'strategically chosen pseudonyms . . . that reveal their true character'.[63] Jezebel's work of deception (*planaō*) links her with the dragon, the beastly false prophet and Babylon (12:9; 13:14; 18:23; 19:20).[64] Some interpreters have argued that John slanders and 'demonizes' his prophetic rivals to maintain his authority and influence within the churches.[65] However, Revelation's staunch

---

[62] Luke 1:67; Acts 2:17–18; 19:6; 28:25; 1 Cor. 12:10; 14:32; Eph. 3:5; 2 Peter 1:21.
[63] DeSilva 2009b: 138.
[64] Ibid. 139.
[65] Royalty 2004: 287.

critique of false prophets and teachers has ample biblical precedent, as God's covenant people are repeatedly warned against believing or following so-called prophets who do not speak for God and who distract or deter people from worshipping the true God.[66] Thus the basic concern of the Apocalypse 'is not personal loyalty to John, but collective loyalty to the "commandments of God and the testimony of Jesus"'.[67]

In Revelation 16:13 John sees 'three unclean spirits [*pneumata tria akatharta*] like frogs' that come out of the mouths of the dragon, beast and false prophet, which he identifies as 'spirits of demons' (*pneumata daimoniōn*). Koester notes that ancient writers likened ignorant speech and flattery 'to the meaningless croaking of frogs'.[68] However, the Old Testament and early Jewish writers consistently associate frogs with God's plagues on Egypt.[69] In 16:14 John identifies these froglike spirits as 'demonic spirits' that perform signs, recalling the counterfeit signs that Pharaoh's magicians produced by their secret arts (Exod. 8:7). In 18:2 the angel identifies fallen Babylon as a dwelling for demons and every unclean spirit.

Thus the enigmatic statement in 19:10 is best interpreted in the light of these competing prophetic claims in the Apocalypse. The angel commands John to worship God alone, the ultimate source of this revelation.[70] The 'testimony of Jesus' that John receives is genuine prophecy from the divine Spirit, which should be embraced as 'the true words of God' (19:9; cf. 22:6–8).[71] In contrast, those holding Balaam's teaching, Jezebel and the false prophet all deceive people and lead them into idolatry and rebellion against God. Koester writes:

> The principal criterion for distinguishing true from false prophecy in Revelation is whether a prophet moves people to worship God or lures people away from God (cf. 1 John 4:1–3; 1 Cor. 12:3).[72]

---

[66] See e.g. Deut. 13:1–5; 18:20–22; Jer. 14:14; 23:21; Ezek. 13:6; Matt. 7:15.

[67] DeSilva 2009b: 69.

[68] Koester 2014: 658. Cf. Philo, *Dreams* 2.259; Dio Chrysostom, *Discourses* 8.36; 66.22.

[69] Exod. 7:27 – 8:5; 8:7–9; Pss 77:45; 104:30; Wis. 19.10; *Jub.* 48.5; Josephus, *Jewish Antiquities* 2.296–298; Philo, *Moses* 1.144.

[70] Dixon 2017: 100. Cf. Stuckenbruck 1995: 252.

[71] Similarly, Dixon 2017: 107–108. For further discussion, see ch. 10, pp. 213–215.

[72] Koester 2014: 740. For further discussion of rivalry between true and false prophets in the Apocalypse, see Duff 2001.

Believers should 'hear what the Spirit says to the churches' (Rev. 2:7) through the Revelation of Jesus Christ.[73] Thus 19:10 establishes that the Apocalypse is true Christian prophecy that communicates the witness of the exalted Christ, and the church must heed and hold fast to this testimony as Jesus' witnesses in the world (11:3; cf. 12:17).[74]

The Spirit's messages to the churches

In Revelation 2 – 3 the risen Christ addresses each of the seven churches in Asia, and these messages all conclude with the saying 'Let the one who has ears hear what the Spirit says to the churches' (*ho echōn ous akousatō ti to pneuma legei tais ekklēsiai*).[75] This formula recalls Jesus' repeated exhortation in the Synoptic Gospels 'Let the one having ears hear' (*ho echōn ōta akouetō*).[76] In Mark 4:9–12 Jesus calls those with ears to 'hear' and then cites Isaiah 6:10 to explain why he speaks in parables. In Isaiah 6 God commissioned the prophet to make the people's heart dull, their ears heavy and their eyes blind, thereby confirming them in their unbelief and making them resemble the unresponsive idols that they worshipped.[77] Moses, Jeremiah and Ezekiel offer similar words of judgment on the rebellious and senseless people who refuse to heed their prophetic warnings (Deut. 29:4; Jer. 5:21; Ezek. 3:27; 12:2). These prophetic texts employ malfunctioning sensory organs as poignant metaphors for Israel's spiritual inability to rightly respond to God, which is closely linked to their misdirected worship of idols that cannot see or hear.[78] Additionally, Jesus and the prophets address their parables and teachings to those with 'ears to hear' in order to affect 'the remnant who have become complacent among the compromising majority',[79] moving them to repent of sin and hold fast to God's Word.

Ezekiel 3 offers an important Old Testament parallel to the Spirit's messages to the seven churches. The Spirit enters into Ezekiel (v. 24) and addresses the prophet:

---

[73] 'The "Spirit of prophecy" suggests that it is the Spirit that provided the truth which Jesus revealed,' according to de Smidt (1994: 229).

[74] See further Bauckham 1993b: 121. Cf. ch. 5, pp. 97–101.

[75] My tr. This hearing formula precedes the promise to 'the one who conquers' in Rev. 2:7, 11, 17; it follows the promise in 2:29; 3:6, 13, 22. Cf. Bruce 1973: 340.

[76] Matt. 11:15; 13:9, 43, my tr. Similar formulations occur in Mark 4:9, 23; Luke 8:8; 14:35.

[77] For extensive discussion of this passage, see Beale 2008: 36–70.

[78] Ibid. 49.

[79] Ibid. 245.

> And when I speak to you, I will open your mouth, and you shall say to them, 'This is what the Lord says.' Let the one who hears hear [*ho akouōn akouetō*], and let the one who refuses refuse, for it is an embittering house. (3:27 NETS)

The phrase *ho akouōn akouetō* in 3:27 LXX is similar to the hearing formula in Revelation 2 – 3 and the Gospels. Further, the Spirit speaks these words to the prophet, and the prophet communicates them to the people as the authoritative message of Yahweh (LXX, *Tade legei kyrios*). Similarly, John writes what he sees and hears in a book of prophecy (Rev. 1:3, 11), yet he presents the messages to the seven churches in chapters 2–3 as the authoritative words of the risen Lord Jesus (*Tade legei . . .*) and also the very words of the Spirit.[80]

Koester observes, 'All the messages to the churches are introduced as words of the risen Jesus, yet in the end it is the Spirit that speaks.'[81] Some interpreters conclude that 'this Spirit . . . is no other than the exalted Lord Himself'.[82] However, the Apocalypse maintains both the unity and the distinctness of the divine persons. For example, the opening salutation communicates grace and peace from God, from the seven Spirits before his throne and from Jesus Christ (1:4–5). Elsewhere Christ sits down with his Father on his throne (3:21) and possesses seven eyes, which represent 'the seven Spirits of God sent out into all the earth' (5:6). Thus:

> It is not that the Spirit is identical with the exalted Lord, but that the exalted Lord speaks to the churches by the Spirit – and the Spirit can scarcely be other than the Spirit of prophecy. The words which John writes to the churches by the Lord's command he writes as a prophet.[83]

Christ highlights serious spiritual problems in five of the seven churches he addresses in Revelation 2 – 3 and calls them to 'repent' (see Table 4.1 on p. 82).[84] Ephesus and Laodicea have grown so spiritually complacent that their very identity as Christian churches is in

---

[80] Ibid. 247.
[81] Koester 2014: 264. Bauckham (1993b: 117) writes, 'Thus what the Spirit says is what the exalted Christ says. He inspires the prophetic oracles in which the prophet John speaks Christ's words to the churches.'
[82] Schweizer 1964: 449.
[83] Bruce 1973: 340. Cf. Fee 2013: 28.
[84] Table adapted from Tabb 2015: 2590.

Table 4.1: The structure of the Christ's messages to the seven churches

(1) Christ commands John to write to the church's angel	All
(2) Christ discloses his divine identity and authority	All
(3) Christ knows the church's works	All
(4) Christ commends the church	Ephesus, Smyrna, Pergamum, Thyatira, Philadelphia
(5) Christ censures the church	Ephesus, Pergamum, Thyatira, Sardis, Laodicea
(6) Christ summons them to repent or persevere	All
(7) Christ calls them to hear what the Spirit says	All
(8) Christ promises to bless conquerors	All

jeopardy.[85] Pergamum and Thyatira have tolerated false teachers, idolatry and immorality in their midst, while Sardis is spiritually 'dead' and must 'wake up'. Conversely, though Smyrna and Philadelphia are 'poor' and have 'little power', Christ commends them for their faithfulness and does not call them to repent. Thus the Spirit speaks to a mixed group of faithful and unfaithful churches. The hearing formula calls Christians to understand their true spiritual situation, to recognize the ultimate danger of false worship and then to respond rightly to Christ's Word (13:9–10).

The Spirit speaks to the churches (2:7), moves upon the prophet John (1:10) and communicates the witness of Jesus (19:10). Remarkably, the Spirit speaks directly and distinctly in 14:13 and 22:17. In 14:13 a heavenly voice instructs John to write a promise of blessing for those who die in the Lord. Then John writes, '"Blessed indeed," says the Spirit, "that they may rest from their labours, for their deeds follow them!"' The Spirit's interjecting voice emphatically confirms the truthfulness and importance of this heavenly promise, following the sober call in 14:12 for God's people to endure in obedience and faith.

In 22:16 Jesus declares that he has sent his angel 'to testify to you about these things for the churches', recalling the introductory words of the Apocalypse (1:1–2). Christ then asserts that he is 'the root and

---

[85] Beale 2008: 243.

the descendant of David, the bright morning star', recalling and interpreting significant messianic titles used earlier in the book (2:28; 5:5). Then in 22:17, 'The Spirit and the Bride say, "Come." And let the one who hears say, "Come."' This repeated appeal to 'come' is followed by the invitation to 'the one who thirsts' to come to receive the water of life without price, alluding to God's entreaty to his people in Isaiah 55:1.[86]

Bauckham reasons that the Spirit in 22:17 'is equivalent to the inspired utterance of the Christian prophets, here in the form of Spirit-inspired prayer'.[87] Swete explains that '"the Spirit and the Bride" is thus practically equivalent to "the Prophets and the Saints" (16:6, 18:24)'.[88] To be sure, Revelation emphasizes that the Spirit is the divine agent of prophecy. However, the formulation 'the Spirit . . . says' in 14:13 and 22:17 emphasizes the divine source more than the human agent.

Interpreters debate whether the initial exhortation in verse 17, 'Come', is addressed to Christ, to the unbelieving world or to believers. Many commentators read the singular *erchou* as a prayer to the risen and returning Christ in response to his repeated promise in the epilogue 'I am coming soon' (22:7, 12, 20).[89] Alternatively, Mounce takes the four invitations in verse 17 to be addressed to the world, as 'the testimony of the church empowered by the Holy Spirit that constitutes the great evangelizing force of this age'.[90] However, three considerations suggest that a third view is most likely, that 'come' enjoins the believing community to respond rightly to Christ's revelation. First, verse 18 resumes the first-person singular 'I' of verse 16, which may suggest that 'verses 16–19 are best understood as a continuous speech of the risen Jesus'.[91] Second, the threefold 'come' in verse 17 likely has the same recipient, rather than shifting from Christ to humanity.[92] Third, Isaiah 55:1 likely serves as the model for the threefold appeal to 'come' in Revelation 22:17.[93] A principle difficulty with this reading is that 'the Bride' that here commands readers is

---

[86] On the allusion to Isa. 55:1, see Fekkes 1994: 260–264; Beale 1999: 1149.

[87] Bauckham 1993a: 160. Cf. Beale 1999: 1149.

[88] Swete 1906: 306. Cf. Bruce 1973: 343.

[89] Bauckham 1993a: 160; Smalley 2005: 577; Wall 2006: 267; Boxall 2006: 318; Koester 2014: 844.

[90] Mounce 1997: 409. Cf. Morris 1987: 249.

[91] Michaels 1997: 256.

[92] However, *Didache* 10.6 sets an appeal to believers ('Let him come') alongside a prayer for Christ's return ('Maranatha'). Cf. Bauckham 1993a: 168.

[93] Beale 1999: 1149.

commonly identified as a reference to the Christian community.[94] Earlier, the angel identifies 'the Bride' (*hē nymphē*) as 'the wife of the Lamb' (21:9), which recalls the wedding feast in 19:7 and John's description of the New Jerusalem in 21:2. 'The Bride' is a corporate image for God's redeemed people in their eschatological purity and joy, representing not the church's *present* reality but its *future* identity from the perspective of Christ's return.[95] Thus in 22:17 the risen Christ appeals to two voices from the visionary world[96] – the revelatory Spirit of God and the eschatological people of God – who together urge the book's readers to 'come' to Christ and persevere in faith so as to lay hold of the eschatological inheritance that Christ promises. Believers in the present must hear and heed the Spirit's voice, which summons them through this book of prophecy 'to become the Bride'.[97]

Conclusion

The Apocalypse records competing claims to prophetic revelation, and the churches must discern who speaks for God by the Spirit and who speaks and acts by another 'spirit' at work in the world. On the one hand, the sevenfold divine Spirit that surrounds the throne of God (Rev. 1:4; 4:5) and rests upon the Davidic king (5:5–6; cf. Isa. 11:1–2 LXX) has been 'sent out into all the earth' (Rev. 5:5). On the other, 'unclean spirits like frogs' spew forth from the lying lips of the beast and its prophet to inspire rebellion among the kings of the whole earth (16:13). The witnesses of Jesus receive his authority to prophesy and perform signs (11:3–6), but the lamblike false prophet receives authority from the beast of the sea and also accomplishes great signs (13:12–13).[98]

Jesus cautioned that false prophets come 'in sheep's clothing' and will 'perform great signs and wonders, so as to lead astray, if possible, even the elect' (Matt. 7:15; 24:24), echoing Old Testament warnings about lying prophets (Deut. 13:1–3; Jer. 14:14; 23:16). The risen Christ rebukes the churches for tolerating false teachers and prophets and failing to recognize them by their fruits. The names 'Balaam' and

[94] E.g. Morris (1987: 249) writes, '*The bride* is the church' (emphasis original).
[95] Bauckham 1993a: 167.
[96] Koester (2014: 844) writes, 'It is preferable . . . to take the Spirit and bride as voices from the visionary world, which readers overhear in John's narration.'
[97] Bauckham 1993a: 167.
[98] The description of the false prophet 'like a lamb' in Rev. 13:11 parodies Jesus as the Lamb. See ch. 6, pp. 121–124.

'Jezebel' in Revelation 2:14, 20 recall the prototypical false prophet and the notorious patroness of false worship in the Old Testament, signalling for readers the true character of these rival teachers who condone idolatry and immorality.

In contrast, John claims that he receives divine visions and is carried along 'in the Spirit' like the prophet Ezekiel (Rev. 1:10; 4:2; 17:3; 21:10; cf. Ezek. 11:24; 37:1). In the Apocalypse John bears witness to 'the word of God and to the testimony of Jesus' (1:2), which he has received from the divine Spirit (19:10). The churches must resist the seductive claims of the false prophet and other prophets and spiritual authorities who deceive people by another 'spirit' (2:14, 20; 13:11–18; 16:13–14). The divine Spirit inspires true prophecy that promotes true worship of God alone.

Part II:
Worship and witness

Chapter Five

Followers of the Lamb: the suffering, witnessing, reigning people of God

To him who loves us and has freed us from our sins by his blood and made us a kingdom, priests to his God and Father, to him be glory and dominion for ever and ever. Amen. (Rev. 1:5–6)

And they have conquered him by the blood of the Lamb and by the word of their testimony, for they loved not their lives even unto death. (Rev. 12:11)

The seer John writes this book of prophecy to the seven churches in Asia (Rev. 1:3–4). Through John's prophetic pen the risen Christ addresses particular challenges these late first-century churches face, such as persecution and slander (2:9–10, 13; 3:8–10), false teaching (2:3, 6, 14–15, 20), spiritual complacency (2:4; 3:1–2, 15–17) and immoral compromise (2:14, 20–21). These historical assemblies in Asia Minor represent the church universal, suggested by the symbolic number seven and the repeated refrain 'Whoever has ears, let them hear what the Spirit says to *the churches*' (2:7, 11, 17, 29; 3:6, 13, 22; cf. 22:16). As the Muratorian Fragment (c. AD 170) states, 'John . . . though he writes to seven churches, nevertheless speaks to all' (lines 57–60). The Apocalypse's symbolic visions recast these believers' present, earthly struggles in the light of heavenly, ultimate realities of cosmic spiritual war and divine judgment and salvation. DeSilva writes:

As a letter, Revelation is anchored firmly in the historical situation of the seven churches it addresses . . . As prophecy, Revelation purports to bring a word from the Lord into a specific situation for specific people . . . As an apocalypse, Revelation spreads before the eyes of the Christians in Asia Minor that larger canopy of space and time that puts their mundane reality, along with its challenges and options, in its 'true' light and proper perspective . . . More than seeking to *be interpreted*, Revelation seeks to interpret the reality of the audience.[1]

This chapter explores Revelation's multifaceted depiction of God's end-time people. Those redeemed by the Lamb's blood serve as priests (Rev. 1:6; 5:10; 20:6; cf. Exod. 19:6), reigning kings (Rev. 1:6; 2:26–27; 3:21; 5:10; 20:6; cf. Ps. 2:9) and prophets testifying to Jesus in the Spirit's power (Rev. 11:3–6; 19:10). The churches are pictured as golden lampstands (1:20), a rich biblical image drawn from Israel's temple that stresses believers' vocation as bearers of divine testimony and presence in an evil, unbelieving world (cf. 11:3–4). They are the new Israel, the people of the Messiah, composed of every tribe, language and nation (5:9–10; 7:4–10). Believers must 'conquer' by resisting the seductive power of sin and holding fast to the testimony of Jesus, that they might share in the Lamb's victory and reign with him for ever in the glorious new creation (12:11; 21:7).[2]

A priestly kingdom

The opening doxology in Revelation 1:5–6 extols Jesus Christ, 'who loves us and has freed us from our sins by his blood and made us a kingdom, priests to his God and Father'. The combination of kingdom (*basileian*) and priests (*hiereis*) likely alludes to Exodus 19:6, where Yahweh calls Israel 'a kingdom of priests' (MT, *mamleket kōhănîm*) or 'priestly kingdom' (LXX, *basileion hierateuma*). Further, the reference to Christ's love and redemptive work conceptually parallel Exodus 19:4–5, where Yahweh reminds Israel that he has rescued them from Egypt and brought them to himself as his 'treasured possession among all peoples'. All the earth belongs to Yahweh as the supreme Creator, but he insists that he has chosen and delivered Israel and entrusts them with his covenant. The expression 'kingdom of priests' aptly summarizes Israel's God-given vocation as priestly mediators of Yahweh's presence, blessing and revelation to all peoples (cf. Isa. 61:6).[3]

---

[1] DeSilva 2009b: 14, emphasis original.

[2] This chapter will not discuss Revelation's presentation of God's people as the bride of the Lamb (19:7–8) and the new Jerusalem (21:2). See ch. 8, pp. 163–186.

[3] The Levitical priesthood does not diminish or supplant Israel as collective royal priesthood, but provides 'a visual model of that vocation' and facilitates it, according to Davies (2004: 240).

The Apocalypse employs the same terms used for Israel in Exodus to refer typologically to the church's identity and vocation in the light of Jesus' consummate act of redemption 'by his blood' (1:5). In 5:9–10 the heavenly worshippers praise Jesus the slain Lamb who ransomed people by his blood and 'made them a kingdom and priests to our God'. In both Exodus and Revelation God's people are redeemed by sacrifice for service as a kingdom of priests.[4]

Daniel 7:13 envisions 'one like a son of man' receiving an indestructible kingdom from the Ancient of Days; then 7:18 promises that God's holy people will 'possess the kingdom for ever'. According to Revelation, Jesus is the Son of Man who receives the promised kingdom that shall never pass away (11:15; cf. Dan. 7:14), and his people 'reign with him' (*basileusousin met' autou*) for a thousand years (20:6) and for ever in the new creation (22:5). As deSilva explains, God shares kingly rule with the saints 'as an extension of the enthronement of God's Anointed'.[5]

Koester argues, 'To be a kingdom does not mean that the redeemed "reign" at present.' Rather, they 'will "reign" only through the resurrection that enables them to participate fully in the benefits of Christ's reign'.[6] Schüssler Fiorenza similarly argues that Revelation does not depict 'a Christian liturgy or priestly liturgical service on earth' while God's throne remains in heaven.[7] However, three considerations suggest that the saints *presently* reign in an inaugurated sense that anticipates their future experience in the consummated kingdom of God and Christ. First, the aorist-tense verb forms *epoiēsen* and *epoiēsas* in 1:6 and 5:10 signal that the risen Christ has already made his people to be a kingdom and priests.[8] Second, John states that he is a fellow partaker with his readers 'in the tribulation and the kingdom [*basileia*] and the patient endurance that are in Jesus' (1:9), which 'implies involvement in three activities and not mere existence in three realms'.[9] Third, while most English translations and many commentators prefer the future tense *basileusousin* in 5:10 (they *shall reign* on the earth), a strong case can be made for the present tense *basileuousin* (they *are reigning* on the earth). The manuscript evidence is evenly divided, with Sinaiticus supporting the future tense and

---

[4] Schüssler Fiorenza 1998: 76; Malone 2017: 163. As Leithart 2018a: 264 writes, 'Passover lurks in the background.'

[5] DeSilva 2009b: 168. Cf. Dan. 7:27.

[6] Koester 2014: 217.

[7] Schüssler Fiorenza 1998: 123–124.

[8] See Beale 1999: 194–195. Bandstra (1992: 17) renders *basileia* 'kingship'.

[9] Beale 1999: 195. Mangina (2012: 102) stresses John's solidarity with the churches.

Alexandrinus the present. The present tense *basileuousin* in 5:10 is the more difficult reading, which scribes may have changed to conform to the future tense in 20:4 and 22:5.[10]

The saints redeemed by Christ's blood constitute a priestly kingdom and confess ultimate allegiance to the Creator God and the Lamb, while resisting the usurping claims of rival authorities aligned with the beast and the dragon. 'Already believer-priest-kings can declare God's praiseworthy acts to the nations and perhaps intercede for the nations.'[11] Yet Christ's followers must also 'keep' his works to the end and 'conquer' (2:26) to share in the promised future reign of Christ in the new creation (22:5). In 2:26–27 Jesus promises that the conqueror will shepherd the nations with an iron rod (*poimanei autous en rhabdō sidēra*), alluding to Psalm 2:9 LXX, 'You shall shepherd them with an iron rod; like a potter's vessel you will shatter them' (NETS). In Revelation 12:5 and 19:15 John clearly applies the promise in Psalm 2:9 to Jesus' messianic reign. Moreover, Jesus introduces himself to this church in Revelation 2:18 as 'the Son of God' – a title derived from Psalm 2:7 – indicating 'he has already begun to fulfill the prophecy of this psalm'.[12] It is noteworthy that Revelation 2:27 follows the Greek translation of Psalm 2:9 (*poimainō*, 'shepherd' or 'rule') rather than the Hebrew (*rʿʿ*, 'smash'), likening this shepherding to clay pots being broken. Moyise comments, 'It is their futile resistance that will be utterly smashed, not the people themselves.'[13] Elsewhere Revelation stresses that believers conquer not by might but by laying down their lives as faithful witnesses as they follow the Lamb (Rev. 14:4; cf. 5:5–6). At the same time, the Lamb who conquered through self-sacrifice will also execute perfect messianic justice, which includes judging his enemies (19:15; cf. Isa. 11:4). Jesus offers believers the very authority he has received from his Father based on the principle of corporate solidarity between the king and his people (Rev. 2:27; cf. 3:21). Jesus the messianic Son fulfils Psalm 2:7–9, and then invites his followers to share in his final rule.[14]

In 20:6 John declares that those who share in the first resurrection 'will be priests of God and of the Messiah and will reign [*basileusousin*] with him for a thousand years' (cf. 20:4). Interpreters have long debated the nature and timing of the thousand-year priestly reign of

---

[10] Bandstra 1992: 18–20.
[11] Malone 2017: 161.
[12] Beale and McDonough 2007: 1095.
[13] Moyise 2004: 234.
[14] Quek 2009: 184–185.

deceased, vindicated believers. Premillennialists interpret 20:4 as portraying the future resurrection and earthly reign of believers after Jesus' return.[15] Conversely, amillennialists typically explain 20:4 as describing the present experience of deceased believers who come to life spiritually and reign with Christ in heaven until his return.[16] Some amillenialists argue that the 'first resurrection' (20:5) denotes the moment of conversion when believers are united to Christ by faith.[17]

On balance, verses 4 and 6 most likely refer to the so-called 'intermediate state' of believers who die and reign in heaven with Christ until his return. The 'souls' John sees in 20:4 are described in nearly identical terms to the martyrs introduced with the fifth seal:[18]

> I saw under the altar *the souls* [*tas psychas*] of those who had been slain *for the word of God and for the witness they had borne* [*dia ton logon tou theou kai dia tēn martyrian hēn eichon*]. (6:9)

> Also I saw *the souls* [*tas psychas*] of those who had been beheaded *for the testimony of Jesus and for the word of God* [*dia tēn martyrian Iēsou kai dia ton logon tou theou*]. (20:4)

In 6:11 the slain saints receive white robes and experience blissful rest in heaven as they await comprehensive divine vindication at the resurrection. The white robes do not refer to their actual glorified resurrection bodies but signify their worthiness and purity as those who have remained faithful to Christ and thus have 'conquered' (3:4–5; 12:11).[19] Revelation 14:13 pronounces that those who die in the Lord are 'blessed' and may 'rest from their labours', which recalls the promise of rest in 6:11 and anticipates the blessing for those who share in 'the first resurrection' in 20:6.[20]

Moreover, 20:4–6 closely parallels Christ's words to the suffering Smyrnan church:

> Be faithful unto death, and I will give you the crown *of life* [*ton stephanon tēs zōēs*] . . . The one who conquers will not be hurt by the *second death* [*tou thanatou tou deuterou*]. (2:10–11)

---

[15] For representative treatments, see Osborne 2002: 703–710; Waymeyer 2016: 207–242.

[16] See Beale 1999: 991–1007; Storms 2013: 451–474.

[17] Riddlebarger 2003: 115.

[18] Storms 2013: 457–458.

[19] Beale 1999: 394. Contra Charles 1920: 1:184–188.

[20] Kline 1975: 373.

They *came to life* [*ezēsan*] and reigned with Christ for a thousand years . . . Blessed and holy is the one who shares in the first resurrection! Over such *the second death* [*ho deuteros thanatos*] has no power. (20:4–6)

Both passages contrast believers' experience of physical death with their exemption from the everlasting 'second death' in the lake of fire (cf. 21:8). 'The crown of life' represents eternal life, which God bestows on his victorious people after death.[21] A crown (*stephanos*) signifies honour, victory in athletics or war, or possession of a high office;[22] crowns have regal connotations frequently in the Apocalypse (cf. 4:4, 10; 6:2; 9:7; 12:1; 14:14). Given the common reference to the 'second death' in 2:10 and 20:6, it is plausible to understand John's depiction of the saints living and reigning with Christ in 20:4 as closely related to the promise of 'the crown of life' in 2:10.[23]

Finally, in 20:4 John sees 'thrones, and seated on them were those to whom the authority to judge was committed'. Amillennialists identify these thrones as in heaven during the inter-Advent period and understand 20:4–6 to offer heavenly perspective on the events in 20:1–3. Alternatively, premillennialists argue that the angel coming from heaven (20:1) and the mention of 'the nations' (v. 3) signal that these 'thrones' are on earth during the thousand years. Thrones in the Apocalypse typically designate places of heavenly authority under the Almighty's supreme rule (4:4; 11:16). Gallusz explains, 'Throughout the book God's throne, along with the Lamb's throne and the thrones of their allies, are located exclusively in the heavenly context, whereas the thrones of God's adversaries are limited to the earth.'[24] The new creation in chapter 21 reverses this pattern 'since it provides a context for the relocation of the heavenly throne to the new earth'.[25] Thus the thrones in 20:4 are most likely situated in heaven, where God reigns and where the victorious Lamb has taken his seat as well (3:21; 4:2).

Interpreters debate whether the thrones' occupants are the heavenly elders, vindicated martyrs or all the saints.[26] The scene in Revelation

---

[21] Blount 2013: 78. Cf. Rev. 3:11; Jas 1:12. The genitive *tēs zōēs* in Rev. 2:10 is likely epexegetical ('the crown which is life'), as noted by *NIDNTTE*, 4: 372; Mathewson 2016: 26.

[22] L&N 6.192.

[23] Kline 1975: 373.

[24] Gallusz 2014: 335.

[25] Ibid.

[26] For representative surveys, see Koester 2014: 771; Gallusz 2014: 195–197.

20:4 likely alludes to Daniel 7:9, 22: Daniel sees 'thrones are set up' around the Ancient of Days, who judges in favour of the saints and awards them the kingdom.[27] Most likely, those sitting on the thrones are specified later in verse 4 as 'the souls of those who had been beheaded', namely 'those who had not worshipped the beast or its image'.[28] This description particularly fits the martyrs (cf. 6:9), who are 'exemplary conquerors' representing the faithful church (cf. 12:11).[29] The Danielic background suggests that *krima edothē autois* in verse 4 means 'judgment was passed in their favor' rather than 'they were given authority to judge'.[30]

In 3:21 Jesus promised conquerors that they would sit with him on his throne as he conquered and took his seat on the Father's throne. This promise is fully realized when the throne of God and the Lamb takes centre stage in the Edenic city of God and the saints reign for ever (22:3, 5). However, 20:4–6 suggests that deceased believers experience life and blessing in heaven with Christ and begin to reign with him during the church age while anticipating the consummation of his kingdom in the new creation.

The Apocalypse presents a glorious future for God's people, who will offer continuous priestly worship as they 'will serve [*latreuousin*] him day and night in his temple' (7:15; cf. 20:6; 22:3).[31] Believers will not only serve as priests and share in Christ's reign (2:26–27; 3:21; 5:10; 20:4, 6; 22:5); they will also experience eternal joy, divine protection and abundant life in God's presence as Jesus the Lamb 'will be their shepherd' (7:16–17).

Lampstands

In the book's opening vision John sees 'one like a son of man' in the midst of seven golden lampstands (Rev. 1:12–13; 2:1). The risen Christ explains that the seven lampstands represent 'the seven churches' to whom John writes (1:20; cf. 1:4, 11). He then identifies himself to the church at Ephesus as the one who holds the seven stars

---

[27] Beale and McDonough 2007: 1146–1147.

[28] The Greek syntax of Rev. 20:4 is difficult and debated. I understand the conjunctions in the phrases *kai tas psychas* and *kai hoitines* as epexegetical, identifying those seated on the throne with the souls of the beheaded and those who refused to worship the beast. Cf. Mathewson 2016: 275–276.

[29] Koester 2014: 771.

[30] Beale 1999: 997.

[31] Cf. ch. 9, pp. 198–201.

and walks among the seven lampstands (2:1), emphasizing his sovereign authority and watchful presence among his people.

The lampstand is rich with biblical-theological associations. A golden lampstand with seven lamps was set up in the holy place of the tabernacle (Exod. 25:31–40; 37:17–24; Heb. 9:2), and was to remain lit 'from evening to morning' (Lev. 24:3). The temple built during Solomon's reign featured ten golden lampstands in front of the inner sanctuary (1 Kgs 7:49; 2 Chr. 4:7, 20). The seven lamps of the lampstand may symbolize the seven heavenly lights created by God that were visible to the naked eye.[32] Further, the original lampstand resembled an almond tree with six 'branches', each with 'bulbs and flowers' (Exod. 25:33–34) and may recall the ancient 'tree of life',[33] which signified God's life-giving presence in Eden.

In Zechariah 4:2 the prophet receives a vision of a golden lampstand and two olive trees, which symbolizes Zerubbabel's rebuilding the temple in reliance on the divine Spirit not human might (4:6, 9). In Revelation 11:3–4 John recalls and develops the imagery in Zechariah 4 by identifying the two witnesses as 'lampstands' and 'olive trees'.[34] Since 1:20 explains that 'lampstands' signify churches, the witnesses in Revelation 11 likewise denote not individuals but the corporate people of God, who testify to Christ and summon the unbelieving world to repent.[35]

The Apocalypse's use of 'lampstands' as a major symbol for the churches is significant for several reasons. First, this symbol highlights the basic contrast between the church and the world, between light and darkness. Light is associated throughout Scripture with God's own presence and his work as Creator, Revealer, and Saviour (e.g. Gen. 1:3; Isa. 9:2; Ps. 27:1; 43:3), while darkness signifies God's absence and human sin and ignorance (Isa. 5:20; John 3:19).[36] Lampstands provide light during the darkness of night (Lev. 24:3). As in the plagues on Egypt, the Apocalypse presents darkness as one of God's most severe judgments on the beast and his kingdom (Rev. 16:10; cf. 8:12).[37] Conversely, John declares that 'there will be no night'

---

[32] Cf. Josephus, *Jewish Antiquities* 3.145; Beale 2004: 34–35.
[33] Beale 2004: 71. Cf. ch. 9, pp. 188–193.
[34] Jauhiainen (2005: 90) calls 11:4 'one of the most obvious OT allusions in Revelation'.
[35] See further ch. 5, pp. 97–101.
[36] Borchert 2000: 644–646.
[37] See further ch. 7, pp. 153–158.

in the New Jerusalem, which will be illuminated completely by the Lord God himself (21:25; 22:5).

Second, the lampstand imagery signals that God's people must bear the light of God's presence and truth in the world through faithful living and speaking in the Spirit's power (11:3; 12:11). In Matthew 5:16 Jesus calls believers 'the light of the world' and summons them to let their 'light shine before others'. As lampstands, God's people do not produce light intrinsically themselves but hold up the illuminating, life-giving presence of God as they speak 'the word of God' and 'the testimony of Jesus' (1:2, 9; 20:4; cf. 12:11). The association between lampstands and witnesses in 11:3–4 informs Jesus' warning to the Ephesian church in 2:5 that he will come and remove their lampstand unless they repent. Removing Ephesus' lampstand may mean losing its identity as a church witnessing to Christ. Christian readers of the Apocalypse should embrace their identity as lampstands and live accordingly, eschewing worldly compromise and cowardice and anticipating the future day when the light of God's glorious presence will eradicate all the darkness.

Prophetic witnesses

The book of Revelation frequently employs the legal terms 'witness' and 'testimony'.[38] John presents Jesus as 'the faithful witness' (1:5; 3:14) who declares divine truth and serves as an example for his followers. The expression 'the testimony of Jesus' occurs six times in the Apocalypse. *Iēsou* may function as an objective genitive – John's testimony *about* Jesus (HCSB, NET) – or, more likely, as a subjective genitive – the testimony borne *by* Jesus.[39] John explains he himself 'bore witness [*emartyrēsen*] to the word of God and to the testimony of Jesus [*tēn martyrian Iēsou Christou*], even to all that he saw' (1:2) and states that he endures present affliction and is relegated to the island of Patmos on account of this 'testimony' (1:9).[40] Thus John presents the revelatory contents of the book as both genuine prophecy and eyewitness testimony. In 20:4 John sees the souls of those beheaded 'for the testimony of Jesus and for the word of God'. Revelation 12:17

---

[38] See ch. 3, pp. 53–55.

[39] Trites 1977: 156–158. See also Bauckham 1993b: 72; Aune 1997: 19. The genitive in 1:2 'includes both subjective and objective aspects', according to Beale (1999: 184). Cf. Bandy 2010b: 120–121; Paul 2018: 59–60.

[40] John's punishment was likely 'relegation to an island' rather than permanent 'deportation', which entailed the loss of property, according to Koester (2014: 242–243).

and 19:10 refer to other believers who 'hold to the testimony of Jesus'; then in 19:10b the angel clarifies that this testimony is 'the spirit/Spirit of prophecy'. Bauckham explains that 'when the Spirit inspires prophecy, its content is the witness of Jesus'.[41]

Jesus' reference to Antipas as 'my faithful witness' (*ho martys mou ho pistos mou*) in 2:13 unmistakably recalls Jesus' own identity as 'the faithful witness' (1:5; 3:14). The context indicates that Antipas remained true to Jesus' name, did not deny faith in him and was executed for his testimony and allegiance to Jesus, 'where Satan lives' (2:13). John, Antipas and other faithful Christians 'follow the Lamb' (14:4) and must testify to the truth amidst political, social and spiritual opposition. Hays writes, 'Their identity as suffering witnesses is patterned on Jesus' identity as Faithful Witness, which finds its definitive embodiment in his own death on a cross.'[42]

Following John's prophetic recommissioning to prophesy 'about many peoples and nations and languages and kings' (10:11), John introduces two witnesses who are authorized to prophesy for 1,260 days (11:3).[43] There are various interpretations of these two witnesses.[44] Ancient and medieval readers typically identified the witnesses as Enoch and Elijah, Old Testament prophets who were taken directly to heaven and might return (Gen. 5:24; 2 Kgs 2:11; Mal. 4:5–6; Sir. 44.16; 48.9–10).[45] Some readers take these witnesses to be Moses and Elijah because they shut the sky, turn water into blood and bring plagues like these pre-eminent Old Testament figures, who are also grouped together at the close of the prophetic books (Mal. 4:4–6) and at the transfiguration (Mark 9:4).[46] Others interpret the two witnesses as symbolic depictions of the whole church or the faithful, persecuted part of the church.[47]

---

[41] Bauckham 1993b: 119. Similarly, Caird 1984: 238. For further discussion, see ch. 4, pp. 76–80.

[42] Hays 2012: 79. Cf. Rev. 12:11, 17, discussed in ch. 5, pp. 102–108.

[43] For discussion of John's commissioning in Rev. 10, see ch. 10, pp. 210–213.

[44] For the brief history of interpretation, see Koester 2014: 439–440, 497–498.

[45] Cf. Tertullian, *The Soul* 50; Hippolytus, *On Christ and Antichrist* 43. For detailed analysis of Christian and Jewish traditions about the return of Enoch and Elijah, see Bauckham 1976: 447–458.

[46] Thomas 1995: 88–89. Wong (1997: 347) reasons that they are unknown individuals 'who will minister in the spirit and power of Moses and Elijah in the future tribulation period'.

[47] Beale 1999: 573–575; Mounce 1997: 217; Witherington 2003: 158–159; Dalrymple 2011: 34–40. Osborne (2002: 417–418) argues the witnesses are historical individuals at the end of history patterned after Elijah and Moses and also corporate representatives of the church.

Most likely, the two witnesses signify the whole church. The decisive evidence for this reading comes in 11:4, where the witnesses are described as 'the two olive trees and the two lampstands that stand before the Lord of the earth'. The combination of lampstands and olive trees alludes to Zechariah's vision of a golden lampstand with an olive tree on either side of it (Zech. 4:2–3).[48] The context suggests that the lampstand in Zechariah 4 signifies the temple, whose foundation had been laid.[49] The olive trees are called 'the two anointed ones who stand by the Lord of the whole earth' (4:14), which many interpreters identify as Joshua the high priest (3:1) and Zerubbabel the governor (4:8–9),[50] who were instrumental in rebuilding of Israel's temple after exile (Hag. 1:14–15). Zechariah's vision offers assurance that Zerubbabel will complete the work in the Spirit's power (Zech. 4:6).[51] Alternatively, these two 'sons of oil' in 4:14 may designate the prophets Zechariah and Haggai, whose ministry is closely linked with the temple rebuilding (8:9; cf. Ezra 5:1–2; 6:14–15).[52] On balance, the latter interpretation is preferable and finds support in Revelation 11:10, which identifies the witnesses as 'two prophets'. The Apocalypse adapts and reinterprets Zechariah's symbols by presenting *two* lampstands and identifying them with the olive trees. In 1:20 the exalted Christ reveals that the seven golden lampstands John saw are *churches* (cf. 2:5). By describing the witnesses as olive trees who 'stand before the Lord of the earth', John further reinforces their divinely authorized prophetic ministry. Additionally, if the lampstand in Zechariah's vision signifies the temple that would be built despite opposition, John is calling his readers to see that the eschatological temple of God, the community of faith among whom God himself dwells, will be established through the church's bold, prophetic witness.

The *two* lampstands in 11:4 may identify these witnesses with the faithful churches of Smyrna and Philadelphia that do not receive an accusation from the risen Christ in chapters 2–3. More likely, the number recalls the Old Testament requirement for at least two witnesses to establish a legal charge (Num. 35:30; Deut. 17:6; 19:15). This symbolic number suggests that John envisions the people of God

---

[48] See Table 5.1 on p. 100, adapted from Tabb 2015: 2605. For additional discussion of the allusion to Zech. 4, see Jauhiainen 2005: 89–93.
[49] Beale and McDonough 2007: 1119.
[50] McComiskey 1992: 1903.
[51] Smith 1984: 204.
[52] Petterson 2015: 156–157.

Table 5.1: The use of the Old Testament in Revelation 11

Two witnesses in Revelation 11	Old Testament background
'my two witnesses' (v. 3)	'testimony of two . . . witnesses' (Deut. 19:15)
'1,260 days' (v. 3; cf. 11:2; 12:6, 14)	'time, times, and half a time' (Dan. 7:25)
'two olive trees' (v. 4)	'two olive trees' (Zech. 4:3, 11)
'two lampstands' (v. 4; cf. 1:20)	'a lampstand all of gold' (Zech. 4:2)
'fire pours from their mouths' (v. 5)	'fire came down from heaven' (2 Kgs 1:10); 'my words in your mouth a fire' (Jer. 5:14)
'shut the sky, that no rain may fall' (v. 6)	'neither dew nor rain . . . except by my word' (1 Kgs 17:1; cf. Luke 4:25)
'waters . . . into blood' (v. 6)	'water . . . into blood' (Exod. 7:17)
'the beast will make war on them and conquer them' (v. 7; cf. 13:5, 7)	the beast's 'horn made war with the saints and prevailed over them' (Dan. 7:21)
'a breath of life . . . entered them, and they stood up on their feet' (v. 11)	'the breath came into them, and they lived and stood on their feet' (Ezek. 37:10)

bearing witness to establish God's legal charge against the unbelieving world that refuses to heed their call to repentance.[53]

The two witnesses are 'identical prophetic twins'.[54] They wear sackcloth to signify their lament over sin and their message of repentance (11:3).[55] The fire from their mouth (11:5) alludes to the depiction of the prophet's word of judgment in Jeremiah 5:14. The witnesses perform signs characteristic of Elijah (shutting the sky) and Moses (turning water into blood) in Revelation 11:6 (cf. 1 Kgs 17:1; Exod. 7:17). They prophesy for three-and-a-half years (Rev. 11:3) – the same length of time that the holy city is trampled (11:2) and that the dragon and the beast oppress God's people (12:6, 14; 13:5).[56] This symbolic forty-two-month period of tribulation recalls 'a time, times and half

---

[53] Beale 1999: 575. Leithart (2018a: 432) posits that the two witnesses represent the Jewish and Gentile church 'united in common testimony to Jesus'.
[54] Beale 1999: 575. Cf. Bauckham 1993a: 275–277.
[55] Smalley 2005: 276.
[56] For discussion of Rev. 12:6, 14, see ch. 5, pp. 105–107.

a time' in Daniel 7:25 and 12:7. Further, Revelation 11:7 states that the beast wars against and conquers the witnesses, and in 13:7 the beast does precisely the same thing to 'the saints'. This alludes to Daniel 7:21, where the beast's horn makes war with the saints.[57] Following the witnesses' apparent defeat, 'a breath of life from God entered them, and they stood up on their feet' (Rev. 11:11). This dramatic reversal alludes to Ezekiel 37:5, 10, the prophet's famous vision of Israel's revival after exile. These Old Testament links offer further support for identifying the two witnesses as a corporate symbol for the people of God.

John's vision of the two witnesses in Revelation 11:3–11 contributes to the Apocalypse's theology of the people of God in at least two key ways. First, this passage illustrates that the church's identity as lampstands (1:20; 2:5) is expressed through prophetic testimony (11:3–6). Such testimony will 'torment' unbelievers who refuse to repent and will prompt vigorous antagonism from the beast and his followers (11:7–10). The church must hold fast to its testimony knowing that God will surely vindicate his people and judge his enemies (11:11–13).

Second, John identifies the witnesses as 'prophets' (11:10; cf. 11:3), thus extending the designation of prophet to the believing community that holds to the 'testimony of Jesus' (19:10). John is uniquely called and authorized to write what he sees in a book of authoritative prophecy in the tradition of the Old Testament prophets (1:1–2, 11, 19; 22:6–7, 18–19).[58] In 22:9 the angel refers to John's 'brothers the prophets', which likely designates a circle of Christian prophets.[59] Nevertheless, the Old Testament anticipated a time when God would pour out his spirit on all his people and they would 'prophesy' (Num. 11:29; Joel 2:28–29 [3:1–2 LXX]; cf. Acts 2:17–18). While Revelation does not designate all individual Christians as prophets like John, the churches as lampstands have a prophetic vocation in the world as they bear witness to Jesus.[60]

[57] Beale 1999: 574.

[58] See ch. 10, pp. 210–213.

[59] Koester 2014: 91, 840. Alternatively, Beale (1999: 1128–1129) takes the phrase 'and those who keep the words of this book' to define further 'your brothers the prophets' (22:9). He concludes, 'To believe and obey the words of John's prophecy is equivalent to holding the testimony of Jesus.'

[60] Bauckham 1993b: 119–120. Waddell (2006: 128) writes, 'Pentecostals easily identify with John's testimony of being in the Spirit. The communal dimension of the Spirit enables the churches to share in John's experience.' However, Rev. 1:10 does not primarily present John as a model for other believers to follow but stresses his unique role as one who receives authoritative prophetic revelation for the churches.

New Israel

'Revelation portrays the church as the new Israel.'[61] We have seen that John identifies followers of Jesus as 'a kingdom' and 'priests' (Rev. 1:6; 5:10), recalling the well-known description of Israel's vocation in Exodus 19:6. The seven churches are also 'lampstands' (Rev. 1:20), an image associated with Israel's tabernacle and temple. Further, the church's role as 'witnesses' (11:3) alludes to Isaiah's frequent appeal to Israel 'You are my witnesses' (Isa. 43:10, 12; 44:8; cf. Luke 24:48; Acts 1:8). Here we consider several further ways that John presents worshippers of the Lamb from every tribe and nation as the new Israel, the true people of God.

First, between the sixth and seventh seals John receives visions of the 144,000 from Israel's tribes (7:1–8) and a redeemed multitude from all nations (7:9–17). Interpreters come to various conclusions on the identity of the 144,000, the great multitude and the relationship between these visions. Some identify the 144,000 as the '"fulness of Israel", the reunified tribes who had been dispersed by the destruction of Israel and Jerusalem'.[62] Many dispensationalist interpreters take the 144,000 to be ethnic Jews saved during the future tribulation, who evangelize the great multitude.[63] More likely, the number 144,000 represents the complete number of the redeemed people of God.[64] Numbers in Revelation are typically symbolic,[65] and the number 144,000 is twelve squared and multiplied by a thousand, which stresses completeness and perfection (see Table 5.2 on p. 103).[66] Further, the list in 7:4–8 may echo the census in Numbers 1 – 2, which numbered Israel's military force, excluding the tribe of Levi (Num. 1:49).[67] In this reading John hears the census of the complete number of God's eschatological army who

---

[61] Schreiner 2013: 629.

[62] Draper 1983: 136. Cf. Kraft 1974: 127.

[63] See e.g. Thomas 1992: 473–478; MacArthur 1999: 219, 223.

[64] Wilcock 1975: 80–81; Beale 1999: 416–417. For the history of interpretation, see Koester 2014: 350–355.

[65] See Beale 1999: 58–64; Webster 2014: 23–27.

[66] Table adapted from Tabb 2015: 2600.

[67] Paul (2018: 159–160) observes that the role of Israel's twelve tribes in Rev. 7:5–8 does not match any of the eighteen listings in the OT. Revelation's list is distinctive in several ways. First, the tribe of Judah – not Rueben, Jacob's firstborn – heads the list because the messianic king descends from Judah (Gen. 49:9–10; Rev. 5:5). Second, Revelation excludes Dan, a tribe notorious for its idolatry (Judg. 18:29–30; 1 Kgs 12:29–30; Amos 8:14) and includes Manasseh, Joseph's firstborn. For discussion, see Osborne 2002: 313–315.

Table 5.2: The number twelve in Revelation

144,000 believers sealed (12 × 12 × 1000)	7:4–8; 14:1, 3
12 stars in the woman's crown	12:1
12 gates and pearls in the holy city Jerusalem	21:12, 21
12 angels	21:12
12 tribes of the sons of Israel	21:12
12 foundations for the city's walls	21:14
12 apostles	21:14
12,000 stadia for the city's dimensions (12 × 1000)	21:16
144 cubits for the walls' height (12 × 12)	21:17
12 kinds of fruit from the tree of life	22:2

will wage war on their spiritual enemies through faithful witness (cf. Rev. 12:11).[68]

The vision of the 144,000 immediately follows the opening of the sixth seal, which brings the terrifying wrath of the Lamb before which no one can stand (6:12–17). The visions in chapter 7 offer an interlude between the final two seals that highlight the situation of God's people. The angels given power to harm the earth (7:1) must wait until God's servants are 'sealed' with 'the seal of the living God' (7:2–3).[69] Sealing conveys both protection and belonging. John's vision likely recalls Ezekiel 9:4–6, where the Lord calls a man clothed in linen to pass through Jerusalem and mark the foreheads of the faithful who lament the city's abominations. When the six executioners pass through the city to execute God's wrath, only those with the mark are spared. In Revelation 9:4 those with God's seal on their foreheads are protected from the tormenting judgment of the locusts. Those sealed are 'the servants of God' (7:3), who receive divine revelation (1:1; 22:6), praise God for his mighty deeds (15:3; 19:5) and will worship him for ever in the new creation (22:3). Those who revere and serve the beast and its image receive a mark (*charagma*) on their foreheads or hands (13:16; 14:9). The redeemed do not receive the beast's mark (20:4) but have the name of the Lamb and the Father written on their foreheads (14:1; 22:4; cf. 3:12). Israel's high priest wore a turban with a golden plate engraved with the words 'Holy to Yahweh' (Exod. 28:36–38), but Revelation identifies all those redeemed by Jesus as 'priests' who are sealed with God's name

---

[68] Bauckham 1993a: 216–220. Cf. 1QM 2.7–8.
[69] For additional discussion of 'sealing' in the Apocalypse, see ch. 10, pp. 213–215.

(1:6; 5:10).[70] The seal identifies those who belong to God rather than to the beast, who are thus protected from divine wrath.

In 7:4–8 John *hears* the number (*arithmon*) of those sealed from every tribe of Israel, but in 7:9–10 the prophet *sees* a great multi-ethnic multitude that no one could number (*arithmēsai*). In Revelation 5:5–6 John *hears* titles that evoke Old Testament messianic promises (the Lion of Judah, the Root of David), but he *sees* a slaughtered, standing Lamb. Similarly, the sight of 'a great multitude that no one could number, from every nation, from all tribes and peoples and languages' reinterprets nationalistic expectation and also recalls God's promise to multiply Abraham's descendants (Gen. 13:16; 15:5; 22:18; 26:4; cf. 32:12).[71]

John sees the great multitude *standing* (*hestōtes*) before the divine throne and the Lamb (7:9), which answers the question of 6:17: 'for the great day of their wrath has come, and who can stand?' While the unredeemed tremble in terror on the day of the Lord's judgment, the redeemed stand securely before the divine throne. This multitude comes from every nation and all tribes, peoples and languages, identifying them with the ransomed people of God described in 5:9. Their white robes recall those given to the martyrs (6:11) and promised to the conquerors (3:4–5, 18). In 7:14 the angel explains that they 'have washed their robes and made them white in the blood of the Lamb' (cf. 22:14). John sees the redeemed throng holding palm branches, which may symbolize victory in athletic contests or battle.[72] More likely, the palm branches in 7·9 recall the feast of tabernacles that memorialized Israel's exodus from Egypt (Lev. 23:40–43; John 12:13; cf. 2 Macc. 10.6–7; Josephus, *Jewish Antiquities* 3.245), which anticipated their future redemption (Zech. 14:16). The worshippers declare, 'Salvation [*sōtēria*] belongs to our God . . . and to the Lamb' (Rev. 7:10), which may be a further nod to the exodus, the paradigmatic occasion of divine salvation in the Old Testament (Exod. 14:13; 15:2).

Therefore, the 144,000 sons of Israel and the great multitude from every nation are most likely two complementary pictures of the same reality – the redeemed people of God.[73] The first picture of the sealed

---

[70] Koester 2014: 416. Rev. 22:3–4 further identifies God's redeemed people as priests in the eschatological temple city, as discussed in ch. 9, pp. 198–201.

[71] Bauckham 1993a: 223; Beale and McDonough 2007: 1108.

[72] See Philo, *Unchangeable* 137; 1 Macc. 13.36; Aristotle, *Magna moralia* 1.33 1196A 36; Plutarch, *Moralia* 723A–724F; Koester 2014: 420.

[73] White (2013: 196) characterizes the 144,000 as '[t]ransformed and restored Israel'.

144,000 stresses that God *protects* and *preserves* the complete number of the people who belong to him. The second picture, of the great crowd, stresses that God *saves* his people from every nation, tribe, people and language, accomplishing a new-exodus deliverance by the blood of the Lamb.[74]

A second major image of the church as new Israel comes in Revelation 12:1–6. John sees 'a woman clothed with the sun, with the moon under her feet, and on her head a crown of twelve stars' (12:1). Interpreters have explained the identity of the woman in Revelation 12 in four primary ways: (1) the people of God living before and after Christ's coming, (2) the church, (3) the Jewish community and (4) Mary, the mother of Christ.[75] The first option is most likely: the woman represents the faithful people of God spanning the Old Testament and New Testament ages.

The imagery of sun, moon and stars in Revelation 12:1 recalls Joseph's famous dream in Genesis 37:9 and indicates that the 'twelve stars' represent Israel's tribes. Further, Philo and Josephus explain the high priest's garments as a 'representation of the universe' (*On the Special Laws* 1.95; *Jewish Antiquities* 3.180): the emeralds on the priest's shoulders signify the sun and moon, while the twelve stones on the ephod engraved with the names of the twelve tribes resemble the twelve stars of the zodiac (*Moses* 1.122–24; *Jewish Antiquities* 3.185–186).[76] The starred crown (*stephanos*) on the woman's head (Rev. 12:1) recalls Christ's promise to give 'the crown of life' (*ton stephanon tēs zōēs*) to his people who conquer (2:10; cf. 3:11).[77] The combination of priestly and regal imagery in 12:1 may have priestly associations, which accords with the description of the church as a priestly kingdom in Revelation 1:6 and 5:10 (cf. Exod. 19:6).[78]

The conflict between the dragon and the woman in Revelation 12:3–4 recalls Genesis 3:15, where God promises enmity between the serpent and the woman, whose offspring shall bruise the serpent's head. This link is confirmed in Revelation 12:9, where the dragon is

---

[74] See ch. 7, pp. 158–160.

[75] For discussion and bibliography see Koester 2014: 542–543. Catholic commentator Williamson (2015: 206) reasons that the woman has multiple levels of meaning and represents 'the faithful people of God of the Old and New Testaments' as well as 'Mary, the mother of the Messiah'.

[76] Interpreters who link the twelve stars with the zodiac include Collins 1976: 71–76; Aune 1998a: 681.

[77] Giesen 1997: 227–228.

[78] See Beale 1999: 626–627.

identified as 'that ancient serpent' and 'the deceiver'.[79] In 12:5 the woman gives birth to 'a male child', who is destined to rule the nations and is 'caught up to God'. This telescopic summary recounts the birth of Jesus the Messiah (cf. Gen. 3:15), the promise of his reign over all the nations (cf. Ps. 2:9) and his ascension to the throne of heaven (cf. Rev. 3:21).

The woman then flees to the wilderness and receives divine protection from the dragon and provision for 1,260 days (12:6, 14). This flight to the wilderness recalls Israel's exodus from Egypt (Exod. 16:32) and Israel's promised restoration after exile (Isa. 40:3; Hos. 2:14–15; cf. Matt. 3:3).[80] The eagle wings given to the woman in Revelation 12:14 recall how God bore Israel on eagle's wings (Exod. 19:4). The woman receives nourishment (*trephō*) in the wilderness (12:6, 14), as 'God spread a table in the wilderness' (Ps. 78:19 [77:19 LXX]) and nourished (*trephō*) Israel even though they forgot him (Deut. 32:18 LXX). 1,260 days (Rev. 12:6) or 'a time, and times, and half a time' (12:14) denotes the symbolic period of tribulation for God's people predicted in Daniel 7:25 and 12:7.[81] During the figurative forty-two months, the holy city is trampled (Rev. 11:2), the two witnesses prophesy (11:3) and the beast exercises authority, blasphemes God and wars against his people (13:5–7). John adds that God will protect and preserve his people during this time of intense opposition from the dragon and the beast (12:6, 14).

After the dragon's defeat in the heavenly war (12:7–8) and his unsuccessful pursuit of the woman on earth (vv. 13–16), he furiously makes war 'on the rest of her offspring' (v. 17). The reference to the woman's singular and plural offspring in 12:5, 17 likely alludes to Isaiah 66:7–8 LXX, where Zion 'delivers a male child' (*eteken arsen*) and also 'suffers birth pains and gives birth to her children'. According to Fekkes, 'the ambiguity of the metaphor in Isaiah 66.7–8 allows for *both* an individual birth (the Messiah), and a collective birth (the salvation community)'.[82] Some dispensationalist interpreters identify the woman as Israel (or believing Israel) and her offspring in verse 17 with a believing Jewish remnant, such as

---

[79] The prophets also characterize Pharaoh as 'the great dragon' (Ezek. 29:3; cf. 32:2; Isa. 27:1) and the king of Babylon as 'a dragon' (Jer. 28:34). On links to the new-exodus theme in Revelation, see ch. 7, pp. 160–162.

[80] See Beale 1999: 643–645.

[81] Cf. ch. 5, pp. 97–101; Beale 1999: 643, 646–647. Leithart (2018a: 426) suggests forty-two months and reckons this time period by the lunar cycle, while 1,260 days calculates the time according to the sun.

[82] Fekkes 1994: 185, emphasis original; cf. Aune 1998a: 708; Beale 1999: 677.

the 144,000.[83] However, the explanatory phrase 'on those who keep the commandments of God and hold to the testimony of Jesus' most naturally refers to the inclusive Christian community, given the parallel description of 'the saints' in Revelation 14:12.[84] In 12:10b–11 the dragon constantly accuses 'our brothers' but 'they have conquered him by the blood of the Lamb and by the word of their testimony'. Thus 'the rest of her offspring' (v. 17) are God's holy people, the followers of Jesus – the royal child (v. 5) – who suffer threats and assaults from the dragon and yet achieve ultimate victory over their ancient enemy (cf. Gen. 3:15) through the Lamb's sacrificial death on the cross and their testimony that aligns them with Jesus the 'faithful witness' and overcomes the dragon's false accusations and deceptions (vv. 10, 15) by speaking the truth.[85]

The cumulative evidence suggests the woman in Revelation 12 links her with the faithful people of God throughout redemptive history. The twelve stars in her crown (v. 1) represent Israel's twelve tribes (Gen. 37:9), and her birth pangs and bearing of the messianic son recall the foundational promise of a deliverer in Genesis 3:15 and the eschatological hope of Zion in Isaiah 66:7–8. At the same time, the dragon's hostile persecution of the woman after she bears the royal child (Rev. 12:13–16) and the reference to 'the rest of her offspring' (v. 17) point beyond Old Testament Israel and Mary the mother of Jesus to the New Testament people of God who receive divine protection and hold fast to the divine Word. Revelation 12 presents the woman adorned 'in heaven' (v. 1) and persecuted 'on earth' (v. 13–16). The woman represents the singular community of faith spanning the Old and New Testament ages. This people as a collective entity is heir to divine promises of salvation and experiences divine protection. From this singular community of faith comes the messianic king who will rule all the nations and crush the head of the serpent (Rev. 12:5; cf. Gen. 3:15; Ps. 2:9), as well as individual believers who follow the Lamb, bear witness to Jesus, and faithfully endure suffering even unto death, thereby conquering their ancient enemy and inheriting their glorious salvation (Rev. 12:10–11, 17).

Revelation 3:9 presents further evidence that the church is true Israel. Jesus declares to the Philadelphian church, 'Behold, I will make those of the synagogue of Satan who say that they are Jews and are

---

[83] Thomas 1995: 142. However, MacArthur (2000: 34) comments that her offspring is 'an all-inclusive phrase, referring to all those who name the name of Jesus Christ'.
[84] Rightly Osborne 2002: 485.
[85] Cf. ch. 3, pp. 53–55.

not, but lie – behold, I will make them come and bow down before your feet [*hina hēxousin kai proskynēsousin enōpion tōn podōn sou*], and they will learn that I have loved you.' Beale argues that this promise is a 'collective allusion' to four Old Testament texts (Isa. 45:14; 49:23; 60:14; Ps. 86:9 [85:9 LXX]) that 'predict that Gentiles will come and bow down before Israel and Israel's God in the last days'.[86] The nearest verbal parallel to Revelation 3:9 may be Isaiah 49:23 LXX: 'With their faces to the ground they shall bow down to you [*proskynēsousin soi*], and lick the dust of your feet [*tōn podōn sou*].'[87] The final phrase of Revelation 3:9, 'they will learn that I have loved you [*egō ēgapēsa se*]', may recall God's declaration to Israel in Isaiah 43:4 LXX, 'I love you' (*kagō se ēgapēsa*). In Isaiah 43 God's love for his chosen people moves him graciously to redeem them even 'from the end of the earth' (v. 7) and grounds his repeated admonition 'Fear not' (vv. 1, 5).

Thus Jesus promises the mostly Gentile church at Philadelphia that they will be vindicated before their Jewish persecutors, a striking reversal of Old Testament expectations.[88] The exalted Christ expresses and enacts Yahweh's declaration of love for his people (Isa. 43:4) by freeing them from their sins by his blood (Rev. 1:5). He alone holds 'the key of David' (Rev. 3:7; cf. Isa. 22:22) and has supreme authority to grant or withhold access to the kingdom of God.[89] Jesus declares that those claiming to be Jews while persecuting Jesus' followers are really 'the synagogue of Satan' (Rev. 3:9; cf. 2:9). Those who keep Jesus' word and know his love will experience eschatological vindication, while those who deny Christ's name and oppose his people will ultimately be put to shame (3:8–9). Thus 'true Israel' is defined not by ethnicity or synagogue participation but by the saving love of Jesus, the Davidic Messiah, and loyalty to his name.

Conquerors

The verb *nikaō* occurs seventeen times in the Apocalypse and is variously translated 'overcome', 'conquer' and 'be victorious'.[90] The

---

[86] Beale 1999: 288.
[87] Fekkes (1994: 134) claims that John in Rev. 3:9 'has in mind particularly Isa. 60.14'.
[88] Beale 1999: 286–288.
[89] On the typological use of Isa. 22:22 in Rev. 3:7, see Beale 1999: 283–285.
[90] Rev. 2:7, 11, 17, 26; 3:5, 12, 21 [twice]; 5:5; 6:2 [twice]; 11:7; 12:11; 13:7; 15:2; 17:14; 21:7.

term draws upon multiple spheres of meaning, including military conquest, victory in athletic competitions and faithfulness amid opposition.[91] In the Apocalypse the 'victory' motif highlights the tension between the earthly and heavenly perspective on the church's situation in the world. On the one hand, John writes from exile to the seven churches as their companion in tribulation (Rev. 1:9).[92] Jesus' followers face poverty and slander (2:9), imprisonment (2:10), weakness and rejection (3:8–9) and even death 'for the word of God and for the witness they had borne' (6:9; cf. 2:10, 13; 20:4). Further, the beast is permitted to war against and conquer (*nikēsai*) the saints (13:7; cf. 11:7). On the other hand, each of the prophetic messages to the seven churches concludes with a promise of eschatological blessing in the new creation for 'the one who conquers' (*tō nikōnti*). In the climactic vision of the New Jerusalem, the Almighty on the throne declares, 'The one who conquers will inherit these things, and I will be his God and he will be my son' (21:7). Thus the Apocalypse presents the people of God ironically as conquered conquerors, who experience present suffering and defeat yet await ultimate victory.

Boxall observes, 'The language of victory . . . reminds us that in the apocalyptic language of this book there is a battle being fought, albeit one whose outcome has already been established.'[93] The Apocalypse fundamentally recasts readers' perception of true victory by presenting Jesus as the Lion of Judah who has conquered (*enikēsen*) as the slain Lamb (5:5–6) and who will conquer those forces who align with the beast when he returns as Lord of lords, accompanied by his people who are 'called and chosen and faithful' (17:14; cf. 19:11–21).

Thus in the world view of the Apocalypse 'victory' is not a matter of military might, political influence or athletic achievement; rather, it entails enduring faithfulness to Christ and his Word and spiritual conquest against sin and evil. According to 12:11, God's people 'have conquered' (*enikēsan*) Satan the great deceiver 'by the word of their testimony, for they loved not their lives even unto death'.

Beale writes, 'It is not just how people die that proves them to be overcomers, but the whole of their Christian lives are to be

---

[91] Koester 2014: 265.

[92] Dixon (2017: 71–85) challenges the traditional interpretation that John was on the island of Patmos because of persecution. More likely, John 'was relegated to Patmos by the provincial authorities', as explained by Koester (2014: 243).

[93] Boxall 2006: 51.

characterized by "overcoming," which is a process completed at death.'[94] Indeed, 'the martyrs are emblematic of the faithful' as they demonstrate the sort of persevering faith that all believers are called to have.[95] The promises to the victors in the messages to the seven churches anticipate believers' glorious future in the New Jerusalem (cf. 21:7). Conquerors will experience eternal life with God (2:7; 3:5; cf. 21:27; 22:2). They will not be hurt by the second death – the lake of fire (2:11; cf. 20:6; 21:8). They will receive a new name and inheritance in the eternal city (2:17; 3:12). They will share in Christ's reign (2:26–28; 3:21). These promises function as incentives and invitations for embattled believers to persevere in following Christ and share in the inheritance in the New Jerusalem.[96]

Thus the Apocalypse redefines 'victory' as faithfulness to Christ, the slain and risen Lamb, who is seated on the divine throne and offers believers a share in his eschatological reign (3:21). Koester writes:

> Revelation transforms the images of conquest and victory, which brought high honor in Graeco-Roman culture, into a call for Christians to resist aspects of that culture. Faithfulness to Jesus could bring dishonor in society, yet in Christ's eyes the faithful are worthy of the victory wreath.[97]

God's people may face scorn, suffering or even slaughter, but they must remember that they will share in the Lamb's victory (17:14) and conquer even now by their faithful testimony to Jesus (12:11).

Conclusion

The Apocalypse clarifies and dramatizes the church's true identity, present struggle and future hope. God's people are presented as lampstands (1:20) who must bear divine light and truth in a dark world. The church expresses this light-bearing vocation as Jesus' witnesses, who proclaim truth about Jesus, follow him in his experience of suffering and rejection and thus establish the legal charge against the unbelieving world that refuses to repent and submit to God's rule (11:3).

---

[94] Beale 1999: 271.
[95] Koester 2014: 552. Cf. Bauckham 1993b: 93–94.
[96] Bauckham 1993a: 213.
[97] Koester 2014: 265.

The church also fulfils the Old Testament offices of king, priest and prophet. The redeemed are designated as a 'kingdom' and 'priests' to God (1:5), who typologically fulfil Israel's vocation as a 'priestly kingdom' (Exod. 19:6). Their true worship and steadfast allegiance to Jesus and his kingdom in the present age anticipates their glorious future in the new creation, in which they will perform unending priestly service in God's presence and will reign with Christ for ever (Rev. 22:3, 5). Further, the church carries out a prophetic vocation as they keep 'the words of this prophecy' (1:3) and hold fast to the testimony of Jesus (19:10) while resisting serpentine prophecies that promote idolatry and immorality (2:20, 24).[98]

Revelation also presents the church, the followers of the Lamb, as the new Israel. The seminal images of the 144,000 sealed from Israel's tribes (7:4–8) and the innumerable multitude from all nations and languages (7:9–14) present complementary depictions of the same reality – the complete number of people that God has redeemed by the Lamb's sacrifice and preserved from coming judgment. In contrast, Christ designates unbelieving Jews who slander the saints as a 'synagogue of Satan' (2:9; 3:9). 'Those who truly belong to the twelve tribes of Israel (21:12) confess the message proclaimed by "the twelve apostles of the Lamb" (21:14).'[99]

John and his Christian brethren are partners 'in the tribulation' (*en tē thlipsei* [1:9]). His authoritative visions offer a sober reminder that followers of the Lamb will face slander, suffering and perhaps the state's sword (2:9–10, 13; 13:10). Nevertheless, the Apocalypse summons God's people to faithful endurance – come what may – and resilient confidence in God's sure promises to execute perfect justice and restore all things.[100] Therefore, those with ears attuned to the Spirit's message to the churches must 'conquer' not by military force or political power but 'by the blood of the Lamb and by the word of their testimony' (12:11).

[98] See ch. 4, pp. 76–80.
[99] Schreiner 2013: 629.
[100] Marriner 2016: 227.

Chapter Six

Every tribe and tongue: the battle for universal worship

After this I looked, and behold, a great multitude that no one could number, from every nation, from all tribes and peoples and languages, standing before the throne and before the Lamb, clothed in white robes, with palm branches in their hands, and crying out with a loud voice, 'Salvation belongs to our God who sits on the throne, and to the Lamb!' (Rev. 7:9–10)

And the beast was given a mouth uttering haughty and blasphemous words, and it was allowed to exercise authority for forty-two months. . . . And authority was given it over every tribe and people and language and nation, and all who dwell on earth will worship it, everyone whose name has not been written before the foundation of the world in the book of life of the Lamb who was slain. (Rev. 13:5–8)

The nations feature prominently in the unfolding drama of the Apocalypse. On the one hand, the book presents every tribe and nation singing the praises of 'the beast' and drunk with Babylon's intoxicating brew (13:7–8; 18:3). On the other hand, John envisions a redeemed multitude from every tribe and nation extolling God and the Lamb in heaven (7:9–10) and eventually serving as royal priests in the new creation (22:3, 5). The nations revile God and incur the Lamb's wrath (19:15), yet they also experience eschatological healing and offer true worship to 'the King of the nations' (15:3–4; 22:2). Revelation stresses that only God and the Lamb are worthy to rule the nations and receive their praise.

This chapter explores Revelation's presentation of this battle for universal worship and allegiance. John's visions evoke God's promises to bless the earth's nations and tribes in Abraham's offspring (Rev. 1:7; 7:9; Gen. 12:3; 28:14). Scenes of all the peoples uniting to praise and serve the God of Israel and his messianic king fulfil Old Testament prophetic hopes. They also offer a crucial corrective to the blasphemous calls to worship with the beast and its image that recall scenes from Daniel. The Apocalypse reorients the churches to their doxological and missiological calling as worshippers *from* all nations and witnesses *to* all nations (Rev. 7:9; 10:11; 11:3).

God and the nations

The book's prologue identifies Jesus as 'ruler of kings on earth' and signals that 'all the tribes of the earth' will see him 'coming with the clouds' (Rev. 1:5, 7). These programmatic declarations of Jesus' universal authority anticipate Christ's ultimate victory as 'King of kings' (17:14; 19:16) and the ultimate destiny of the nations and their kings as worshippers in the New Jerusalem (21:24, 26; 22:2). They also recall several major Old Testament promises and prophecies concerning the nations.

As discussed earlier, Revelation frequently alludes to Daniel's famous prophecy in which 'one like a son of man' approaches the Ancient of Days and receives an everlasting kingdom 'that all peoples, nations, and languages should serve him' (Dan. 7:13–14).[1] Revelation 1:7 alludes to Daniel 7:13 ('Look, he is coming with the clouds'), but the remainder of the verse invokes Zechariah 12:

> every eye will see him, even those who pierced him, and all tribes of the earth will wail on account of him. Even so. Amen. (Rev. 1:7b)

> And I will pour out on the house of David and the inhabitants of Jerusalem a spirit of grace and pleas for mercy, so that, when they look on me, on him whom they have pierced, they shall mourn for him . . . The land shall mourn, each family by itself. (Zech. 12:10, 12)

The Apocalypse universalizes Zechariah's prophecy in several ways. First, Revelation 1:7 refers to 'every eye' (*pas ophthalmos*) seeing him, while Zechariah 12:10 refers to the house of David and residents of Jerusalem looking on Yahweh in a time of eschatological repentance

---

[1] See ch. 3, pp. 48–53.

after sinfully rejecting Yahweh and his representative, 'whom they have pierced'.[2] Second, Revelation presents 'all the tribes of the earth' (*pasai hai phylai tēs gēs*) mourning, while in Zechariah 12:12 the land of Israel shall mourn, each family by itself. Some interpreters have argued that the Zechariah background signals that *gē* in Revelation 1:7 refers to Israel's land, not to the earth.[3] However, *gē* elsewhere in the Apocalypse consistently refers to 'the earth', not the land of Canaan. Further, Revelation's reference to 'all the tribes of the earth' likely derives from Zechariah 14:17, where the survivors 'from all the tribes of the earth' (*ek pasōn tōn phylōn tēs gēs*) shall go up to worship Yahweh the King and keep the feast of booths or else face punishment, plagues and drought. This scene in which the nations go up to worship Yahweh as their King fulfils Zechariah's earlier prophecy that many nations and peoples will seek Yahweh in Jerusalem, and men 'from the nations of every tongue' will join with Jews because God is with them (8:22–23). Thus Revelation 1:7 universalizes the eschatological mourning in Zechariah 12:10 by applying it to Christ's 'coming' as depicted in Daniel 7:13 (cf. Matt. 24:30) and also by using universal language from elsewhere in the book of Zechariah.

The phrase 'all the tribes of the earth' (*pasai hai phylai tēs gēs*) in Revelation 1:7 may also recall the divine promise that 'all the tribes of the earth shall be blessed' in Abraham and his offspring (Gen. 12:3).[4] In Genesis 28:14 Yahweh reiterates to Jacob his intention to bless the earth's families. Within the book of Genesis the reference to 'tribes' or 'families' (Hebr. *mišpĕḥôt*) in these patriarchal promises recalls the Table of Nations, in which Noah's descendants spread 'in their own land, each with his own language, by their tribes, in their nations' (Gen. 10:5; cf. 10:32).[5] Amos 3:2 highlights Yahweh's unique covenant relationship with his people Israel 'from all the tribes of the earth', recalling Genesis 12:3.[6] Additionally, Psalm 72 (71 LXX) envisions the earth's families uniting to praise 'the God of Israel'

---

[2] Beale and McDonough 2007: 1090. The references to 'piercing' in Rev. 1:7 and John 19:37 follow the Hebrew textual tradition of Zech. 12:10 over against the LXX, which mistakenly reads 'mocked' (*katōrchēsanto*). For nuanced discussion of John's textual use of Zech. 12:10, see Jauhiainen 2005: 102–105.

[3] Walvoord 1985: 929.

[4] Bauckham (1993a: 321) notes that Rev. 1:7 alludes to the promise to Abraham in Gen. 12:3, which is associated by the interpretive principle of verbal analogy (*gezerah shawah*) with Zech. 12:12 and may interpret Zechariah's prophecy.

[5] DeRouchie 2013: 241.

[6] Stuart 1987: 322.

(vv. 17–18). Thus while Yahweh has uniquely chosen and called Israel from among all peoples, 'all the tribes of the earth' will one day experience blessing in Abraham's promised descendant and will join in worshipping the true God of Israel. The Apocalypse signals the ultimate fulfilment of the promise to Abraham that an innumerable multitude from every tribe will gather to worship the true God and the Lamb (7:9), even though for a time the earth's peoples will idolatrously worship the beast and submit to its usurping authority.

True worship: God and the Lamb

The Apocalypse presents glorious visions of the believers from all peoples offering unceasing praise to God and the Lamb in heaven and ultimately in the New Jerusalem. These scenes establish the foundational reality that only God and the Lamb deserve the nations' acclaim because they alone are able to redeem and are worthy to rule. These visions of genuine worship prepare for and contrast with the beast's counterfeit claims to sovereignty (Rev. 13). The book presents readers with a critical choice: Who is worthy to receive the nations' worship – God and the Lamb, or the dragon and the beast?[7]

John's heavenly vision in Revelation 4 establishes the absolute centrality of the divine throne – a potent image of God's rule as supreme King and Judge over all that he has created. The four living creatures and the twenty-four elders offer unceasing thanks and adulation to the one seated on the throne (4:8–11).[8] These doxologies establish that 'all things' (*ta panta*) owe their lives and loyalties to the Creator God, who alone is worthy to receive glory, honour and power (4:11). Seen through the lens of Revelation 4, 'the throne of Satan' (2:13) and 'the throne of the beast' (16:10; cf. 13:2) are brazen attempts to usurp the authority and status that rightfully belongs to God alone.

In Revelation 5:7 the worthy Lamb approaches the divine throne and receives the sealed scroll, which recalls Daniel's prophecy of a messianic figure approaching the Ancient of Days to receive authority, glory and power (Dan. 7:13–14).[9] The living creatures and twenty-four elders then 'fall down before the Lamb' (*epesan enōpion tou arniou* [Rev. 5:8]), as they 'fall down before the one seated on the throne' (*pesountai . . . enōpion tou kathēmenou epi tou thronou*) in 4:10. The living creatures and elders' physical acts of homage signal

---

[7] Similarly, Grabiner 2015: 111.
[8] See ch. 2, pp. 37–40.
[9] On this allusion to Dan. 7:13, see Beale 1999: 356.

their total submission and allegiance to the heavenly sovereign.[10] They extol the Lamb as 'worthy' (*axios ei*), echoing praise to God in 4:11 (*axios ei*) and answering the question in 5:2 ('Who is worthy [*tis axios*] to open the scroll?'). These parallels signal that 'Christ is being adored on absolutely equal terms with God the creator!'[11]

The heavenly beings sing 'a new song' (5:9), a phrase in Scripture that regularly connotes worship for God's marvellous acts of salvation.[12] Elsewhere in the Apocalypse the term 'new' (*kainos*) is closely tied to God's work of new creation (21:1–2, 5) and the end-time inheritance of those who conquer (2:17; 3:12). The 'new song' in 5:9–10 combines these themes of salvation and new creation.[13] The Lamb is worthy because by his blood he purchased people 'from every tribe, language, people and nation' (*ek pasēs phylēs kai glōssēs kai laou kai ethnous*) and made (*poieō*) them 'a kingdom and priests for God'. This description of the redeemed anticipates the book's consummate vision of worship in the new Eden (22:3–5). The presentation of the Lamb's redeemed people in 5:9–10 combines Old Testament language for universal humanity with a designation for Israel's vocation as God's chosen, redeemed people.[14] In Exodus 19:5–6 Yahweh declares that 'all the earth' (*pasa hē gē*) belongs to him, and he has chosen Israel as his special people 'from all the peoples' (*apo pantōn tōn ethnōn*) and called them to be 'a kingdom of priests and a holy nation'. While Exodus 19:5–6 originally stresses that Yahweh has saved and selected a single ethnic group (Israel) 'from' (*apo*) all the earth's peoples, Revelation 5:9–10 applies this description typologically to God's choice of a multi-ethnic people with representatives 'from' (*ek*) every tribe and tongue, redeemed by Jesus the eschatological Passover Lamb and set apart to serve as God's royal priesthood in the new creation.[15]

In Revelation 7:9 John sees 'a great multitude that no one could number, from every nation, from all tribes and peoples and languages'. This reference to an incalculable throng (*ochlos polys, hon arithmēsai auton oudeis edynato*) invokes ancient promises to the patriarchs.[16] Yahweh likens Abraham's future offspring to the innumerable stars

---

[10] The elders and living creatures 'fall down' (*piptō*) and 'worship' (*proskyneō*) in Rev. 4:10; 5:14; 7:11; 11:16; 19:4. On these terms, see Peterson 1992: 270.
[11] Peterson 1992: 272.
[12] See Pss 96:1–2; 98:1–2; Isa. 42:10; Rev. 14:3.
[13] Similarly, Beale 1999: 358.
[14] See ch. 5, pp. 90–95.
[15] Bauckham 1993a: 327.
[16] Bauckham 1993a: 223; Beale and McDonough 2007: 1108.

in Genesis 15:5. The angel reassures Hagar that her descendants 'shall not be counted for multitude' (*ouk arithmēthēsetai apo tou plēthous*). Similarly, in Genesis 32:12 (32:13 LXX) Jacob expresses God's promise to 'make your offspring as the sand of the sea, which cannot be numbered for multitude' (*hē ouk arithmēthēsetai apo tou plēthous*). The crowd's multi-ethnic make-up in Revelation 7:9 further recalls God's promises to bless 'all the tribes' (*pasai hai phylai* [Gen. 12:3; 28:14]) and 'all the nations of the earth' (*panta ta ethnē tēs gēs* [22:18; cf. 17:4]).

Earlier the prophet depicts the triumphant Lamb's 'standing' (*hestēkos*) in the midst of the throne (5:6), and in 7:9 he presents the multi-ethnic multitude similarly 'standing before the throne and before the Lamb' (*stōtes enōpion tou thronou kai enōpion tou arniou*). Their standing posture also answers the question of the unredeemed in 6:17 ('who can stand?'). This throng wears the white robes promised to all victors (3:4–5, 18) and given to vindicated martyrs (6:11).[17] In 7:14 the angel explains that their robes are made white 'in the blood of the Lamb', echoing the heavenly praise in 5:9. The palm branches in their hands and the cries of 'salvation' complete the picture of new-exodus deliverance for this redeemed multitude (7:9–10).[18] The links between Revelation 5 and 7 suggest that 'the Lamb's victory is continued by his people'.[19] These scenes of heavenly praise stress that only God and the Lamb are worthy of the nations' worship because they alone exercise rightful sovereignty and accomplish salvation. Thus readers from every nation should identify with the multi-ethnic throng of worshippers in 7:9, persisting in praise for the true sovereign while resisting calls to revere the beast (13:4, 8).

In Revelation 15:2–4 conquering believers extol the Almighty as 'King of the nations', whose amazing deeds and righteous acts call all nations to fear and worship him alone. John introduces the worshippers as those who 'had conquered the beast and its image and the number of its name', expanding the saints' victory over the dragon in 12:11 to include the beasts from sea and land who threaten God's people in 13:1–17. Like the multi-ethnic throng of 7:9, the victors in 15:2 are standing (*hestōtas*). Like the 144,000 redeemed followers of the Lamb in 14:1–3, these victors carry harps and sing (15:2–3). While the 144,000 'sing a new song' (14:3), the victors in 15:3 'sing the song

[17] Grabiner 2015: 114.
[18] See further ch. 5, pp. 102–108; ch. 7, pp. 158–160.
[19] Bauckham 1993a: 333.

118

of Moses . . . and the song of the Lamb', praising God for judging his enemies and saving his people not only at the exodus (Exod. 15:1–18; cf. Deut. 31:30 – 32:43) but climactically in the new exodus by the Lamb's blood (cf. Rev. 5:9).[20]

The victors' song reverberates with Old Testament declarations of God's sovereign rule and mighty deeds among the peoples, particularly Exodus 15:11, Jeremiah 10:7 and Psalm 86:9–10.[21] It is fitting that the hymn introduced as 'the song of Moses' resonates with Exodus 15.[22] After recounting Yahweh's works of judgment and salvation in the exodus, Moses exclaims, 'Who is like you among the gods, O Lord? Who is like you, glorified among holy ones [*dedoxasmenos en hagiois*], awesome in glorious deeds [*thaumastos en doxais*], doing wonders?' (Exod. 15:11 NETS). Similarly, the triumphant worshippers in Revelation 15:3–4 praise the Almighty for his 'amazing' (*thaumasta*) deeds and declare that all should 'glorify' (*doxasei*) his name. The appellation 'King of the nations' (*ho basileus tōn ethnōn*) recalls the concluding note of Moses' song: 'Yahweh will reign [*basileuōn*] for ever and ever' (Exod. 15:18).

Bauckham suggests that Revelation 15 links Exodus 15 with several other Old Testament passages by the interpretive principle of verbal analogy (*gezerah shawah*).[23] First, the divine title 'King of the nations' (15:3) and the question 'Who will not fear . . . and glorify your name?' (15:4a) recall Jeremiah 10:7a, 'Who would not fear you, O King of the nations?'[24] Thompson comments, 'A king both deserves and commands allegiance, and Yahweh is king over all.'[25] Jeremiah celebrates Yahweh as 'the living God and the everlasting King' (10:10), in contrast to the nations' futile, foolish idols (10:8, 11).

Second, the hymn of praise in Revelation 15:3–4 alludes extensively to Psalm 86 [85 LXX]. In Revelation 15:3, 'Great and amazing are your works' (*megala kai thaumasta ta erga sou*) combines the reference to Yahweh's incomparable 'works' (*ta erga sou*) with the praise 'You are great and do wondrous things' (*megas ei sy kai poiōn thaumasia*) in

---

[20] See ch. 7, pp. 158–160.

[21] Bauckham 1993a: 303–304. He also suggests an allusion to Ps. 98:1–2. See also Schnabel 2002: 262–265; Grabiner 2015: 182–183.

[22] Following Bauckham 1993a: 297, 302–303. Contra Schüssler Fiorenza (1998: 135), who claims that the song in Rev. 15:3–4 'is an amalgam of various OT themes' and is unconnected to Moses' 'songs' in Exod. 15 or Deut. 32.

[23] Bauckham 1993a: 302.

[24] The LXX version of Jeremiah lacks this verse. For discussion, see McKane 1986: 216–228.

[25] Thompson 1980: 328.

Psalm 86:8, 10. In Revelation 15:4 'All nations will come and worship you' (*panta ta ethnē hēxousin kai proskynēsousin enōpion sou*) restates the promise in Psalm 86:9 (*panta ta ethnē . . . hēxousin kai proskynēsousin enōpion sou*). The victors' call to fear and glorify God's name (Rev. 15:4; cf. 14:7) recalls the psalmist's confidence that all nations 'shall glorify your name' (*doxasousin to onoma sou* [Ps. 86:9]) and his own resolve to 'fear your name' and 'glorify your name for ever' (vv. 11–12). The phrase 'you alone [*monos*] are holy' (Rev. 15:4) is similar to the psalmist's words 'You alone [*monos*] are God' (Ps. 86:10).

The prophetic hope that all nations will come and worship the true God (Rev. 15:4) is ultimately fulfilled in the New Jerusalem. In Revelation 21:3 a voice from the throne says, 'Behold, the dwelling place [*skēnē*] of God is with humanity [*meta tōn anthrōpōn*]. He will dwell with them, and they will be his peoples, and God himself will be with them as their God' (*autoi laoi autou esontai, kai autos ho theos met' autōn estai autōn theos*, my tr.). This remarkable declaration recalls the repeated Old Testament promise that Yahweh will dwell among his covenant people for ever, particularly Ezekiel 37:27: 'My dwelling place [*kataskēnōsis*] shall be with them, and I will be their God, and they shall be my people [*esomai autois theos, kai autoi mou esontai laos*].'[26] Revelation 21:3 appears to combine this covenantal promise with the expansive prophecy in Zechariah 2:10–11 [2:14–15 LXX] that Yahweh will come to dwell in Zion, and 'many nations' (*ethnē polla*) shall join themselves to him and be his 'people' (*esontai autō eis laon*). Remarkably, Revelation 21:3 expands the singular 'people' (*laos*) common in the Old Testament covenantal promises and designates human beings as his 'peoples' (*laoi*).[27] Bauckham explains, 'In its combination of the language of God's commitment to his covenant people with the most universalistic reference to all humanity, this verse is programmatic for the whole account of the New Jerusalem that follows.'[28] Revelation's vision is both universal and particular: God's covenant people includes men and women from every nation, language and tribe, who are ransomed and cleansed by the Lamb's blood to declare his praises for ever (1:5–6; 5:9–10; 7:9–14; 22:14).[29]

[26] Cf. Lev. 26:11–12; Jer. 32:38; Zech. 8:8.
[27] Following the NA28 Greek text of Rev. 21:3. For discussion of the textual variants in this text, see McNicol 2011: 73–74, n. 47; Aune 1998b: 1110–1111.
[28] Bauckham 1993a: 311. Similarly, McNicol 2011: 73–75. Cf. ch. 9, pp. 198–201. Muller rightly cautions, 'The reference to the peoples does not annul the restriction to the Christians, who come, precisely, from all peoples and nations.'
[29] For a similar emphasis, see Schnabel 2002: 265–268.

Counterfeit worship: the beast and his image

In Revelation 13:1 John sees 'a beast rising out of the sea [*ek tēs thalassēs thērion anabainon*], with ten horns and seven heads, with ten diadems on its horns and blasphemous names on its heads.' In 11:7 and 17:8 this beast rises 'out of the abyss' (*ek tēs abyssou*), the bottomless pit where demons dwell (9:1–2, 11; cf. Luke 8:31). The beast unmistakably resembles the great red dragon with its seven heads and ten horns (12:3). The beast receives power and authority from the dragon (13:2), is worshipped along with the dragon (13:4) and follows the dragon's lead in making war against the saints (12:17; 13:7; cf. 11:7; Dan. 7:21).

The beast of Revelation 13 is a composite of the 'four great beasts coming up out of the sea' (*tessara thēria anebainon ek tēs thalassēs*) in Daniel 7:3 LXX.[30] John portrays this beast having features like a leopard, bear and lion (Rev. 13:2), corresponding to the first three beasts in Daniel 7:4–6, while its ten horns link it to the fourth beast in Daniel 7:7.[31] In Daniel's vision the four great beasts represent four kings and kingdoms (7:17, 23). The fourth beast is the most terrifying and the most hostile, and his horn wars against and conquers the saints until the Ancient of Days comes to vindicate his people and establish his everlasting kingdom (7:21–22, 26–27). In the book of Daniel these beasts correspond to king Nebuchadnezzar's dream of 'a great image' of different metals that signify four kingdoms (2:31–43).[32] Interpreters have traditionally identified these four kingdoms as (1) Babylonia, (2) the Medo-Persian empire, (3) Greece or Macedonia and (4) Rome.[33] In the Jewish apocalypse *4 Ezra* the seer receives a dream of an eagle from the sea that spread its wings over all the earth (11.1–2), a likely symbol for Rome. In *4 Ezra* 12.11 the angel interprets this eagle as 'the fourth kingdom which appeared in a vision to your brother Daniel'.[34]

---

[30] Beale (1999: 683) suggests that Revelation's two beasts may also be partially based on Job 40–41. Cf. Collins 1976: 164.

[31] Beale 1999: 683.

[32] Hamilton 2014: 88–91. 'There is general agreement that the kings in question correspond to the four kingdoms of chap. 2', according to Collins (1993: 312). Alternatively, Goldingay (1989: 174) argues that the four regimes in Dan. 2 correspond to the rulers in Dan. 1–6, not to the four beasts of Dan. 7.

[33] Hill 2008: 137; Baldwin 1978: 163–164. Cf. Josephus, *Jewish Antiquities* 10.272–276. Critical scholars typically identify these kingdoms as (1) Babylonia, (2) Media, (3) Persia and (4) Greece or Macedonia. See Lucas 2002: 188–191; Collins 1993: 312.

[34] Stone (1994: 366) writes, 'Various symbolic identifications were used for Rome in this book, clearly showing how central the Roman Empire was for our author. Thus this verse sets up the triple equivalation of eagle/fourth empire/Rome.'

Revelation's poignant image of 'a beast', inspired by Daniel's prophecy of four kingdoms, recasts the empire's political power and military muscle as ugly, ruthless, violent and fearsome. It also conveys a subtle yet crucial truth: the state's mighty rulers who order total allegiance, oppress the saints and oppose God are themselves *creatures*, categorically distinct from the *sui generis* Creator. God alone 'created all things' and is thus worthy to receive glory, honour and power (Rev. 4:11). Those familiar with the biblical story recall that 'God made the beasts [*ta thēria*] of the earth according to their kinds' (Gen. 1:25), and even the seducing serpent was among the beasts (3:1, 14). When King Nebuchadnezzar boasted about 'this great Babylon' built by *his* power for the glory of *his* majesty, the Most High took away his kingdom and gave him the mind of a beast and a portion with the beasts (Dan. 4:14–16; 4:30–33). The beastification of Babylon's most famous sovereign illustrates that the King of heaven will humble any creature who proudly claims divine praise and prerogatives (4:37).

Revelation 13 recounts how the diabolical beasts from the sea and the earth parody Jesus, the victorious slain Lamb. The first beast, with its seven heads and ten horns, takes on the image of the dragon (13:1; cf. 12:3) and receives the dragon's power, throne and authority (13:2). This parallels Jesus' assertions that he has received from his Father supreme authority and has sat down on his throne (2:27; 3:21).[35] According to 13:3, the beast had a head 'as slain unto death' (*hōs esphagmenēn eis thanaton*), which mimics John's description of 'a Lamb standing as though slain' (*arnion hestēkos hōs esphagmenon*) in 5:6 (cf. 5:9, 12; 13:8).[36] The slain beast is then 'healed' (*etherapeuthē*) after being wounded by the sword and 'came to life' (*ezēsen*; 13:3–4, 12, 14), which parodies Christ's resurrection (1:18; 2:8). Bauckham writes, 'The beast's death and resurrection are and are not like Christ's. In other words, they are a deceitful imitation.'[37] After seeing that the beast is healed, the whole earth worships the beast and the dragon (13:4; cf. 13:12), aping the heavenly praise that 'every creature' gives to God and the Lamb in 5:13.[38]

Revelation 13:11 introduces an insidious beast from the earth with 'two horns like a lamb' (*homoia arniō*) that 'spoke like a dragon'. This beast deliberately parodies Jesus, whom the Apocalypse repeatedly

---

[35] Bauckham 1993a: 434. Cf. Gallusz 2014: 222.
[36] Bauckham 1993a: 432.
[37] Ibid. 433.
[38] DeSilva 2009b: 201.

calls 'the Lamb' (*to arnion*).[39] Mounce suggests that Revelation 13 presents an 'evil triumvirate' that parodies the triune God: 'As Christ received authority from the Father (Matt 11:27), so Antichrist receives authority from the dragon (Rev 13:4); and as the Holy Spirit glorifies Christ (John 16:14), so the false prophet glorifies the Antichrist (Rev 13:12).'[40] However, Bauckham argues that the second beast's role corresponds to that of Christian prophets, not the Spirit.[41] This beast's imitation of the two witnesses in Revelation 11 is particularly striking. This beast is later called 'the false prophet' (16:13; 19:20; 20:10), contrasting with Jesus' witnesses who prophesy in sackcloth (11:3; cf. 11:6, 10). Further, the second beast performs signs and exercises authority (*tēn exousian*) in the presence of (*enōpion*) the first beast, even 'making fire come down from heaven' (13:13–14). Similarly, the two witnesses stand before (*enōpion*) the Lord, fire pours from their mouths and they have authority (*tēn exousian*) to perform miraculous deeds (11:4–5). Moreover, according to Revelation 13:15, the beast from the earth 'was allowed to give breath [*pneuma*] to the image of the beast, so that the image of the beast might even speak and might cause those who would not worship the image of the beast to be slain'. This may parody 11:11, where 'a breath/Spirit of life' enters into the two witnesses and raises them to life.[42]

Those who refuse to worship the image of the beast will face the state's wrath (13:15), which recalls the famous court story in Daniel 3. Likely inspired by his dream of a massive image in which the head of gold represented his glorious empire (2:31–32, 38), King Nebuchadnezzar erects a massive golden image sixty cubits high (3:1). He then gathers all the officials and issues a decree that the 'peoples, nations and languages' must 'fall down and worship the golden image that King Nebuchadnezzar has set up' when the Babylonian band begins to play (Dan. 3:4–5).[43] Those who refuse to worship the colossal idol will face the flames (3:6). Bauckham rightly states that Nebuchadnezzar's coercive call for the nations to worship this image 'must have

---

[39] Osborne 2002: 511. In contrast, Mounce (1997: 255) argues that only the first beast parodies Christ.

[40] Mounce 1997: 255.

[41] Bauckham 1993a: 434.

[42] For further discussion of Rev. 11:11, see ch. 4, pp. 76–80.

[43] Except for the harp or lyre (*kithara*), Israelite worshippers used none of the instruments named in Dan. 3:5, and 'most are foreign terms for instruments used in secular contexts. They thus imply a double judgment on the alien, pagan nature of the ceremony Nebuchadnezzar is inaugurating', according to Goldingay (1989: 70).

seemed to John to prefigure the universal worship of the image of the beast'.[44]

The Apocalypse refers to 'the throne of Satan' (2:13) and 'the throne of the beast', which it receives from the dragon (16:10; cf. 13:2). While scholars debate the background and referent of Satan's throne in Pergamum, Gallusz plausibly identifies it with the presence of Roman power in that great Asian city, expressed chiefly through its imperial cults.[45] The seven cities of Asia Minor mentioned in Revelation were all official centres for the imperial cult by the late first and early second century.[46] Loyal citizens expressed their gratitude for the benefits of Roman peace and prosperity by offering divine honours in temples and before statues of living emperors.[47] Romans considered the emperors to have authority derived from the gods,[48] and Domitian expected to be referred to as 'our master and god'.[49] However, Revelation 13 makes clear that the beast from the sea 'received its power, throne, and great authority from the Dragon, not from Jupiter or some other Olympian'.[50]

The first Christian readers of the Apocalypse faced tremendous social and economic pressure to participate in these public displays of loyalty and gratitude to the emperors. According to Revelation 13:15, those who refuse to worship the beast and its image face the prospect of death.[51] This again recalls Nebuchadnezzar's decree to worship the golden image under threat of execution by fire (Dan. 3:4–6). In Daniel three faithful Jews refuse to heed the king's order to bow down to the image, yet they are miraculously delivered from the flames (3:28). Revelation makes clear that some believers will be slain like Antipas for their allegiance to Jesus (2:13; 13:10; 20:4). Nevertheless, God's people will ultimately 'conquer' the beast and its image (15:2), while the beast and its allies will be thrown into the lake of fire (19:20; 20:10).

---

[44] Bauckham 1993b: 329.

[45] Gallusz 2014: 206. Alternatively Friesen (2005: 366) interprets Satan's throne as 'a reference to tensions in that city between the assembly and mainstream society'.

[46] Slater 1999: 253. Cf. Tabb 2016.

[47] Winter 2015: 2.

[48] Koester 2014: 570. Cf. Pliny the Younger, *Epistle* 10.102; Horace, *Odes* 1.12.49–52.

[49] Suetonius, *Domitian* 13.2 (*dominus et deus noster*).

[50] Friesen 2006: 202.

[51] According to Pliny the Younger's correspondence with the emperor Trajan (*Epistles* 96–97) in the early second century AD, those charged with being Christians were summoned under threat of death to pray to Roman deities, make offerings to the emperor's image and repudiate Christ's name.

The beast and Babylon

John's vision of the great prostitute clarifies the relationship between the beast and Babylon the great. In Revelation 17:3 John sees 'a woman sitting on a scarlet beast that was full of blasphemous names, and it had seven heads and ten horns'. This woman is 'the great prostitute' (v. 2), 'Babylon the great' (v. 5) and 'the great city that has dominion over the kings of the earth' (v. 18). The beast's seven heads and ten horns identify it as the same terrifying beast that rises from the abyss and the sea (11:7; 13:1), and its scarlet colour and hideous features also recall the great red dragon (12:3). The Harlot and her scarlet mount are a 'mystery', which the angel interprets beginning in 17:7. The seven heads of the beast represent 'seven mountains' and also 'seven kings', while its horns signify 'ten kings who have not yet received royal power' and the beast itself is an eighth king that belongs to the seven (17:9–11). These ten 'will receive authority as kings for one hour' and they proceed to 'deliver over their power and authority to the beast' (17:12–13).

Interpreters have attempted to untangle these images in various ways. Koester writes, 'The dual imagery of mountains and kings underscores the beast embodying the power of both the city of Rome and its emperors.'[52] Most readers understand 'seven mountains' (*hepta orē*) in 17:9 as an unmistakable reference to Rome, widely known as 'the city on seven hills'.[53] The 'seven kings' in 17:10 are commonly taken as Roman emperors, though interpreters debate whether the list is comprehensive or selective and whether it begins with Julius Caesar, Augustus or Galba.[54]

While acknowledging Rome as the dominant and oppressive empire of John's day, some readers question a tidy identification between 'the beast' and Roman rule. Thomas identifies the beast as 'the false Christ of the last times', an individual who leads a final world empire and deceives the earth.[55] However, this specific identification of the beast with a future antichrist seems at odds with Thomas's own claim that 'no historical situation, including John's own, can fully satisfy all the criteria regarding the beast'.[56] Further, a strictly futurist reading does

[52] Koester 2014: 677.
[53] Cf. Cicero, *Letters to Atticus* 6.5; Pliny the Elder, *Natural History* 3.9, Virgil, *Aeneid* 6.782–785; *Georgica* 2.534–535.
[54] Boxall 2006: 246–247. The recent historical study by Winter (2015: 289–296) identifies the sixth king ('the one is') with Nero.
[55] Thomas 1995: 153–154.
[56] Ibid. 152–153.

not adequately account for John's 'call for the endurance and faith of the saints' (13:10).

Alternatively, Beale stresses 'the temporal transcendence of the oppressive beast'. Thus 'the dragon and the beast include world empires of the past and the present and potentially of the future'.[57] Caird reasons that for John 'the current embodiment of the chaos monster is Rome, but he sees Rome as the residual legatee of all the pagan empires in the past', and his depiction of the beast during Domitian's reign 'is equally applicable to totalitarian and tyrannical power at any other period of the world's history'.[58] In this approach the 'seven kings' of 17:10 represent the completeness of the beast's power, rather than a precise list of first-century sovereigns.[59] Koester asserts, 'The issue is not whether readers can identify the kings, but whether they identify *with* them.'[60]

Thus 'the beast' likely signifies the state's political and military might that commands total allegiance and even worship, while 'Babylon the great' is its cultural and economic system that seductively promises affluence.[61] In John's vision Babylon the Harlot rides on the beast, illustrating that the state's coercive power supports its cultural prosperity. Rome certainly fits this beastly bill for Apocalypse's first readers, who faced political, social, religious and economic pressures to express their loyalty to Caesar.[62] Yet the Danielic background of the monsters rising from the sea signals that Rome is the latest in a line of imperial powers that coerce and threaten the faithful to fall down and worship the state-authorized image (cf. Dan. 3:5) but whose dominion shall be taken away. For a time, Babylon controls and cons peoples, multitudes, nations and languages and their kings (17:15, 18; 18:3). Similarly, the beast is given (*edothē*) authority 'over every tribe, people language and nation' and receives worship from all the earth dwellers (13:7–8). The verb *edothē* signals that the beast is not self-determining but rules with derivative authority for a limited duration under God's sovereign decree.[63] As Babylon's mighty king famously

---

[57] Beale 1999: 685.

[58] Caird 1997: 229.

[59] Mounce (1997: 316) concludes that the reference to seven kings in 17:10 'is symbolic and stands for the power of the Roman Empire as a historic whole'.

[60] Koester 2014: 692, emphasis original.

[61] See further ch. 8, pp. 164–168.

[62] For recent discussions of the significance of the imperial cult for interpreting Revelation, see Winter 2015: 286–306; Friesen 2005; Naylor 2010: 207–239.

[63] The divine passive *edothē* 'stresses that the ultimate power, throne and authority is derived from God', according to Gallusz (2014: 215).

learned, 'The Most High rules the kingdom of humanity and *gives* it to whom he will' (Dan. 4:17). Thus believers must not be beguiled by the beast's blasphemies and bluster.

At various points in Revelation the nations align with Babylon and the beast. They trample the holy city (11:2) and 'rage' against God (11:18), recalling the international conspiracy against God and his king in Psalm 2:1. The nations become intoxicated by Babylon's maddening wine (Rev. 14:8; 17:2; 18:3), an evocative image for her deceptive economic, political and religious influence that alludes to Jeremiah 51:7. Further, Babylon deceives the nations by her sorceries (Rev. 18:23) like the harlot city Nineveh (Nah. 3:4). Jesus at his return will strike down and rule the nations with an iron rod in fulfilment of messianic expectation (Rev. 19:15; Isa. 11:4; Ps. 2:9; cf. *Pss Sol.* 17.21–25). Yet Revelation also positively presents the nations being ransomed by Christ (5:9), healed in the New Jerusalem (22:2), offering true worship to God, the 'King of the nations' (15:3–4).

Witness to the nations

In Revelation 10:8–11 John takes and eats a little scroll from the angel's hand and receives instructions to 'prophesy about [*prophēteusai epi*] many peoples and nations and languages and kings'. This symbolic action deliberately echoes the prophetic commissioning of Ezekiel (Ezek. 2:8 – 3:3).[64] The scroll is sweet as honey in John's mouth as the true word of God, yet the bitterness in his stomach may parallel Ezekiel's prophecy of lament, mourning and woe (Rev. 10:10; Ezek. 2:10; 3:14) or may portend suffering for Jesus' followers. Nevertheless, God does not send Ezekiel 'to many peoples of obscure speech and strange language' who would listen to the prophet's words (3:6); in contrast, John must 'prophesy about [*prophēteusai epi*] many peoples and nations and languages and kings' (Rev. 10:11). John's prophetic commissioning is then immediately applied to God's two witnesses, who 'will prophesy' (*prophēteusousin*) among many peoples, nations and languages (11:3, 9).[65]

Interpreters debate whether *prophēteusai epi* in 10:11 has a primarily positive connotation ('prophesy *about*' or '*to*') or primarily negative sense ('prophesy *against*'). Bauckham adopts the former position and writes that 'John's prophecy is "to many peoples" – with the

---

[64] See ch. 10, pp. 210–213; cf. Beale 2011a: 4–6.
[65] Beale 1999: 599. On the two witnesses, see ch. 5, pp. 97–101.

implication, therefore, that they will listen.'[66] Alternatively, Beale reasons that 'prophesy *against*' more precisely reflects the LXX usage of the phrase and the negative portrayal of the nations and kings in the remaining chapters of the Apocalypse.[67] Osborne renders *prophēteusai epi* more generally as 'prophesy *about*' and plausibly suggests that the phrase contains 'both positive and negative elements', since 'warning and witness are hardly mutually exclusive categories in prophetic witness'.[68]

Within LXX Ezekiel, *prophēteusai epi* frequently introduces a message of correction or judgment against Israel (4:7; 6:2; 21:2), Israel's false prophets and leaders (11:4; 13:2, 16, 17; 24:2) or the surrounding nations (25:2; 28:21; 29:2; 38:2; 39:1). However, the same phrase announces comfort and promised restoration for God's people (36:6; 37:4, 9). The visions of Revelation do not directly address the unbelieving nations but the seven churches (1:4, 11; 22:16). Thus John 'prophesies *about* the nations but *to* his readers'.[69] At the same time, John proclaims the culmination of biblical prophecy as he announces that 'in the days of the trumpet call to be sounded by the seventh angel, the mystery of God would be fulfilled, just as he announced to his servants the prophets' (10:7). This trumpet call comes in 11:15, when loud voices in heaven proclaim, 'The kingdom of the world has become the kingdom of our Lord and of his Christ', bringing wrath against his enemies and reward for his servants (11:18).

Bauckham closely links John's commission with the prophetic ministry of the two witnesses in Revelation 11:3, and argues that the witnesses do not primarily preach a word of judgment, but a call to repentance. Bauckham concludes that the church's witness is ultimately successful, as the nations 'give glory to God' in 11:13 as a sign of 'genuine repentance and worship of God'.[70] However, in 11:10 'the people flatly reject the witnesses' and gloat over their deaths.[71] They fear and give glory to God not in response to the witnesses' preaching but only after the great earthquake (11:13).[72] Bauckham correctly reasons that 'the church was drawn from all nations (5:9; 7:9) . . . so that it can bear witness to all nations'.[73]

---

[66] Bauckham 1993a: 264.
[67] Beale 1999: 554. Similarly, Schnabel 2002: 251–253.
[68] Osborne 2002: 405.
[69] Koester 2014: 483.
[70] Bauckham 1993a: 278.
[71] McNicol 2011: 125.
[72] Ibid.
[73] Bauckham 1993a: 265.

However, as 'witnesses', the church not only calls the nations to repent of their idolatry and immorality, but it also establishes the legal charge against the unbelieving nations that refuse to repent and glorify God as the true sovereign.

In 14:6–7 an angel proclaims an eternal gospel 'to those who dwell on earth, to every nation and tribe and language and people', summoning them to 'fear God and give him glory, because the hour of his judgment has come, and worship him who made heaven and earth, the sea and the springs of water'. Bauckham observes that these verses contain multiple allusions to Psalm 96 [95 LXX], a psalm that calls 'all nations to worship the one true God who is coming to judge the world and to establish his universal rule'.[74] The reference to 'gospel' in Revelation 14:6 parallels *euangelizesthe* (proclaim good news) in Psalm 96:2 [95:2 LXX], and the psalmist calls worshippers to declare Yahweh's glory among the nations because he alone is worthy of praise and fear (96:3–4). The psalmist climaxes with the affirmation 'Yahweh reigns' (v. 10), and celebrates his coming righteous judgment (v. 13). The proclamation in Revelation 14:6–7 is immediately followed by the declaration of Babylon's fall (v. 8) and the warning that worshippers of the beast and its image will incur God's wrath (vv. 9–11). Thus the angel's announcement in verses 6–7 'functions as a final warning to the totality of the whole world, that it is time to shift allegiance from idolatry to the one Creator God'.[75]

The last battle

'Why did nations grow insolent, and peoples contemplate vain things? The kings of the earth stood side by side, and the rulers gathered together, against the Lord and against his anointed' (Ps. 2:1–2 NETS). The kings of the nations have long resisted God's righteous rule, and their hubris and hostility culminates in a final battle 'on the great day of God the Almighty . . . at the place that in Hebrew is called Armageddon' (Rev. 16:14, 16). 'Armaggedon' occurs only here in the Scriptures and likely combines the Hebrew words *har měgiddôn*, 'mountain of Megiddo'.[76] Some interpret 16:16 as the precise location of the last battle, but 'more likely a general reference is intended, building on the Old Testament connection of Megiddo

[74] Ibid. 288.
[75] McNicol 2011: 33.
[76] Blount 2013: 307.

with warfare'.[77] While Megiddo is located on a plain (Zech. 12:11), *har* in Armaggedon links this famous battlefield with the 'mountains of Israel', where Ezekiel prophesied that the enemies of God's people would gather for a great eschatological conflict (Ezek. 38:8; 39:2, 4, 17).

The nations' rage reflects the diabolical influence of the dragon, the beast and the false prophet, the unholy trinity of the Apocalypse, whose lying words and devious signs move their allies to arm against the Almighty (16:13–14). Revelation 17:12–14 pictures these kings of the earth as 'ten horns' on the beast, who

> receive authority as kings for one hour, together with the beast. These are of one mind, and they hand over their power and authority to the beast. They will make war on the Lamb, and the Lamb will conquer them, for he is Lord of lords and King of kings, and those with him are called and chosen and faithful.

The kings' support for the beast's regime lasts only 'until the words of God are fulfilled' (17:17), signalling that even in their rebellious support for the beast they ironically carry out the Almighty's sovereign decree.

The Apocalypse returns to the last battle in 19:11–21. In verses 11–16 John sees Christ seated on his battle steed leading the armies of heaven. The divine title 'King of kings and Lord of lords' in verse 16 occurs elsewhere in the book only in 17:14, where Christ's status as supreme King and Lord explains why he achieves victory over the beast and its allies. Surprisingly, John does not describe the actual conflict in any detail. One expects a fierce fight, but instead an angel summons fowl to feast on flesh: 'Come, gather for the great supper of God, to eat the flesh of kings, the flesh of captains, the flesh of mighty men, the flesh of horses and their riders, and the flesh of all men, both free and slave, both small and great' (19:17–18).

This strange supper scene clearly alludes to the graphic curse against Gog in Ezekiel 38 – 39.[78] In between Ezekiel's famous dry bones prophecy in chapter 37 and his expansive vision of the new temple in chapters 40–48, the prophet speaks against 'Gog, of the land of Magog' (38:1), a prince marching against Israel with armies composed of 'nations from all parts of the known world'.[79] God's

[77] Osborne 2002: 596. Cf. Zech. 12:11; Judg. 5:19–21; 2 Kgs 23:29; 2 Chr. 35:22.
[78] See the careful study by Bøe (2001).
[79] Ibid. 384.

wrath is roused and he promises to reveal his greatness and holiness by executing judgment on this proud prince and his formidable forces (38:19, 21–23). In 39:4 Yahweh declares that Gog and his hosts shall fall on Israel's mountains and shall be devoured while Magog is burned. In 39:17–20 Yahweh summons birds and beasts to 'gather' for 'a great sacrificial feast', where they shall eat the flesh and drink the blood of Israel's fallen assailants.

The invitation for the birds to 'gather' (*synachthēte*) to dine in Revelation 19:17 reaffirms Ezekiel's prophecy that the foes of God's people will be utterly defeated and destroyed. The angelic command 'gather' ironically anticipates verse 19: 'And I saw the beast and the kings of the earth with their armies gathered [*synēgmena*] to make war against him who was sitting on the horse and against his army.' This recapitulates John's earlier description of the Armageddon assembly in 16:14, 16 and again alludes to the prophecy of Gog's gathering nations for battle (Ezek. 38:13). Once again 'Ps. 2:2 rings in the background' as mighty rulers 'gathered themselves' (*synēchthēsan*) to oppose Yahweh.[80] The concluding verses of chapter 19 summarize the results of Christ's landslide victory: the beast and false prophet are seized and thrown alive into the fiery lake, while Christ slays their compatriots with the sword of his mouth (19:20–21; cf. v. 15).

Revelation 20 has perplexed interpreters for nearly two millennia. Premillennialists argue that verses 1–6 describe events that follow Jesus' return and victory over the beast and its allies (19:11–21).[81] Alternatively, amillennialists hold that the events of 20:1–6 do not chronologically follow the last battle in chapter 19 but rather recapitulate the church age.[82] Interpreters divide sharply concerning the timing and nature of Satan's binding in 20:3. Verse 2 reintroduces 'the dragon, that ancient serpent, who is the devil and Satan', which closely parallels the comprehensive naming of the great dragon in 12:9. While 12:9 identifies the dragon as 'the deceiver [*planōn*] of the whole world', in chapter 20 Satan is restricted from deceiving the nations until the thousand years are finished (v. 3), at which time he 'will come out to deceive [*planēsai*] the nations that are at the four corners of the earth, Gog and Magog, to gather them for battle' (v. 8). While the beast and false prophet are 'seized' and 'hurled' to their eternal deaths at the last battle (19:20), the dragon – the final member of the terrible trio – is 'bound' and 'hurled' into the abyss (20:3). Only

---

[80] Beale and McDonough 2007: 1144.
[81] Blomberg 2013: 80–82.
[82] Storms 2013: 428.

after his postmillennial effort to deceive the nations is the ancient foe flung alive into the fiery lake (20:10).

Interpreters have proposed various identifications of 'the nations' in 20:8, including (1) the people who did not fight in the battle in 19:19–21,[83] (2) ghosts and demons who inhabit the underworld[84] and (3) the unrepentant nations previously slain in 19:21 who have been raised from the dead.[85] Most likely, 'the nations' are ordinary nations of human beings as elsewhere in the Apocalypse.[86] Satan goes forth 'to deceive' (*planēsai*) these nations and 'to gather them for the battle' (*synagagein autous eis ton polemon*) in 20:8, which closely parallels the earlier accounts of the beast and false prophet deceiving through demonic spirits and gathering the kings of the earth for battle (16:13–14; 19:19).

John's reference to 'Gog and Magog' in 20:8 signals further dependence on Ezekiel 38 – 39 (see Table 6.1 on p. 133).[87] The formulation 'Gog *and* Magog' differs from 'Gog, *of the land of* Magog' (Ezek. 38:2) but reflects the conventions of early Jewish texts that present the terms as a pair.[88] Moreover, while the prince Gog leads the coalition of nations against Israel in Ezekiel 38 – 39, the Apocalypse universalizes the reference to Israel's eschatological enemy by setting 'Gog and Magog' in apposition to 'the nations that are at the four corners of the earth'.[89] In addition to employing the names 'Gog' and 'Magog' clearly associated with Ezekiel 38 – 39, Revelation 20:8–9 includes several additional allusions to Ezekiel's prophecy.[90] In both passages the innumerable armies are 'gathered' (*synagō*), they 'march' or 'come up' (*anabainō*) and the Lord sends fire (*pyr*) on Gog and the hostile nations. Moreover, both Ezekiel and Revelation stress that God permits and superintends this ultimate conflict with the hostile nations: he 'brings out' Gog (Ezek. 38:5) and frees the ancient serpent from bondage, though fully aware of his evil aims (Rev. 20:7).[91]

---

[83] Osborne 2002: 713.

[84] Rissi 1972: 35–36.

[85] Mealy 1992: 131–135. For extensive critical engagement with Mealy's thesis, see Beale 1994: 229–249.

[86] Bøe 2001: 322; Koester 2014: 776–777.

[87] Table adapted from Tabb 2015: 2621.

[88] Cf. *3 En.* 45.5; *Sib. Or.* 3.319; 5.512; 4Q523 2.5. See Bøe 2001: 140–234.

[89] Bøe 2001: 312–315; Beale 1999: 1022.

[90] Bøe (2001: 342–343) lists thirteen correspondences between Rev. 20:7–10 and Ezek. 38 – 39. Alternatively, Mangina (2010: 231) claims that the names 'Gog and Magog' carry 'no particular significance' aside from serving as 'a suitably barbaric-sounding designation for the enemies of God'.

[91] Bøe 2001: 342.

Table 6.1: The use of Ezekiel 38 – 39 in Revelation 19 – 20

Final battle(s) in Revelation 19 – 20	Prophecy against Gog in Ezekiel 38 – 39
birds called to 'gather' (*synachthēte*) for the great supper of God (19:17)	birds and beasts called to 'gather' (*synachthēte*) for the sacrifice (39:17)
'eat the flesh of kings . . . captains . . . mighty men . . . horses and their riders' (19:18)	'eat the flesh of the mighty . . . princes . . . horses and charioteers' (39:18, 20)
'Gog and Magog' (20:8)	'Gog . . . Magog' (38:2)
deceived nations gathered for battle (20:8)	many nations come against Israel (38:15–16)
innumerable army like 'sand' (20:8)	innumerable army like a 'cloud' (38:9, 16)
the nations 'went up' (*anebēsan*, 20:9)	Gog and his troops 'will go up' (*anabēsetai*, 38:9, 16, 18)
'Fire came down from heaven' (20:9)	'fire on Magog' (39:6; cf. 38:22)

Some interpreters propose a 'two-stage use of Ezekiel' in Revelation 19 – 20 in which the battle, and judgment of Satan in 20:7–10, corresponds to Ezekiel 38 and follows the earlier battle in 19:19–21 that corresponds to Ezekiel 39.[92] Mealy asserts that Ezekiel presents two distinct oracles against Gog and that John recognizes 'these two entirely different contexts for the battles of Ezekiel 38 and 39'.[93] However, Block argues that Ezekiel 38:1 – 39:21 is a single, clearly defined oracle that depicts Gog's invasion of Israel and Yahweh's complete annihilation of these enemies.[94] Bøe remarks, 'It is hard to imagine how John can have read Ezekiel 38 and 39 as two completely different prophecies which chronologically were expected to take place in the reverse order.'[95] The cumulative evidence suggests that Revelation 20:7–10 does not describe another later conflict but the very same battle of Armageddon depicted in 16:12–16 and 19:11–21, now focusing on Satan's deceptive role and consummate defeat.

---

[92] Koester 2014: 778.
[93] Mealy 1992: 132.
[94] Block 1998: 424. Similarly, Allen 1990: 202.
[95] Bøe 2001: 321.

Conclusion

The Apocalypse weaves together various biblical threads regarding the nations into a remarkable prophetic tapestry. God is the Creator, Sustainer and Sovereign of all things (4:11). In the biblical story God confused the languages and scattered rebellious humanity at Babel (Gen. 11:7–9) and promised to bless all the earth's families in Abraham and his seed (12:3; 22:18). Revelation offers a stark, binary division of the nations as either allies and worshippers of the dragon and the beast or of God and Lamb. Grabiner writes, 'The acclaim that God ultimately receives from the nations is in opposition to the universal acclaim given to the beast.'[96] Those who follow the beast are the children of Babel, loyal citizens of Babylon who gladly fall down and worship the image at the emperor's command in order to share in Babylon's rewards (Rev. 13:12; 18:3; cf. Dan. 3:7). Those who follow the Lamb are God's redeemed people (Rev. 14:1–5). Like Hananiah, Mishael and Azariah they refuse to venerate a lie and resolve to endure the beast's fiery fury no matter the cost (Rev. 13:15; cf. Dan. 3:16–18).

Revelation's first readers faced substantial pressure to conform to and compromise with the expectations of the surrounding culture, aptly called 'Babylon'. Some leaders within the church encouraged the faithful to eat food sacrificed to idols and practise sexual immorality (2:14, 20) – as one does in Babylon – but the risen Christ exposes such teachings as false and deadly.[97] The rivalry between the Lamb and the murderous beast presses Christians to choose whom they will serve. Followers of the Lamb will celebrate his consummate victory over his foes and serve him for ever in paradise (19:14; 22:3–5), while the nations under the serpent's sway who bind themselves to the beast will face the same terrible judgment in the lake of fire (19:21; 20:10; 21:8).

The visions of the redeemed from every nation worshipping God and the Lamb depict the doxological destiny of God's people and challenge coercive calls to revere the beast and its image. The bliss, purity and security of the Lamb's multi-ethnic multitude (7:9–17; 14:1–5) contrast sharply with the distress and destruction that await all who worship the beast and live for Babylon's luxury (14:9–11; 18:3). These visions celebrate the truth, beauty and worthiness of the

---

[96] Grabiner 2015: 222.

[97] For discussion of competing claims to prophetic revelation in Revelation, see ch. 4, pp. 84–85.

'King of the nations' (15:3), while exposing the falsity, ugliness and unworthiness of all rivals for the peoples' praises. Readers of the Apocalypse must 'worship God' alone (19:10; 22:9).

Part III:
Judgment, salvation and restoration

Chapter Seven

The wrath of the Lamb: the plagues of judgment and the new exodus

> Fall on us and hide us from the face of him who is seated on the throne, and from the wrath of the Lamb, for the great day of their wrath has come, and who can stand? (Rev. 6:16–17)

> And they sing the song of Moses, the servant of God, and the song of the Lamb, saying, 'Great and amazing are your deeds, O Lord God the Almighty! Just and true are your ways, O King of the nations! Who will not fear, O Lord, and glorify your name? For you alone are holy. All nations will come and worship you, for your righteous acts have been revealed.' (Rev. 15:3–4)

The Apocalypse depicts the deliverance of God's people and the demise of his enemies in terms of a new exodus. Jesus the Lamb saves sinners, stands triumphant over death and sits on the divine throne to enact God's righteous judgment on the rebellious world. The divine plagues against the ungodly and redemption of his people follow the script of the exodus and fulfil Old Testament longings for the day when God would again bare his holy arm to dry up the sea, pierce the dragon and lead his people to experience everlasting joy (Isa. 51:9–11).

This chapter examines various aspects of the new-exodus motif in Revelation. The book repeatedly depicts the revelation of God's awesome and holy presence in terms reminiscent of the storm theophany at Mount Sinai in Exodus 19. When the victorious Lamb unseals the secret scroll of the Almighty, he unleashes God's eschatological plans to judge his foes and redeem his followers. Revelation presents God's mighty acts of judgment and salvation as a response to the petitions of his people that ascend to the divine throne as sweet-smelling incense. The seven trumpets and the seven bowls of wrath typologically follow the pattern of the plagues against Egypt at the exodus and prompt heavenly praise. The ungodly curse God and hide in terror on the day of his wrath (Rev. 6:17; 16:9), while the redeemed hail the God of the exodus as 'King of the nations' (15:3–4). The book also presents Jesus as the final Passover Lamb whose blood redeems his multi-ethnic people from their sins and makes them 'a kingdom and priests' (5:9–10; cf. Exod. 19:6).

The prayers of the saints

The Apocalypse refers explicitly to 'the prayers of the saints' (*hai proseuchai tōn hagiōn*) only three times (5:8; 8:3–4). However, these petitions – along with the cries of the martyrs in 6:10 – play a crucial role in the book's unfolding drama of new-exodus salvation and judgment.

First, in 5:8 John describes the four living creatures and twenty-four elders falling down before the Lamb, who is found worthy to take the sealed scroll. Each of these heavenly worshippers holds 'a harp, and golden bowls full of incense, which are the prayers of the saints'. The harp (*kithara*) frequently accompanies praise and thanksgiving to God in the Old Testament,[1] and elsewhere in Revelation the redeemed hold harps as they sing 'a new song' and 'the song of Moses . . . and the song of the Lamb' (14:2–3; 15:2–3). The golden bowls in their hands contain incense (*thymiamata*), a staple of Jewish worship in the tabernacle and the temple (Exod. 30:1, 7–8; 1 Chr. 28:18; Luke 1:9). John explains that the incense represents the prayers of God's people.[2] In Luke 1:10 the faithful gather to pray at the hour of incense, and in Psalm 141:2 (140:2 LXX) the psalmist asks that his prayer 'be counted as incense' (cf. *4 Bar.* 9.3–4; Jdt. 9.1). Revelation 5:8 draws upon this symbolic association of incense and prayer but goes further by presenting heavenly beings bringing the saints' sweet-smelling prayers directly into the divine throne room as the worthy Lamb prepares to break the seals of the divine scroll. Moreover, they bring these prayers before the Lamb, who shares God's praise and carries out God's purposes (5:8–9).[3]

---

[1] Cf. Pss 33:2; 43:4; 57:8; 71:22; 81:2; 92:3; 98:5; 108:2; 147:7; 150:3.

[2] The relative clause 'which are the prayers of the saints' is grammatically difficult, as the feminine relative pronoun *hai* does not agree with its likely antecedent 'incense' (*thymiamatōn*), which is neuter. *Hai* may modify the feminine noun 'bowls' (*phialas*), but its feminine gender is likely due to attraction to 'prayers' (*proseuchai*) in its own clause. See Thomas 1992: 397; Mathewson 2016: 77.

[3] Similarly, Koester 2014: 388.

The next prayer scene in the Apocalypse comes in 6:9–11. When the Lamb opens the scroll's fifth seal, John sees under the altar the souls of martyrs who cry out, 'O Sovereign Lord, holy and true, how long before you will judge and avenge our blood on those who dwell on the earth?' (6:9–10).[4] Interpreters debate whether the 'altar' here refers to the altar of burnt offering or the altar of incense. The sacrificial connotations of 'blood' and the location 'under the altar' relate most closely to the Old Testament description of the altar of burnt offering, where the blood of slain animals was poured out at the altar's base (Lev. 4:18, 30, 34).[5] However, the Apocalypse seems to present only one altar in the heavenly sanctuary.[6] John's reference to the souls as 'slain' (*sphazō*) recalls the repeated depiction of the 'slain' Lamb (5:6, 9, 12), which may imply 'a kind of participation in the shed blood of the Lamb',[7] or that Christ's followers 'will have their sacrificial suffering and apparent defeat turned into ultimate victory'.[8]

Heil claims that their prayer for judgment and vindication 'sets the agenda for the remainder of the book'.[9] They do not appeal for personal revenge but for God's righteous justice to be revealed on a cosmic scale,[10] for 'the Judge of all the earth [to] do what is just' (Gen. 18:25). Their question 'how long?' resonates with Old Testament appeals for God to judge evildoers and save his suffering people (e.g. Pss 6:3; 13:1–2; 79:4–6, 10). Their urgent petitions are heard, but God responds initially with a call to 'rest a little while' (Rev. 6:11). Yet the martyrs' prayers are decisively answered later in the Apocalypse. In the midst of the bowl judgments an angel declares, 'Just are you, O Holy One, who is and who was, for you brought these judgments. For they have shed the blood of saints and prophets, and you have given them blood to drink. It is what they deserve!' (16:5–6). Then the altar speaks, 'Yes, Lord God the Almighty, true and just are your judgments!' (16:7). The judgment reflects the principle of *lex talionis*: those who shed blood now drink blood. The Almighty 'gives to people only what they have given to others, and his judgment is testimony to

---

[4] *1 En.* 47.1–2 likewise refers to the blood of the righteous and repeated prayers that ascend to the Lord until 'judgement is executed for them'.
[5] Bauckham 2001a: 260. Alternatively, Beale (1999: 391–392) identifies the altar with the altar of incense and associates this altar with God's throne.
[6] See Rev. 6:9; 8:3, 5; 9:13; 11:1; 14:18; 16:7; Osborne 2002: 284–285; Koester 2014: 398.
[7] Bauckham 2001a: 260–261.
[8] Beale 1999: 392.
[9] Heil 1993: 242.
[10] Bauckham 2001a: 261.

his justice and equity'.[11] The voice here may come from the angel presenting their prayers at the altar (8:3–4; 9:13);[12] most likely, 'the altar' refers by metonymy to the martyrs 'under the altar' (6:9).[13] The victims who cried out at the altar are now the victors consenting to God's true judgments.

The Apocalypse returns to the saints' prayers in chapter 8 in a transitional scene marking the conclusion of the seven seals and the introduction of the seven trumpets (8:1–2, 6). John writes:

> And another angel came and stood at the altar with a golden censer, and he was given much incense to offer with the prayers of all the saints on the golden altar before the throne, and the smoke of the incense, with the prayers of the saints, rose before God from the hand of the angel. Then the angel took the censer and filled it with fire from the altar and threw it on the earth, and there were peals of thunder, rumblings, flashes of lightning, and an earthquake. (8:3–5)

When the Lamb takes the sealed scroll in Revelation 5, the elders bring incense-prayers in golden bowls. Here in Revelation 8 the angel offers those prayers with incense on the altar, like a priest ministering in the tabernacle (Lev. 16:12). This is presumably the same heavenly altar sprinkled by the martyrs' blood in Revelation 6:9. The mingled prayers and incense rise before God, signalling that the petitions of God's people – including the martyrs' appeals for justice in 6:10 – reach God's throne with angelic authorization.[14] The direct answer to these prayers comes in 8:5, where the same priestly angel who offered the prayers in 8:3 fills his censer with fire from the altar and hurls it to the earth. The storm theophany in 8:5 recalls God's awesome presence at Sinai and prepares for the next septet of judgments on the earth.[15] The first two trumpets in 8:7–8 include 'fire' (*pyr*), further linking these divine acts with the prayers offered on the heavenly altar in 8:5.

The Apocalypse reinforces the connection between prayer and divine judgment in several ways. In 9:13 the voice from the altar at the

---

[11] Paul 2018: 46.

[12] Osborne 2002: 584–585.

[13] Koester 2014: 648.

[14] Beale 1999: 455.

[15] 'It is the manifestation of God's numinous holiness that effects the final judgment of the world,' according to Bauckham (2001a: 257). The theophany in 8:5 is discussed further in ch. 7, pp. 143–146.

sixth trumpet blast further links the martyrs' blood and the saints' petitions with God's righteous acts of judgment.[16] In 14:18 an angel with 'authority over the fire' comes from the altar and announces the time for gathering the grapes for the winepress of God's wrath (v. 19; cf. 19:15).[17] This may be the same priestly angel who offers the saints' prayers and takes fire from the altar in 8:3–5 who now prepares for the 'blood' to flow from the winepress of divine wrath (14:20) to avenge the 'blood' of God's people (6:10; 16:6; 18:24; 19:2). Finally, in 15:7, 'one of the four living creatures gave to the seven angels seven golden bowls full of the wrath of God'. Elsewhere in Revelation 'golden bowls' (*phialas chrysas*) appear only in 5:8, where they are filled with incense-prayers. Whether or not the golden bowls full of wrath in 15:7 are precisely the same as those in 5:8, the unique lexical repetition of 'golden bowls' implies that the last septet of judgments is a further, more definitive, answer to the petitions of God's people in 5:8 and 8:3–4 (cf. 6:9–11).[18]

Thus the Apocalypse presents the judgment cycles of seals, trumpets and bowls as God's direct response to the effective prayers of the saints.[19] The heavenly altar under which the slain martyrs cry (6:9–10) and on which the angel presents believers' petitions as a fragrant offering (8:3–4) is also the place from which divine fire falls, bringing righteous retribution (8:5; 9:13) and leading to approving praise for the Almighty (16:7).

The God of thunder

John's foundational vision of the heavenly throne room depicts 'flashes of lightning, and rumblings and peals of thunder' (*astrapai kai phōnai kai brontai*) emanating from the divine throne (4:5). Revelation employs the same phrase following the seventh seal (8:5), the seventh trumpet (11:19) and the seventh bowl (16:18):

> Then the angel took the censer and filled it with fire from the altar and threw it on the earth, and there were *peals of thunder, rumblings,*

---

[16] Similarly, Bauckham 2001a: 258.

[17] 'Angels with power over fire and water (16:5) reflect Jewish traditions that linked angels to fire, wind, clouds, and thunder,' according to Koester (2014: 625). Cf. *Jub.* 2.2; *1 En.* 60.11–21; *LAB* 38.3; *T. Ab.* 12.14; 13.11; Aune 1998a: 846.

[18] Giesen 1997: 346; Mounce 1997: 289; Beale 1999: 806; Bauckham 2001a: 257.

[19] Similarly, Bauckham 2001a: 259.

flashes of lightning [brontai kai phōnai kai astrapai], and an earthquake. (8:5)

Then God's temple in heaven was opened, and the ark of his covenant was seen within his temple. There were *flashes of lightning, rumblings, peals of thunder [astrapai kai phōnai kai brontai]*, an earthquake, and heavy hail. (11:19)

And there were *flashes of lightning, rumblings, peals of thunder [astrapai kai phōnai kai brontai]*, and a great earthquake such as there had never been since man was on the earth, so great was that earthquake. (16:18)

Each of these scenes recalls Yahweh's awesome theophany at Mount Sinai:[20]

Now on the third day, early in the morning, rumblings and lightning *[phōnai kai astrapai]* and a dark cloud came upon Mount Sinai; there was a loud sound *[phōnē]* of the trumpet, and all the people in the camp were terrified. Now Mount Sinai was smoking in its entirety, because God had come down upon it in fire, and the smoke was rising up like the smoke of a furnace. And all the people were greatly amazed. Now the sounds *[hai phōnai]* of the trumpet increased and became much stronger. Moses spoke, and God answered him with a sound *[phōnē]*. (Exod 19:16–19 LXX; cf. 20:18)[21]

The Hebrew text of Exodus 19:18 refers to the mountain trembling (*hrd*), which the LXX interprets as the people's astonishment. However, both storms and quakes feature prominently in later Old Testament and Jewish depictions of the exodus and Sinai. For example, the psalmist writes, 'O God, when you went out before your people, when you marched through the wilderness, the earth quaked *[eseisthē]*, the heavens poured down rain, before God, the One of Sinai, before God, the God of Israel' (Ps. 68:7–8 [67:7–8 LXX]). Psalm 77:17–18 (76:17–18 LXX) refers to rumbling (*phōnē*), thunder (*brontē*), lightnings (*astrapai*)

---

[20] Cf. Bauckham 1993a: 202–204; Beale 1999: 124; Gallusz 2014: 125–126.

[21] While the term 'thunders' (*brontai*) does not occur in Exod. 19 LXX, Philo includes *brontai* in his depiction of Sinai in *Decalogue* 44. Josephus combines the Sinai storm theophany and the exodus judgments as he depicts thunders (*brontai*) and lightning (*astrapēs*) coming upon the Egyptians as the sea crashed upon them at the exodus (*Jewish Antiquities* 2.343).

and the earth shaking and trembling (*esaleuthē kai entromos*). *4 Ezra* stresses the cosmic implications of God's appearance at Sinai: 'And when you led his descendants out of Egypt, you brought them to Mount Sinai. You bent down the heavens and shook the earth, and moved the world, and made the depths to tremble, and trouble the times' (3.17–18).[22] Pseudo-Philo similarly expands upon the Sinai theophany by presenting the burning of the mountains, the shaking of earth and every habitable place and the gathering of the stars until God establishes his covenant with Israel (*LAB* 11.4–5). Thus the thunder, lightning and tremors associated with Yahweh's awesome self-revelation after the exodus are paradigmatic for Old Testament and later Jewish depictions of God's coming appearance to execute eschatological judgment.

In Revelation 4:5 the presence of lightning, rumblings and thunder establish the divine throne as the central place where 'God's holiness and power are openly revealed'.[23] The Apocalypse reintroduces these theophanic phenomena at three crucial junctures within the book to conclude each of the major septets of judgment.[24] The storm theophany in 4:5 is focused on the heavenly throne room and does not describe eschatological judgment on earth but rather underscores the awesome authority of the supreme Creator and Judge of all. This God of thunder who rules from his heavenly throne executes righteous judgment on earth in the cycles of seals, trumpets and bowls of wrath. While there is no quake in 4:5, the Apocalypse's subsequent storm theophanies conclude with 'an earthquake' (*seismos* [8:5]), 'an earthquake and great hail' (*seismos kai chalaza megalē* [11:19]) and a 'great earthquake' (*seismos. . . megas* [16:18]).[25] These verses each recall the awesome theophany in Exodus 19, and each depicts 'the climactic destruction of the world'.[26] Bauckham writes:

The progressive expansion of the formula accords with the increasing severity of each series of judgments, as the visions focus

[22] Bauckham 1993a: 200. Cf. Ps. 114:1, 3, 7; Isa. 64:3; *LAB* 23.10.

[23] Gallusz 2014: 125.

[24] This repetition is one of the strongest evidences for progressive parallelism or recapitulation in the seals, trumpets and bowls, as noted by Beale (1999: 124). Alternatively, Thomas (1995: 527–542) rejects the recapitulation reading in favour of a telescopic or 'dove-tailing' view in which the seventh seal contains the seven trumpets, and the seventh trumpet contains the seven bowls.

[25] 'A great earthquake' also accompanies the sixth seal's cosmic conflagration imagery (Rev. 6:12–14).

[26] Beale 1999: 459.

more closely on the End itself and the limited warning judgments of the trumpets give place to the seven last plagues of God's wrath on the finally unrepentant.[27]

The inclusion of 'great hail' in Revelation 11:19 suggests that John combines the Sinai imagery with the seventh plague on Egypt (Exod. 9:18–25).[28] Moreover, this reference to hail following the seventh trumpet blast (11:15) recalls the destructive hail of the first trumpet (8:7) and anticipates the seventh and last bowl of wrath, which brings the severe 'plague of the hail' with its massive hundred-pound hailstones (16:20–21).

Thus the Apocalypse returns repeatedly to the sights and sounds of Sinai to convey the transcendent holiness and thundering power of God. The refrain of lightning, rumblings, thunder and quake drawn from Exodus 19:16 signals that God is executing his new-exodus plans for judgment and salvation. The cycles of seven seals, trumpets and bowls of wrath each conclude with theophanic imagery first introduced in Revelation 4:5 to make clear that the heavenly throne is the ultimate source of the climactic plagues of judgment – the throne inhabited by the one true God and the Lamb (3:21; 7:17). Those who are loyal to the throne of God and the Lamb take comfort and rejoice in their dramatic judgments, while the rest of humanity will curse and cower at 'the great day of their wrath' (6:16–17; cf. 16:9, 11, 21).

The seven seals

The enthronement of the Lamb in Revelation 5 initiates the first of the book's major cycles of judgment in 6:1 – 8:1. In 5:1 the scroll in the Almighty's hand recalls the double-sided scroll containing 'words of lamentation, mourning and woe' in Ezekiel 2:9–10 and the sealed books in Isaiah 29:11 and Daniel 12:4. The triumphant Lamb takes the scroll and opens its seven seals, beginning in Revelation 6:1 to indicate that he alone is worthy to reveal and enact God's hidden plans for consummate judgment and salvation. The successive announcements from the four living creatures suggest a close connection between the initial four seals (6:1, 3, 5, 7). Further, the four coloured horses in Revelation 6:1–8 likely recall Zechariah 6:1–8, where the

[27] Bauckham 1993a: 204.
[28] The mention of 'the ark of his covenant' in 11:19 offers a further nod to Sinai (Exod. 25:10).

Lord sends chariots pulled by red, black, white and dapple-gray horses to patrol the earth.[29] The four horsemen have been variously interpreted as references to first-century threats, future events during a coming 'tribulation' (cf. Matt. 24:6–8, 21) or realities throughout the church age.[30] The first horseman comes forth 'conquering and to conquer' (Rev. 6:2), anticipating the beast's hostility towards God's people in 11:7 and 13:7. Its crown and white horse signify military conquest and do not identify this horseman with Christ but suggest a parody of his righteous war against evil (19:11). The rider of the red horse takes peace from the earth, and its 'great sword' conveys violent bloodshed and prepares for the sober call for endurance in 13:10. The scales in the third rider's hand symbolize commerce, and the dramatically inflated prices for food staples wheat and barley suggest scarcity or famine, perhaps as a consequence of war (2 Kgs 6:24–33). The fourth horseman, identified as 'Death', inflicts violence by the sword, famine, pestilence and wild beasts. This recalls God's 'four dreadful judgments' that God promises to bring against unfaithful Israel (Ezek. 14:21 NIV; cf. 14:12–20; Lev. 26:22–26; Deut. 32:24–26; Jer. 24:10).

The fifth seal in Revelation 6:9–11 reveals the martyrs' appeals for divine justice after they were 'slain' like the Lamb (5:6, 9, 12), perhaps as a consequence of the previous four seals that bring violence and slaughter (6:4, 8).[31] The definitive answer to their petitions for God to 'judge the inhabitants of the earth' comes when Christ opens the sixth seal (6:12–17).[32] The result is cosmic upheaval associated with 'the day of the Lord' (Isa. 13:9–13; Joel 2:10, 31) and utter terror for 'the kings of the earth' and other classes of unrepentant humanity who hide from the wrath of God and the Lamb (cf. Isa. 2:19–21; Hos. 10:8). Their despairing question 'who can stand?' (Rev. 6:17) anticipates the vision of the redeemed multitude 'standing before the throne and before the Lamb' (7:9).[33]

The opening of the seventh seal in 8:1 brings a brief period of heavenly silence. This silence has been variously interpreted to denote God's creative rest, a pause in divine revelation, reverence and awe in God's presence, preparation for the impending trumpet judgments

---

[29] For discussion, see Beale and McDonough 2007: 1102–1103. Alternatively, Jauhiainen (2005: 63–64) argues that Rev. 6 corresponds more closely to Zech. 1:8–17.

[30] Koester (2014: 353–355) provides a useful history of interpretation.

[31] Heil 1993: 222–223.

[32] Ibid. 230; Beale 1999: 395–396.

[33] Cf. ch. 5, pp. 102–108.

or a context for prayer.[34] Zephaniah calls for 'silence' before Yahweh's holy presence as the wrath, distress and trumpet blast of judgment day draws near (Zeph. 1:7, 14–16; cf. Hab. 2:20; Zech. 2:13). Further, in Exodus 14:13–14 LXX Moses commands, 'Take heart, stand and see the salvation from God, which he will work for you today. For the Egyptians whom you see today, you shall never see again. Yahweh will fight for you, and you will be silent [*sigēsete*].' The call for silence answers the people's fearful cries (14:10–12) and prepares for Israel's dramatic deliverance from the hand of the Egyptians (14:30–31).

The seven trumpets

The links to the exodus in Revelation 8:1 become more pronounced in the septet of trumpets in 8:2 – 11:19. Beale writes, 'The exodus plagues are both a literary and a theological model for the trumpets.'[35] In the Old Testament the priests sound trumpets in worship and warfare (Num. 10:8–10). The seven angels with seven trumpets standing before the Lord in Revelation 8:2 may recall Joshua 6, where seven priests go before the ark of the Lord and sound seven trumpets, signalling the imminent fall of Jericho.[36] Bauckham suggests that the Apocalypse interprets 'the whole Exodus event from the plagues of Egypt to the conquest of Canaan as one great manifestation of God's power to judge the nations and to deliver his people'.[37] Throughout Revelation the number seven signifies completion or fullness,[38] so the septets of seals, trumpets and bowls of wrath reveal the comprehensiveness of divine judgment on the earth.

At the first trumpet blast, hail and fire, mixed with blood are hurled upon the earth, bringing destruction to a third of the earth, its trees and grass (Rev. 8:7). This unmistakably recalls the seventh plague, where Yahweh gave sounds of thunder, 'hail' (*chalazan*) and 'fire to the earth' (*to pyr epi tēs gēs* [Exod. 9:23 LXX]). Later Old Testament texts recall these displays of awesome power at the exodus (Pss 78:47; 105:32), and Ezekiel 38:22–23 announces that God will again rain down hail, fire and sulphur to display his greatness and holiness in the eyes of the nations.

---

[34] For representative surveys, see Osborne 2002: 336–338; Koester 2014: 431.
[35] Beale 1999: 466–467. Cf. Paulien 1988: 43.
[36] Beale and McDonough 2007: 1112.
[37] Bauckham 1993a: 205.
[38] See ch. 1, pp. 9–15.

In the second trumpet judgment a great burning mountain is hurled into the sea, turning a third of the sea to blood and destroying a third of the sea's creatures and ships (8:8–9). This alludes to the initial plague against Egypt in Exodus 7:20–21, where the water of the Nile turned into blood and its fish died. The partial destruction contrasts with the complete devastation of the second bowl judgment in Revelation 16:3 in which the entire sea becomes like blood and every sea creature dies. John's description of 'a great mountain, burning with fire' reflects the prophecy that Babylon will be 'a burned-out mountain' (Jer. 51:25). The Apocalypse stresses that Babylon the harlot city will be consumed by fire (Rev. 17:16; 18:8) and 'will be thrown down with violence' like a great millstone hurled into the sea (18:21), which recalls Jeremiah 51:63–64.[39] The destruction of ships in Revelation 8:9 similarly prepares for 18:17–19, where the sea captains, travellers and sailors behold Babylon's burning and lament the loss of wealth through her sea trade.

At the third trumpet blast a great burning star – 'Wormwood' – falls on a third of the rivers and water springs, making them bitter and deadly (8:10–11). In the Old Testament 'wormwood' is consistently used metaphorically for the bitterness of suffering (Lam. 3:15, 19), the effects of sin (Deut. 29:19; Prov. 5:4) and retributive judgment (Jer. 9:15; 23:15).[40] Like the second trumpet, this judgment recalls the first plague that makes the Nile and Egypt's other waters, canals and ponds become putrid and impotable (Exod. 7:19–21; cf. Ps. 78:44). This bitter water of death contrasts with the 'springs of living water' promised to the Lamb's followers (Rev. 7:17).

Following the judgments upon the earth and the waters, the fourth trumpet blast disturbs the heavenly lights: 'a third of the sun was struck, and a third of the moon, and a third of the stars, so that a third of their light might be darkened' (Rev. 8:12). This recalls the penultimate plague in which a palpable darkness enveloped Egypt for three days (Exod. 10:21–23). Similarly, the beast's kingdom is 'plunged into darkness' in Revelation 16:10. The disturbance of the sun, moon and stars is a staple of prophetic and apocalyptic descriptions of the Day of the Lord, which brings natural disasters and destruction of earthly kingdoms.[41] The fourth trumpet particularly recalls Isaiah's

[39] See ch. 8, pp. 168–174.
[40] The Hebrew term *la 'ănâ* (wormwood) is rendered *pikros* (bitter [Prov. 5:4]), *pikria* (bitterness [Lam. 3:15, 19; Amos 6:12]) and omitted from Amos 5:7 in the LXX.
[41] Isa. 13:10; 24:23; Ezek. 32:7–8; Joel 2:10, 31; 3:15; Matt. 24:29; cf. *1 En.* 80.4–8. See Storms 2013: 263–264.

oracle concerning Babylon (13:1), in which the darkening of the celestial bodies accompanies the divine destruction of the lawless and proud (Isa. 13:10–11). The scene in Revelation 8:12 also strongly resembles the book's first depiction of the final judgment in the sixth seal, in which the sun goes black, the moon turns red and the stars fall to earth.

Five of the seven trumpets depict severe yet restrained judgment on 'a third' (*tritos*) of various parts of the created order described in Genesis 1 – 2. The effect is a partial destruction or de-creation of the earth, the sea and freshwaters, the heavenly lights and finally humankind (see Table 7.1 below).[42] This limitation recalls God's promise to never again destroy *all* living creatures as in the great flood (Gen. 8:21), while anticipating the total devastation, destruction and darkness of the bowls of divine wrath (Rev. 16:2–4, 10).

Table 7.1: The de-creation of the created order in the trumpets

Creation (Gen. 1 – 2)	De-creation (Rev. 8 – 9)
Day 3: Plants and trees sprout on the earth (Gen. 1:11–12)	Trumpet 1: A third of the earth and trees are burned (Rev. 8:7)
Day 5: Living creatures swarm in the sea (Gen. 1:20–21)	Trumpet 2: A third of the sea turns to blood, a third of the sea's living creatures are destroyed (Rev. 8:8–9)
A spring from the ground and a river from Eden water the garden (Gen. 2:6, 10)	Trumpet 3: A third of the rivers and springs of water become wormwood (Rev. 8:10 11)
Day 1: God separates the light from the darkness (Gen. 1:3–5) Day 4: God makes the sun, moon and stars to rule the day and night (Gen. 1:14–16)	Trumpet 4: A third of the sun, moon and stars are struck, affecting a third of the day and the night (Rev. 8:12)
Day 6: God creates mankind in his image and gives them dominion (Gen. 1:26–27)	Trumpet 6: A third of mankind is killed by three plagues (Rev. 9:15, 18)

In 8:13 John looks and hears an eagle proclaiming a threefold 'woe' to earth dwellers. This ominous warning introduces the final three trumpets, which receive longer descriptions than the initial four and

---

[42] The theme of de-creation is also noted by Ellul (1977: 74) and McDonough (2000: 242).

bring more intensified judgment. The fifth trumpet opens with a star falling from heaven, as in 8:10. Elsewhere in Revelation stars signify angels (see 1:20), and interpreters have identified the star in 9:1 as either a fallen angel – perhaps Satan himself – or an angel carrying out God's bidding. Some reason that the word 'fallen' (*peptōkota*) clearly designates this heavenly being as an evil agent under divine judgment.[43] Luke 10:18 similarly depicts Satan's fall, and Revelation 12:9 recounts how the dragon and his angels are 'thrown down' (*eblēthē*) to the earth. Alternatively, others argue that it is unlikely that an evil angel would be entrusted with 'the key of the shaft of the abyss' in 9:1 when in 20:1–3 one of God's angels 'descends' from heaven holding 'the key of the abyss' and binds Satan for a millennium.[44] On balance, the latter option is preferable: the star in 9:1 refers to an angel to whom God entrusts authority to open the abyss and release destructive agents on the earth. The fifth trumpet once again builds upon the pattern of the exodus plagues. The darkening of the sun and air in 9:2 again recall the ninth plague on Egypt (Exod. 10:21–23; cf. Rev. 8:12), while the destructive locusts allude to the eighth plague in which locusts cover the whole land of Egypt and consume all its plants and fruit such that 'not a green thing remained' (Exod. 10:12–15; cf. Ps. 78:46). Locusts are included among the covenant curses Yahweh threatens to send against Israel (Deut. 28:38; cf. 2 Chr. 7:13; Joel 1:4; Amos 4:9). Locusts always devour vegetation, but in Revelation 9:4 they are instructed not to harm the grass, plants or trees (contrast 8:7) but instead to torture people without God's protective seal for five months.[45]

The sixth trumpet blast unleashes four angels prepared to kill a third of humanity (9:13–15). These angels are not the same angels who hold back the four winds in 7:1; rather, they are evil agents equivalent to the four winds formerly restrained but now released for destruction. Their location at the Euphrates (9:14) recalls Old Testament prophecies of foes invading from the north, particularly Jeremiah 46:2, 10.[46] It also prepares for the sixth bowl judgment in

[43] Beale 1999: 491–493; Blount 2013: 173. Cf. Isa. 14:12; *1 En.* 88.1–3.
[44] Osborne 2002: 362–363; Koester 2014: 456.
[45] The green grass is consumed in Rev. 8:7 yet preserved from devouring locusts in 9:4. Thomas (1995: 31) posits, 'The grass damaged under the first trumpet has regrown by now, but the locusts are to leave it alone.' More likely, this apparent inconsistency between 8:7 and 9:4 signals that the trumpets do not relate future events in strict chronological succession but may be temporally parallel while reflecting different emphases. Cf. Beale 1999: 496; Koester 2001: 97.
[46] Cf. Isa. 8:7–8; Jer. 1:14–15; Beale 1999: 506–507.

which the great river's water is dried up so that the kings may assemble for Armageddon (Rev. 16:12–16). The 'three plagues' in 9:18 – fire, smoke and sulphur – allude to the archetypal destruction of Sodom and Gomorrah (Gen. 19:24, 28; cf. Luke 17:29) and anticipate God's climactic judgment on his enemies (Rev. 14:10–11; 18:9; 20:10; 21:8). The sixth trumpet is not clearly patterned after the exodus plagues like the previous five, though the unrepentant response to the plagues by 'the rest of humankind' parallels Pharaoh's hard-hearted refusal to submit to Yawheh despite the ten plagues (Exod. 4:21; 14:4).

Following the important 'literary and theological parenthesis' of Revelation 10:1 – 11:13,[47] John announces that the second woe has passed and 'the third is coming quickly' (11:14). Because the seventh trumpet blast in 11:15 does not bring destructive judgment but heavenly praise, many interpreters resist identifying the third woe with the seventh trumpet.[48] However, as Koester explains, 'given the pattern of connecting the three woes to the last three trumpets, it seems best to identify the final woe with the seventh trumpet, since the coming of God's kingdom does bring woe to those who destroy the earth'.[49]

The twenty-four elders worship God because the establishment of his reign (*ebasileusas*) brings divine wrath (*orgē*) on the raging nations (11:17–18). This hour of judgment promises reward for those who fear God's name and destruction for those who destroy the earth (*diaphtheirai tous diaphtheirontas tēn gēn* [11:18]).[50] Morris comments, 'The punishment fits the crime. God's *wrath* is not irrational, but the fitting response to the conduct of *the nations*.'[51] This heavenly praise reflects the pattern of Psalm 2: the nations rage and plot against the Lord and his Messiah (2:1),[52] but God sits enthroned in heaven and speaks to them 'in his anger' (*en orgē autou* [2:4–5]). The Lord's anointed is installed as king on Zion (2:6) and will inherit the nations and rule them with an iron rod (2:8–9; cf. Rev. 12:5; 19:15). The earth's kings are warned to fear the Lord and celebrate his rule or else face divine anger and destruction (2:10–12). Moreover, the final trumpet recalls Exodus 15, where Moses and Israel praise God following the

---

[47] Beale 1999: 609.

[48] Charles 1920: 1:292–298; Thomas 1995: 99–100; Smalley 2005: 288–289.

[49] Koester 2014: 504. Cf. Bauckham 1993a: 11; Blount 2013: 219.

[50] Beale (1999: 616) posits that this destruction in Rev. 11:18 alludes to the announcement of judgment on Babylon in Jer. 51:25 [28:25 LXX].

[51] Morris 1987: 149, emphases original.

[52] Moyise (2004: 232–233) suggests that Rev. 11:15 employs the verb *ōrgisthēsan* for the nations' fury under the influence of Exod. 15:14 LXX (*ēkousan ethnē kai ōrgisthēsan*) or Ps. 99:1 (98:1 LXX, *orgizesthōsan laoi*).

rescue from Egypt.[53] Nations became angry (*ethnē . . . ōrgisthēsan*) when they heard how Yahweh led his redeemed and brought them into his sanctuary (15:13–14, 17). The song of the seventh trumpet begins precisely where the Song of Moses concludes: the Lord 'will reign for ever and ever'.[54]

The trumpet judgments conclude with lightning flashes, rumblings, thunders and an earthquake (Rev. 11:19), recalling the theophanic finale of the seals (8:5).[55] The 'great hail' after the seventh trumpet recalls the seventh plague (Exod. 9:18–25), while also creating an inclusio with the initial trumpet judgment (Rev. 8:7). Further, the reference to the ark of God's covenant in his heavenly temple (11:19) reinforces the associations with Sinai (Exod. 25:10) and signifies God's holy and gracious presence with his people.

The seven bowls of wrath

Interpreters debate the relationship and timing of Revelation's septets of judgment. Some hold to a non-chronological *literary* relationship between the seals, trumpets and bowls; others discern a strict or modified *sequential* relationship; while still others hold to some form of *parallelism* or *recapitulation*.[56] Further, interpreters debate whether these judgments concern the fall of Jerusalem or Rome (preterists), the end of history (futurists) or the church age between Christ's first and second comings (idealists).[57] The repetition of flashes of lightning, rumblings, peals of thunder and an earthquake following the seventh seal (8:5), the seventh trumpet (11:19) and the seventh bowl (16:18) strongly suggests a parallel relationship of the cycles. The striking similarities between the trumpets and bowls and their common exodus background further signal parallelism.[58] At the same time, many have noted an intensification of the judgment between the three septets. For example, the second trumpet depicts a third of the sea becoming blood and a third of sea creatures dying, but in the

---

[53] Beale 1999: 618–619.

[54] Rev. 11:15 (*basileusei eis tous aiōnas tōn aiōnōn*); Exod. 15:18 LXX (*kyrios basileuōn ton aiōna kai ep' aiōna kai eti*).

[55] For additional discussion, see ch. 7, pp. 143–146.

[56] Storms (2013: 394–406) presents and analyses five interpretive schemes. For a concise history of interpretation, see Koester 2014: 437–438.

[57] Cf. ch. 1, pp. 9–15.

[58] E.g. Steinmann (1992: 76) convincingly argues that 'the sixth seal, trumpet, and bowl are each a tripartite unity' and concludes that the three cycles 'are to be understood as parallel, not sequential'.

Table 7.2: The Exodus plagues and Revelation's trumpets and bowls

Trumpets in Revelation 8 – 11	Bowls in Revelation 16	Plagues in Exodus 7 – 10
1st trumpet (8:7): on earth (*gē*); hail and fire	**1st bowl** (16:2): on earth (*gē*); festering sores	**6th and 7th plagues** (9:8–12, 22–25): dust over the land; festering boils; hail
2nd trumpet (8:8–9): on sea; water turns to blood; a third of sea creatures die	**2nd bowl** (16:3): on sea; sea to blood; all sea creatures die	**1st plague** (7:20–21): Nile to blood; fish die
3rd trumpet (8:10–11): on rivers and springs; turn bitter	**3rd bowl** (16:4): on rivers and springs; blood	**1st plague** (7:20–21): Nile to blood
4th trumpet (8:12): on sun, moon and stars; third of sun, moon and stars turn dark	**4th bowl** (16:8–9): on sun; people scorched	**9th plague** (10:21–23): darkness
5th trumpet (9:1–11): the abyss opened; darkness; locusts *torment* people	**5th bowl** (16:10–11): on the throne of the beast; darkness; people in *agony*	**8th and 9th plagues** (10:12–15, 21–23): locusts; darkness
6th trumpet (9:13–21): four angels released at the Euphrates; third of people killed	**6th bowl** (16:12–14): on Euphrates; river dried up; deceptive demonic spirits like frogs	**2nd plague** (8:2–7): frogs from the Nile River; magicians' secret arts
7th trumpet (11:15–19): lightning, rumblings, thunder, earthquake, severe hailstorm	**7th bowl** (16:17–21): into the air; lightning, rumblings, thunder, severe earthquake, huge hailstones	**7th plague** (9:22–25): thunder, hail, lightning

second bowl judgment the whole turns to blood and every creature dies (8:8–9; 16:3; see Table 7.2 above).[59] Further, the sun is darkened in the fourth trumpet, but the fourth bowl results in the sun scorching people with fire and the fifth bowl plunges the beast's kingdom into darkness (8:12; 16:8–10). The correspondence and escalation between cycles – particularly the trumpets and bowls – is in my view

[59] Table adapted from Tabb 2015: 2613.

best explained as 'progressive parallelism' or 'recapitulation'.[60] Storms explains that 'in the vision of the trumpets John sees the preliminary, introductory aspect of a judgment, of which the corresponding bowl is the intensified and consummate expression'.[61]

The third and final cycle of judgments – the seven bowls of divine wrath – brings definitive devastation on unrepentant humanity allied with the beast (16:2, 10). The seven bowls substantially parallel the seven trumpets (8:6 – 11:19) and likewise continue to follow the script of the exodus plagues.[62] Beale explains:

> Both trumpets and bowls present the plagues in the same order: plagues striking (1) the earth, (2) the sea, (3) rivers, (4) the sun, (5) the realm of the wicked with darkness, (6) the Euphrates (together with influencing the wicked by demons), and (7) the world with the final judgment . . . The overwhelming likeness of the trumpets and the bowls is a result of both being modeled on the exodus plagues.[63]

The Apocalypse introduces the bowl judgments as 'seven plagues, which are the last, for in them God's wrath is completed' (15:1; cf. 15:6, 8; 21:9). The designation 'plagues' (*plēgai*) recalls the divine punishments against Pharaoh and Egypt, from which Israel was spared (Exod. 11:1; 12:13 LXX). It also closely resembles God's warning to Israel in Leviticus 26:21 LXX: 'If after this you walk treacherously and are unwilling to obey me, I will add to you seven plagues [*plēgas hepta*] in accordance with your sins.' As noted earlier, the fourth seal recalls the threat of wild beasts, sword, pestilence and famine in Leviticus 26:22–26. In context, 'seven plagues' (26:21) is equivalent to 'sevenfold' (*heptakis*) chastisement for Israel's sins (26:18, 24, 28), a figurative designation for increasingly severe judgments that would result in scattering for Israel and 'sabbaths' for the land (26:35). If Leviticus 26 stands behind the bowls full of seven plagues in Revelation, these consummate judgments against idolatry and immorality 'not only purge and punish but also serve as warnings to repent'.[64] Koester asserts that 'Revelation's final plagues press the beast's allies to repent.'[65] DeSilva reasons that Revelation's plagues,

---

[60] See Beale 1999: 121–132, 144–145, 809; Storms 2013: 400–406.
[61] Storms 2013: 400.
[62] Casey 1987: 36–37.
[63] Beale 1999: 808–809.
[64] Ibid. 803.
[65] Koester 2014: 631.

like those against Egypt, 'were meant to induce repentance' but 'are simply unsuccessful in this regard'.[66] However, Revelation 16 does not hint at unbelievers' contrition and change in response to these divine blows. Rather, just like the beast, they repeatedly 'blaspheme' God (16:9, 11, 21; cf. 13:5–6), and 'they did not repent' (16:9, 11; cf. 9:20). The angels pour out the bowls of wrath 'with unimpeded rapidity', signalling that 'the time for repentance is past'.[67] Further, the bowls offer fitting retribution on God's enemies who now reap what they have sown to avenge the blood of God's people (16:6). Thus the bowls seem designed not to induce the beast and its loyal allies to repent but to reassure suffering saints of their future vindication (cf. 3:9; 6:10) while warning those within the covenant community about the calamitous consequences of compromise.

The initial four bowl judgments – like the trumpets – target the earth, sea, springs and sky (8:7–12; 16:2–9), demonstrating God's unrivalled glory and sovereign authority over these four spheres of creation (14:7).[68] When the first angel pours his bowl on the earth, 'harmful and painful sores' (*helkos kakon kai poněron*) afflict those who worship the beast's image and bear his mark (16:2; cf. 13:15–16). This clearly recalls the sixth plague, when 'sores' (*helkē*) break out on man and beast throughout all Egypt (Exod. 9:9–10). When the second angel pours out his bowl, the sea becomes 'like blood of a corpse', and every sea creature perishes (Rev. 16:3). Similarly, the third bowl turns the rivers and springs to blood (16:4). This escalates the earlier partial judgments on the sea and springs (8:8–9) and again alludes to the first plague when all the Nile's water turns into blood and the fish die (Exod. 7:20–21; cf. Pss 78:44; 105:29). The fourth angel pours out his bowl on the sun. The sun goes black in the sixth seal and is partially darkened in the fourth trumpet, but now the sun scorches humanity with fire (Rev. 16:8–9).[69] In contrast, 7:16 depicts the redeemed before God's throne being protected from the sun's scorching heat.

The angel over the waters explains the fittingness of these plagues: 'For the blood [*haima*] of saints and prophets they poured out, and blood [*haima*] you have given them to drink. They are worthy of this' (16:6). This exemplifies the principle of *lex talionis*, as the punishment

---

[66] DeSilva 2009b: 163.
[67] Bauckham 1993a: 14.
[68] Ibid. 31.
[69] 4 Macc. 14.9–10 reflects on the unsurpassed pains and agonies of fire. Cf. Tabb 2017: 119; de Silva 2009a: 348–349.

(blood drinking) corresponds to the crime (blood shedding).[70] It also answers the martyrs' cries for God to avenge their blood (6:10).

The fifth angel pours his bowl of divine wrath directly on the beast's throne (16:10), which was given him by the dragon (13:2). The beast's kingdom is plunged into darkness, alluding to the pitch darkness covering Pharaoh's dominion in Exodus 10:22. Beale notes that some early Jewish texts interpret the plague of darkness against Egypt as 'a theological metaphor'.[71] For example, Wisdom 17.2 depicts the Egyptians as 'captives of darkness and prisoners of long night', a fitting sentence for those who kept God's people in captivity (18.4). In Revelation 16:10–11 the people of the beast's kingdom revile God for their pain and sores (cf. 16:2).

The sixth bowl is poured out on the great river (16:12), from which the four angels are released in 9:14. The drying up of Euphrates recalls the parting of the waters at the Red Sea (Exod. 14:21–22) and later at the Jordan River (Josh. 3:15–17). Various prophetic texts warned that God would dry up the Euphrates and waters of Babylon (Isa. 11:15; 44:27; Jer. 50:38; 51:36). Yet in Revelation 16:12, the drying up waters does not prepare the way for God's people but for the formidable 'kings from the east' to pass safely. The pouring out of the penultimate bowl prompts the false trinity – the dragon, beast and false prophet – to produce their decisive deception. John sees 'three unclean spirits like frogs' come from their mouths to assemble the world's kings for battle (16:13–14). The Old Testament and early Jewish writings consistently associate frogs with the second plague on Egypt.[72] The sorcerers of Egypt 'by their sorceries' (*tais pharmakeiais autōn*) were able to parody the frog plague (Exod. 8:7 [8:3 LXX]), and such counterfeit signs characterize the deceptive practices of the false prophet (Rev. 13:13–14; 19:20) and Babylon (18:23). The assembling (*synēgagen*) of the world's rulers in 16:16 may recall the concerted opposition to the Lord and his anointed in Psalm 2:2, and prepares for the gathering for war against Christ and his army in Revelation 19:19.[73]

When the final angel pours out his bowl, a voice from the divine throne says, 'It is done!' (*gegonen*; 16:17). This pronouncement signals that God has accomplished his mysterious plan (10:7), established his

---

[70] Bauckham 2001a: 262; deSilva 2009b: 163. Cf. Ps. 79:3, 10, 12.
[71] Beale 1999: 482.
[72] Exod. 8:2–13; Pss 78:45; 105:30; Wis. 19.10; Jub. 48.5; Philo, *Moses* 1.101, 144; Josephus, *Jewish Antiquities* 2.296–298.
[73] See ch. 6, pp. 129–133.

kingdom (11:15) and now consummated his wrath (15:1, 8). In 21:5–6 God declares that he is making all things new and reiterates, 'It is done!' The bowl sequence concludes with another storm theophany, as in 8:5 and 11:19. However, the 'great earthquake' in 16:18–19 creates a catastrophe of unprecedented proportions: 'The great city was split into three parts, and the cities of the nations fell, and God remembered Babylon the great, to make her drain the cup of the wine of the fury of his wrath.' The final bowl judgment shakes and shatters the sinful city of man. Once again, the punishment fits the crime: since Babylon 'made all nations drink the wine of the passion of her sexual immorality' (14:8), she must now swallow the wine of divine wrath (16:19; cf. 14:10; 18:3; Jer. 51:7). The next visionary cycle in Revelation 17:1 – 19:10 dramatically expands on this concise description of Babylon's demise.[74]

The cycle of bowl judgments concludes with a scene of cosmic dissolution in 16:20: 'And every island fled away, and no mountains were to be found.' This closely parallels the displacement of islands and mountains following the sixth seal (6:14) and the flight of heaven and earth at the final judgment (20:11).[75] The scene culminates in 16:21 with 100-pound hailstones falling upon people, which ironically answers unbelievers' frantic request for rocks to fall on them in the day of wrath (6:16). The superlative storm of hail recalls the seventh plague in which 'Yahweh sent thunder and hail, and lightning flashed down to the ground' (Exod. 9:23). Of the ten plagues of the exodus, only the seventh plague involves a storm with thunder and lightning. Thus Revelation fittingly fuses features of the storm plague with the storm theophany at Sinai (Exod. 19:16; 20:18) in presenting the thunderous presence of God in judgment.

New-exodus salvation

We have seen that the Exodus account of the plagues against Egypt and the Sinai storm theophany significantly shape Revelation's presentation of God's thunderous presence in judgment. In the exodus God destroys his oppressive adversaries in order to deliver his people and bring them into their promised inheritance. The Apocalypse follows a similar script as it discloses God's consummate plans for judgment and salvation through Jesus, the slain Lamb and returning King.

---

[74] See ch. 8, pp. 168–174.
[75] For additional discussion of these parallels, see Beale 1999: 844.

The foundational vision in Revelation 5 presents Jesus as the slain Lamb, an evocative image that recalls the Old Testament sacrifices and particularly the slaughter of the Passover lamb at the exodus (Exod. 12:6).[76] Casey writes, 'Jesus' sacrifice is that of a new and greater paschal lamb, whose redemptive death effects a new and greater exodus.'[77] The Lamb's blood ransoms people for God from the nations and makes them a kingdom and priests (Rev. 5:9–10), which recalls Israel's vocation as 'a kingdom of priests and a holy nation' (Exod. 19:6).[78] Jesus 'has freed us from our sins', invoking the new-exodus hope of Isaiah 40:2 LXX. Further, he accomplishes 'salvation' (*sōtēria*) for a multi-ethnic multitude (Rev. 7:10), a term associated with the exodus from Egypt (Exod. 14:13; 15:2) and the ultimate deliverance he promised to bring (Isa. 49:6; 52:7; 52:10). The palm branches in the worshippers' hands (Rev. 7:9) recall the feast of booths, which celebrated Israel's rescue from Egypt and anticipated their future return from exile (Lev. 23:40–43; Zech. 14:16; cf. John 12:13).[79]

In Revelation 15:3 the victors 'sing the song of Moses, the servant of God, and [*kai*] the song of the Lamb'. Most translations render *kai* 'and' in 15:3, but the conjunction may function epexegetically ('that is'), identifying the songs of Moses and the Lamb as a single hymn.[80] 'The song of Moses' likely recalls either the song Moses and Israel sang at the Red Sea (Exod. 15:1–18) or the song that God instructs Moses to teach the people at the end of his life (Deut. 31:30 – 32:43; cf. 31:19–22). The victors in Revelation 15:2 stand 'on the sea of glass', which refers to the floor of heaven (4:6) but may also recall the seaside location of Israel's song in Exodus 15.[81] The reference to Moses as 'the servant of God' (Rev. 15:3) likely alludes to Exodus 14:31 and further strengthens the connection to the song in Exodus 15.[82] As noted in the previous chapter, this song in Revelation 15:3–4 resounds with Old Testament affirmations of God's rule and righteous

---

[76] See ch. 3, pp. 59–61.

[77] Casey 1987: 35.

[78] See ch. 5, pp. 90–95.

[79] Jauhiainen (2005: 127) questions this identification of palm branches with the feast of tabernacles and suggests that they are 'symbols of victory in the ancient Mediterranean world'. In support of an allusion to the feast of booths in Rev. 7:9, see Beale and McDonough 2007: 1108–1109; Leithart 2018a: 334.

[80] Cf. Beale 1999: 793; Osborne 2002: 564; Smalley 2005: 385–386; Grabiner 2015: 186. Aune (1998a: 873) claims that '"the song of the Lamb" is very probably an editorial addition to an earlier form of the text', but this judgment lacks both textual support and contextual warrant.

[81] Bauckham 1993a: 296–297.

[82] Osborne 2002: 562.

acts among the nations.[83] The association of 'the song of Moses' with 'the song of the Lamb' in 15:3 calls to mind the Old Testament's paradigmatic act of redemption in the exodus and celebrates the new-exodus deliverance from sin and the eschatological victory over God's enemies that the Lamb achieves.

A final subtle yet significant affirmation of the eschatological new exodus comes in 21:1, when John says, 'the sea was no more'. The sea in Revelation is part of the created order, along with the heavens and earth (5:13; 10:6), and also carries rich symbolic associations with evil and enmity towards God and his people. The Apocalypse pronounces 'woe' on the earth and sea because the devil has come down in great wrath (12:12), and several verses later John beholds a beast rising from the sea (13:1). Later Babylon's economic prosperity is linked to its bustling sea trade, and the captains and sailors bitterly lament the great city's collapse that portends their own financial ruin (18:17–19).[84] God first demonstrates his power over the sea by separating the seas from the dry land and commanding creatures to fill the waters (Gen. 1:10, 22). In the exodus Yahweh 'turned the sea into dry land' to allow his people to pass safely through before tossing the Egyptians into the sea (Exod. 14:21, 26). The prophets assert that God will dry up Babylon's sea in judgment (Jer. 50:38; 51:36) and once again make a way in the sea for the redeemed to cross over to experience freedom from threats and enjoyment of eschatological blessing (Isa. 51:10–11; Zech. 10:11; cf. Isa. 43:16; 50:2).[85] Isaiah 43:19 LXX depicts this new-exodus redemption as an act of new creation: 'Look, I am doing new things [*idou poiō kaina*] that will now spring forth, and you will know them, and I will make a way in the wilderness and rivers in the dry land' (NETS). Likewise, in the Apocalypse God declares that he makes all things new (*idou kaina poiō panta*) shortly after John highlights the sea's absence (21:1, 5). Mathewson reasons that this allusion to Isaiah 43:19 signals that 'John conceives of eschatological deliverance as a new Exodus.'[86]

Conclusion

The theme of divine judgment looms large in the Apocalypse. The seven trumpets and seven bowls recall many of the plagues against

---

[83] See esp. Exod. 15:11; Jer. 10:7; Pss 86:9–10; 98:1–2. For discussion, see ch. 6, pp. 116–120.
[84] See ch. 8, pp. 168–174.
[85] Cf. ch. 9, pp. 193–195; Mathewson 2003a: 253.
[86] Ibid. 256.

Pharaoh and Egypt that expose the weakness and futility of the Egyptian gods and disclose the glory and power of Israel's God.[87] The exodus narrative exemplifies the biblical pattern of salvation through judgment as Yahweh defeats and destroys Israel's enemies in order to deliver his people.[88] Echoes of the exodus reverberate throughout the Prophets and the Psalms, and faithful reflection on Yahweh's mighty deeds in Egypt cultivated hopeful expectation that their God 'who makes a way in the sea' would return with omnipotent strength to dispose of their foes, deliver them from exile and direct them into fullness of joy (Isa. 43:16; cf. 51:9–11; Jer. 23:8).[89]

The Apocalypse discloses the last and greatest exodus. As the Israelites groaned for deliverance from Egyptian bondage (Exod. 2:23), so the martyrs cry out for justice and vindication before their oppressors (Rev. 6:10). In the exodus narrative God hears, sees and knows the cries of his troubled people, remembers his covenant promises and comes down to rescue them from their enemies (Exod. 2:24–25; 3:7–8). Likewise, in Revelation the prayers of the faithful ascend like incense to the heavenly throne and prompt a divine outpouring of judgment on the earth (Rev. 5:8; 8:3–5). The seven trumpets recall the plagues against Egypt as God destroys the earth's vegetation, turns water to blood, darkens the sun and unleashes tormenting locusts. The seven bowls are the last 'plagues' that recapitulate the restrained judgments of the trumpets and bring definitive devastation on those who align with the beast and curse the true God (15:1; 16:2, 10–11). Jesus the slain Lamb secures consummate salvation by his sacrificial blood (5:9–10), which inspires the redeemed to sing 'the song of Moses . . . and the song of the Lamb' (15:3).

This ultimate exodus spells decisive defeat for the most formidable foes of God's people. At the exodus Yahweh triumphs over Pharaoh's army, hurling horse and rider into the sea (Exod. 15:1). Yet the wilderness generation soon craves Egypt's comforts, and their descendants clamour for Egypt's protection and help (Exod. 16:3; Isa. 30:7; 31:1). The prophet depicts Pharaoh as 'the great dragon [*ton drakonta ton megan*] that lies in the midst of his rivers' (Ezek. 29:3 LXX;

---

[87] According to Exod. 12:12, Yahweh brings judgment 'on all the gods of Egypt'. Cf. Num. 33:4.

[88] On the interrelationship of salvation and judgment throughout the biblical story, see Hamilton 2010.

[89] For recent treatments of the biblical-theological significance of the exodus, see Estelle 2017; Roberts and Wilson 2018.

cf. Isa. 27:1).[90] In the Apocalypse 'the great dragon' (*ho drakōn ho megas*) is hurled down from heaven (Rev. 12:9), bound for a thousand years (20:2) and finally banished to unending torment in the lake of fire and sulphur along with the beast and false prophet (20:10). Though the Lamb's followers must endure the dragon's fury and the beast's oppression (12:17; 13:7), they will experience everlasting security and satisfaction in God's sanctuary (7:15–17) and will sing of the Almighty's glorious salvation and just judgments (19:1–3).

---

[90] Beale (1999: 632–633) discusses additional OT and Jewish depictions of Egypt as a dragon or sea monster.

Chapter Eight

Babylon the harlot and Jerusalem the bride

Then one of the seven angels who had the seven bowls came and said to me, 'Come, I will show you the judgement of the great prostitute who is seated on many waters, with whom the kings of the earth have committed sexual immorality, and with the wine of whose sexual immorality the dwellers on earth have become drunk.' (Rev. 17:1–2)

Then came one of the seven angels who had the seven bowls full of the seven last plagues and spoke to me, saying, 'Come, I will show you the Bride, the wife of the Lamb.' (Rev. 21:9)

Charles Dickens's classic *A Tale of Two Cities* memorably opens with a series of contrasts:

It was the best of times, it was the worst of times, it was the age of wisdom, it was the age of foolishness, it was the epoch of belief, it was the epoch of incredulity, it was the season of Light, it was the season of Darkness, it was the spring of hope, it was the winter of despair, we had everything before us, we had nothing before us, we were all going direct to Heaven, we were all going direct the other way . . .[1]

The Apocalypse concludes with its own tale of two cities – not England and France but Babylon and the New Jerusalem, which Augustine calls 'the city of this world' and 'the city of God'.[2] The former is called 'the great city' and depicted as a tawdry whore mounted on a beast, sipping holy blood from a golden goblet (16:19; 17:1–6). The latter is called 'the holy city' and cast as a radiant 'bride adorned for her husband', the Lamb (21:2, 9). The Apocalypse discloses to embattled believers that while it appears

---

[1] Dickens 1999: 1.
[2] Augustine, *The City of God* 18.1–2.

163

to be 'the best of times' for Babylon and 'the worst of times' for God's people, a great reversal is coming. John's visions of cosmic judgment and salvation culminate with the destinies of these two cities.[3]

This chapter compares and contrasts Revelation's presentation of the woman-cities Babylon and the New Jerusalem. Interpreters have regularly identified Babylon with Rome, the city on seven hills (17:9). However, Babylon is not simply a cipher for Rome but is a rich biblical-theological symbol for the world's idolatrous, seductive political economy – the archetypal godless city, which Rome embodied in the first century. Babylon's dramatic demise represents the culmination of God's judgment on ungodly human society, beginning with Babel (Gen. 11:1–9). Alternatively, Revelation 21 presents the New Jerusalem as the holy, everlasting temple city that represents God's redeemed people and fulfils Old Testament prophecies and patterns of God's enduring fellowship with his people, which was lost in Eden (Gen. 3:8, 24), anticipated by the Old Testament tabernacle (Exod. 25:8) and the temple (2 Chr. 6:18) and promised by Isaiah and Ezekiel.

Unlike Dickens's tale, the Apocalypse does not delineate a historical contrast with contemporary analogues but an eschatological contrast that highlights our ultimate allegiances and calls for action. The seer urgently summons readers to 'come out' of Babylon (18:4) and, in the book's final beatitude, depicts the blessedness of those who wash their robes, have access to the tree of life and 'enter' the city by the gates (22:14).

Babylon: the great city

The Apocalypse introduces 'the great city' as a place of antagonism, humiliation and death for God's people. After the beast kills the two witnesses, 'their bodies will lie in the street of the great city that symbolically is called Sodom and Egypt, where their Lord was crucified' (Rev. 11:8). This verse presents 'the great city' as the alternative to 'the holy city' (11:2), which some interpret as Jerusalem but which most likely denotes the afflicted people of God who are heirs of the 'New Jerusalem' (21:2).[4] The Apocalypse mentions 'the great

---

[3] There are several structural markers in 17:1–3 and 21:9–10 that signal new major visionary sections; see Table 1.4 on p. 23.

[4] For discussion of Rev. 11:2, see ch. 8, pp. 174–175.

city' eight times,[5] consistently designating it as 'Babylon the great' (16:19) or 'Babylon' (18:10, 21).

In the initial mention of this 'great city' in 11:8 the seer offers a symbolic or spiritual interpretation. The adverb *pneumatikōs* is variously translated 'symbolically' (ESV), 'figuratively' (NIV), 'prophetically' (NRSV), 'mystically' (NASB) and 'spiritually' (NKJV). Most likely, 'it refers to Spirit-given perception', as the prophetic Spirit discloses the great city's true character.[6] 'Sodom' is proverbial for an immoral, debased society deserving God's judgment. In Genesis 19:24 the Lord destroyed Sodom and Gomorrah with fire and sulphur in response to the 'outcry' against those cities and their grave sin (18:20).[7] The Old Testament prophets indict Judah for her Sodomesque laundry list of transgressions, including sexual immorality, deceit, rebellion, disgraceful abominations, haughty self-reliance and neglect of the needy (Isa. 1:9–10; 3:9; Jer. 23:14; Ezek. 16:46–50).[8] They also liken Jerusalem's devastating destruction (Lam. 4:6) and Babylon's future fate (Isa. 13:19; Jer. 49:18; 50:40) to the paradigmatic overthrow of Sodom and Gomorrah.

Egypt, the next 'spiritual' appellation for the great city in Revelation 11:8, recalls the powerful nation that oppressed and enslaved Israel before God brought his people 'out of the iron furnace' (Deut. 4:20; 1 Kgs 8:51; Jer. 11:4). The wilderness generation longed for the meat and delicacies of Egypt (Num. 11:5), and Judah later 'sought shelter in the shadow of Egypt' because of her famous horses and chariots (Isa. 30:2; 31:1). Egypt's luxuries and might offered an alluring but empty alternative to trusting the Lord (30:7).

Finally, John spiritually perceives that the great city is the place 'where also their Lord was crucified', presumably referring to Jerusalem (Rev. 11:8). Jesus lamented over Jerusalem as 'the city that kills the prophets and stones those who are sent to it' (Luke 13:34). The link with Jesus' crucifixion also reiterates the explicit connection between the message and suffering ministry of Jesus and *his* two witnesses (11:3).

Many interpreters have sought to identify 'the great city' as a reference to a particular geographic locale. Dispensationalists and historical critics commonly read 11:8 as a futuristic or historical

---

[5] *Hē polis hē megalē* (Rev. 11:8; 16:19; 17:18; 18:10, 16, 18, 19); *hē megalē polis* (18:21).

[6] Bauckham 1993a: 169.

[7] For recent discussion of Sodom's sin in Gen. 19, see Peterson 2016: 17–31.

[8] Cf. Koester 2014: 500–501.

reference to Jerusalem, respectively.[9] For example, Thomas boldly asserts, 'If language has any meaning at all, it is hard to identify "the great city" as anywhere else but Jerusalem.'[10] He correctly notes that Jerusalem is called 'this great city' once in the Old Testament (Jer. 22:8), but the same designation is used for Calah (Gen. 10:12), Gibeon (Josh. 10:2) and Nineveh (Jon. 1:2; 3:2; 4:11). The basic challenge with Thomas's position is that it neatly classifies references to Sodom and Egypt as 'allegory or metaphor' while insisting the immediately following clause ('where also their Lord was crucified') must be a historical location.[11] However, 'where' (*hopou*) in the Apocalypse regularly introduces 'symbolic, spiritual geography' and is best read as a further 'description of the city's spiritual character, adding the crucifixion alongside "Sodom and Egypt"'.[12] Further, Thomas and other interpreters unnecessarily distinguish 'the great city' in 11:8 from Revelation's references elsewhere to Babylon as 'the great city', which he similarly takes to be a literal reference to 'the city on the Euphrates by that name'.[13]

Others understand 'the great city' in Revelation 11:8 and elsewhere in the Apocalypse as a clear reference to Rome, the vast, prosperous empire of John's day. Christians and Jews from the first two centuries AD applied the moniker 'Babylon' to Rome (1 Peter 5:13; *4 Ezra* 3.1–2; 16.1; *2 Bar.* 11.1; 33.2). Further, the description of Babylon ruling over many nations with vast commercial influence and affluence is apropos for Rome in John's time.[14] The vision of the scarlet-clad harlot in Revelation 17 satirizes popular depictions of the goddess Roma as a virtuous woman dressed for battle, lounging on Rome's seven hills.[15]

---

[9] Those identifying 'the great city' as *future* Jerusalem include Thomas 1995: 94; MacArthur 1999: 303–304. Those interpreting Rev. 11:8 as a reference to *historical* Jerusalem include Ford 1975: 180; Chilton 1990: 281; Giesen 1997: 255; Aune 1998a: 619–621; Leithart 2018b: 170–177.

[10] Thomas 1995: 94; cf. MacArthur 1999: 303–34.

[11] Thomas 1995: 93–94.

[12] Beale 1999: 592.

[13] Thomas 1995: 207; cf. Walvoord 1966: 240–241. Swete (1906: 135) acknowledges, 'In the ultimate meaning of the symbols, the City is doubtless not Jerusalem, but Rome, the persecutor of the Saints, the mystic Sodom and Egypt of the early centuries, where Christ was crucified afresh in His Saints. But this line of thought has not yet come into view; for the present Jerusalem, the city of the Crucifixion and of the earliest Christian martyrdoms, by a strange irony represents the antagonist of the *civitas Dei*.'

[14] See esp. Bauckham 1993a: 338–383 ('The Economic Critique of Rome in Revelation 18'); Biguzzi 2006: 371–386.

[15] Koester 2001: 158–159; Osborne 2002: 608–609.

For John's first readers, 'the great city' looks much more like Rome than Jerusalem – particularly if one follows the traditional dating of the book to Domitian's reign.[16] However, Rome is not 'Babylon' without remainder. The seer names the city *spiritually* in 11:8, and the apparently contradictory links to Calvary and Caesar's hills are clues that 'Revelation's great city can never be located on a terrestrial map.'[17]

The moniker 'Babylon' is thick with biblical associations. 'Babylon strikes a chord, not a single note.'[18] In King Nebuchadnezzar's day it was the most advanced, powerful civilization the world had seen – 'the head of gold' ruling over all (Dan. 2:38). Babylon was also the 'enduring' and 'ancient nation' of 'mighty warriors' that God raised up to execute covenant judgment on his unfaithful people (Jer. 5:15–16; cf. Deut. 28:49–52; Hab. 1:5–12). The ancient prophecies were fulfilled when Nebuchadnezzar's army besieged David's city from 588 to 586 BC. They starved the people, scattered the army, slaughtered the royal sons, smashed the walls, set fire to the Lord's house and seized its treasures (2 Kgs 25:1–17). This ruthless, bitter enemy left the land in ruins and took Judah into exile (2 Kgs 25:21), where God's people wept 'by the waters of Babylon' and served the foreign despot for three score and ten (Ps. 137:1; Jer. 25:11–12). Revelation 16:19 identifies 'the great city' as 'Babylon the great', a title adapted from Nebuchadnezzar's boast 'Is not this *great Babylon*, which I have built by my mighty power as a royal residence and for the glory of my majesty?' (Dan. 4:30 [4:27 MT]).[19] Such bragging about kingdom building recalls ancient humanity's arrogant quest to make a name for themselves in 'the land of Shinar' (Gen. 11:2, 4; Dan. 1:2). Significantly, Babel's founder is the mighty man and kingdom-builder Nimrod, whose name means 'rebel' (Gen. 10:8–10).[20] At 'Babel' or 'Babylon' (MT, *bābel*) God 'muddled' (*bālal*) languages and scattered peoples for their rebellion (Gen. 11:9).[21] Already in Genesis, Babel/Babylon represents the idolatrous quest for human glory in revolt against God. 'Babylon the great' in the Apocalypse is the seed of Nimrod in full flower. It is the world's idolatrous, seductive, political economy – the quintessential pagan city. Caird aptly writes, 'Rome is

---

[16] E.g. Irenaeus, *Against Heresies* 5.30.3; Eusebius, *Ecclesiastical History* 3.18.1–5; Victorinus, *Commentary on the Apocalypse* 10.3. Cf. Carson and Moo 2005: 707–711.
[17] Boxall 2006: 165–166.
[18] Leithart 2018a: 9.
[19] Beale and McDonough 2007: 1132.
[20] Dempster 2003: 75, n. 39.
[21] Fokkelman 2004: 12.

simply the latest embodiment of something that is a recurrent feature of human history. The great city is the spiritual home of those John dubs inhabitants of earth; it is the tower of Babel, the city of this world, Vanity Fair.'[22]

Thus John's spiritual explanation of the 'great city' challenges the church to see their location aright – Jesus' witnesses reside and testify in hostile territory. Behind Rome's lavishness is Sodom's corrupting licentiousness. Caesar's 'peace' secured through violence amounts to Pharaoh's 'house of bondage' from which God's people must flee lest they 'share in her plagues' (Exod. 20:2; Rev. 18:4). Christians follow the Lamb on the Calvary road, yet God will avenge their blood shed in Babylon (Rev. 19:2).

Babylon: the great harlot

John's final two visions 'in the Spirit' (Rev. 17:3; 21:10) are tightly connected by a number of literary markers and related motifs.[23]

1. The speaker in both visions is identical: 'one of the seven angels who had the seven bowls came and spoke with me' (17:1; 21:9).
2. Both visions begin with the invitation 'Come, I will show you' (*deuro, deixō soi*), unique to 17:1; 21:9.
3. The visions focus on two women: 'the great harlot seated on many waters' (17:1) and 'the bride, the wife of the lamb' (21:9).
4. The angel carries John away 'in the Spirit' (*apēnenken me en pneumati* [17:3; 21:10]).
5. The seer moves to different symbolic locations: 'into a wilderness' (17:3) and 'to a great and high mountain' (21:10).
6. Each woman *(gynē)* represents a city (*polis*): 'the great city that has dominion over the kings of the earth' (17:18) and 'the holy city Jerusalem coming down out of heaven from God' (21:10).

These notable parallels accentuate the pointed differences between the two woman-cities that John sees.[24]

The vision concerning Babylon's demise in Revelation 17:1 – 19:10 expands upon the final bowl judgment in 16:17–21.[25] The seer makes

---

[22] Caird 1984: 138.
[23] Giblin 1974; Bauckham 1993a: 4.
[24] See Table 8.3 on p. 183.
[25] This unit is 'a large interpretive review of the sixth and seventh bowls', according to Beale (1999: 847).

this connection explicit by reintroducing 'one of the seven angels who had the seven bowls' (17:1) and referring to the woman as 'Babylon the great', as in 16:19. Additionally, another angel declares, 'Fallen, fallen is Babylon the great!' in 18:2, recalling the same pronouncement in 14:8 (cf. Isa. 21:9).

The angel reveals to John 'the judgement of the great prostitute' (Rev. 17:1), later identified as 'the great city that has dominion over the kings of the earth' (17:18). The seer describes the woman's beastly mount (v. 3), her lavish clothing, charms and cup (v. 4) and her iniquitous intoxication (v. 6).[26] The name on her forehead discloses the woman's true identity: 'Babylon the great, mother of prostitutes and of earth's abominations' (v. 5). Beale and Gladd note, 'Names written on "foreheads" in the book reveal the true character of people and their ultimate allegiance'; so too with the harlot (17:5) and the bride of the Lamb (22:4).[27] John calls the harlot's name 'a mystery' (*mystērion* [17:5]), a technical term drawn from Daniel's prophecy.[28] 'Mystery' denotes spiritual and eschatological realities hidden from human understanding that only God may 'uncover' (*anakalyptō*), 'reveal' (*ekphainō*) and 'show' (*dēloō*) in his time.[29] In Daniel these mysteries concern things that 'must happen at the end of the days' (2:29 LXX). Further, 'the term mystery highlights the ironic nature of the fulfillment and its reversal of expectations'.[30] Thus, by calling the harlot's name 'a mystery', John signals the divine disclosure of the woman's identity and the surprising way that her judgment will occur in accord with God's plan (Rev. 17:16–17).

Revelation's portrayal of Babylon as 'the great prostitute' (17:1; 19:2) moves hearers to disgust, repulsion and critical distance from this deplorable counterfeit society.[31] This identification is also rich with biblical echoes, particularly to the Old Testament prophets, who persistently likened Israel's idolatry and immorality to adultery and prostitution.[32] Hosea famously took Gomer, 'a wife of whoredom', signifying Israel as God's unfaithful covenant partner (Hos. 1:2).

---

[26] For discussion of 'the beast', see ch. 6, pp. 121–124.

[27] Beale and Gladd 2014: 281.

[28] Beale and Gladd 2014: 286. *Mystērion* occurs eight times in Dan. 2 LXX (vv. 18, 19, 27, 28, 29, 30, 47 [twice]) and once in Dan. 4:9 TH, consistently rendering the Aramaic *roz*.

[29] *Anakalyptō*: Dan. 2:28–29 LXX; *ekphainō*: Dan. 2:19, 30 LXX; *dēloō*: Dan. 2:28–30, 47 LXX.

[30] Beale and Gladd 2014: 287.

[31] DeSilva 2008: 18–19. Cf. Quintilian, *The Orator's Education* 6.1.15.

[32] See the excellent study by Ortlund (1996).

Isaiah lamented 'how the faithful city has become a whore' (1:21).
Jeremiah said that Judah has 'the forehead of a whore', refusing
to be ashamed for her abominations (3:3). Ezekiel chided Jerusalem
for committing 'the deeds of a brazen whore', yet refusing payment for
her illicit services (16:30–31). Some interpreters take Israel's history
of whoredom as corroborating evidence that 'the great prostitute' is
in fact Jerusalem, not Rome.[33] This reading is implausible, as noted
above in the discussion of Revelation 11:8. Notably, the prophets
elsewhere depict the pagan cities Tyre and Nineveh as prostitutes:

> In that day Tyre will be forgotten for seventy years, like the days
> of one king. At the end of seventy years, it will happen to Tyre as
> in the song of the prostitute: 'Take a harp; go about the city, O
> forgotten prostitute! Make sweet melody; sing many songs, that
> you may be remembered.' At the end of seventy years, Yahweh will
> visit Tyre, and she will return to her wages and will prostitute
> herself with all the kingdoms of the world on the face of the earth.
> (Isa. 23:15–17)

> And all for the countless whorings of the prostitute, graceful
> and of deadly charms, who betrays nations with her whorings, and
> peoples with her charms . . . And all who look at you will shrink
> from you and say, 'Wasted is Nineveh; who will grieve for her?'
> Where shall I seek comforters for you? (Nah. 3:4–7)

In the Apocalypse Babylon resembles these ancient whore-cities –
especially Tyre – who exerted immoral influence on other nations and
accrued massive wealth through vast economic networks, much like
Rome did in John's time.[34]

The angel explains to John that the great prostitute commits sexual
immorality with the earth's kings and intoxicates earth dwellers with
her immoral brew (Rev. 17:2). The Apocalypse presents Babylon's
enticing, inebriating, immoral influence among the nations as the
basis for her swift and total judgment by God:

> 'Fallen! Fallen is Babylon the great!' . . .
> *For* [*hoti*] all the nations have drunk the maddening wine of
> her adulteries. The kings of the earth committed adultery with her,

---

[33] See e.g. Chilton 1990: 421–423; Campbell 2012: 234, 299, 308.
[34] Koester 2014: 671; Bauckham 1993a: 347. On the allusion to Isa. 23:17, see Beale
1999: 849–850.

and the merchants of the earth grew rich from her excessive luxuries. (18:2–3; cf. 14:8)

In 18:3 and extensively in 18:9–19 the nations' immoral passion for the harlot city is presented as iniquitous commercial, material interest. 'The nations' loyalty to Babylon lay in her ability to provide economic prosperity for them.'[35] In this regard, 'the great city' is the successor of Tyre, 'the greatest trading centre of the Old Testament period, notable not, like Babylon, for her political empire, but for her economic empire'.[36]

The depiction of Babylon's fall and its devastating effects draws extensively on Old Testament prophecies concerning the fall of Babylon and Tyre.[37] 'Fallen, fallen is Babylon the great!' in 18:2 reiterates the angelic pronouncement in 14:8, where it follows the summons to fear and glorify God 'because the hour of his judgement has come' (14:7). This repeated proclamation of the great city's demise alludes to Isaiah 21:9, 'Fallen, fallen is Babylon; and all the carved images of her gods he has shattered to the ground.'[38] The true God does not share his praise with idols (Isa. 42:8), so he will destroy pompous Babylon, 'the glory of kingdoms' (13:19). As noted above, the Apocalypse's designation 'Babylon the great' also recalls the king's hubristic admiration of 'great Babylon' in Daniel 4:30, swiftly followed by Nebuchadnezzar's humiliation (4:31–37). The Apocalypse further depicts the ruined whore city as 'a dwelling place for demons, a haunt for every unclean spirit, a haunt for every unclean bird, a haunt for every unclean and detestable beast' (Rev. 18:2), recalling prophecies of Babylon's total desolation (Isa. 13:21; Jer. 50:39; 51:37).

Babylon's dramatic fall prompts contrasting responses of earthly mourning (18:9–19) and heavenly rejoicing (18:20; 19:1–3). The earth's kings (18:9–10), merchants (18:11–17a) and sea captains (18:17b–19) who once profited from the whore city now bitterly lament her judgment, which signals their own economic demise. Revelation 18 extensively parallels Ezekiel's prophecy against Tyre, suggesting that Ezekiel 26 – 27 serves as a blueprint or prototype for

---

[35] Beale and Gladd 2014: 280.
[36] Bauckham 1993a: 346.
[37] Ibid. 345.
[38] Rev. 14:8 and 18:2 more closely resemble the textual tradition preserved in Isa. 21:9 MT (*noplâ noplâ bābel*) than the LXX, which reads *Peptōken Babylōn*, 'Babylon has fallen.'

Table 8.1: Laments over Babylon and Tyre

Lament over Babylon (Rev. 18)	Lament over Tyre (Ezek. 26 – 27)
'The kings of the earth . . . lived in luxury with' Babylon (v. 9)	Tyre 'enriched the kings of the earth' (27:33)
'gold, silver' (v. 12)	'silver . . . gold' (27:12, 22)
'jewels, pearls' (v. 12)	'all precious stones' (27:22; cf. 28:13)
'fine linen, purple cloth' (v. 12)	'purple . . . fine linen' (27:16)
'ivory . . . costly wood, bronze, iron' (v. 12)	'vessels of bronze . . . ivory tusks and ebony . . . wrought iron, cassia' (27:13, 15, 19)
'cinnamon, spice' (v. 13)	'the best of all kinds of spices' (27:22)
'wine, oil' (v. 13)	'oil . . . wine' (27:17, 18)
'cattle and sheep, horses and chariots' (v. 13)	'horses, war horses . . . lambs, rams and goats' (27:14, 21)
'slaves, that is, human souls' (v. 13)	'they exchanged human beings' (27:13)
Babylon's wealth 'laid waste' (v. 17)	'a city laid waste' (26:19)
'What city was like this great city?' (v. 18)	'Who is like Tyre . . .?' (27:32; cf. 26:17)
shipmasters, sailors and traders 'threw dust on their heads as they wept and mourned' (v. 19)	mariners and sea pilots 'cast dust on their heads' and 'weep . . . with bitter mourning' (27:27–31)
'all who had ships at sea grew rich by her wealth' (v. 19)	'all the ships of the sea with their mariners were in you to barter for your wares' (27:9)
Babylon 'will be found no more' (v. 21)	'you will never be found again' (26:21)
'the sound of harpists and musicians . . . will be heard in you no more' (v. 22)	'I will stop the music of your songs, and the sound of your lyres shall be heard no more' (26:13)

this lament over Babylon's fall (see Table 8.1 above).[39] Babylon and Tyre seek glory and live luxuriously (Rev. 18:7; Ezek. 28:1–6) and enrich 'kings of the earth' (Rev. 18:9; Ezek. 27:33). The extensive list of cargo that the earth's merchants trade with Babylon (Rev. 18:12–13)

---

[39] 'John seems to have drawn his sketch of fallen Rome with dust and soot from the ruins of Tyre itself', according to Kraybill (1996: 152–153). Cf. Vogelgesang 1985: 31. Table adapted from Tabb 2015: 2618.

closely resembles Tyre's wares (Ezek. 27:12–25): gold, silver, various precious stones, purple cloth and fine linen, costly wood, ivory, bronze, iron, numerous spices, oil and wine, horses, sheep and trafficked human beings. Yet Babylon 'this great city', like Tyre the 'city of renown', is 'made desolate' (*erēmoō*), 'never again to be found' (Rev. 18:17–18, 21; Ezek. 26:17, 19, 21). In response, the sea captains (*kybernētai*) and other seafarers 'throw dust on their heads' and cry out in mourning (Rev. 18:17–19; Ezek. 27:27–30).

Revelation follows the weeping and woe of the earth's kings and merchants and the sea's captains (18:6–19) with the rejoicing of three corresponding groups in heaven: the saints, apostles and prophets (18:20). This recalls the contrasting exhortations in Revelation 12:12, 'Therefore rejoice, you heavens and you who dwell in them! But woe to the earth and the sea, because the devil has gone down to you!' The injunction in 18:20 – 'Rejoice over her, O heaven' – echoes the closing lines of Moses's song 'Rejoice, O heavens [*euphranthēte, ouranoi*] with him' (Deut. 32:43 LXX), which commands praise to God for executing vengeance on his adversaries. Jeremiah employs similar language when prophesying Babylon's fall: 'Then the heavens and the earth, and all that is in them, shall sing for joy over Babylon' (Jer. 51:48).[40] The particular combination of saints, apostles and prophets is found only in Revelation 18:20, where it likely denotes believers in general and two groups of leaders in the early church.[41] Elsewhere in the Apocalypse, the saints and prophets are persecuted and opposed yet await divine vindication and reward (11:18; 16:6; 18:24). Their blood stains the streets of Babylon (18:24; cf. 11:8), and God's true and just judgments against the violent whore city serve as answers to the prayers of his slain saints (6:10; 19:2; cf. 5:8; 8:3–4).[42]

In Revelation 18:21 a mighty angel throws a millstone into the sea to signify Babylon's irreversible, decisive judgment. This parabolic action recalls Jeremiah 51:63, where the prophet instructs his servant to tie a stone to the scroll containing Babylon's judgment and hurl it into the Euphrates. The angel explains, 'So will Babylon the great city be thrown down with violence, and will be found no more' (Rev. 18:21, echoing Jer. 51:64). Verses 22–23a poetically expand upon verse 21b

---

[40] Revelation reflects awareness of the textual tradition preserved in Jer. 51:48 MT, as Jeremiah LXX omits this verse.

[41] Osborne 2002: 654. Beale (1999: 916) identifies the three terms in Rev. 18:20 as 'believers in general and not particular groups of the Christian community', based on the allusion to Jer. 51:48.

[42] Cf. ch. 7, pp. 139–162.

with five things that 'will be . . . no more' (*ou mē . . . eti*) in Babylon: the sounds of musicians, mills and marriage and the sights of artisans and lighted lamps. This list of special and commonplace lost joys is a patchwork of Old Testament allusions headlined by Jeremiah 25:10, 'Moreover, I will banish from them the voice of mirth and the voice of gladness, the voice of the bridegroom and the voice of the bride, the grinding of the millstones and the light of the lamp.'[43] Ironically, Jeremiah's word of judgment prophesied the losses Judah would experience at the hands of Babylon until God would punish their oppressors (25:12). The absence of 'harpists and musicians, of flute players and trumpeters' in Revelation 18:22 most closely reflects the judgment on the earth in Isaiah 24:8 LXX ('the sound of the harp has ceased') and on Tyre in Ezekiel 26:13 ('And I will stop the music of your songs, and the sound of your lyres shall be heard no more'). The list of losses culminates poignantly with the cessation of weddings in the great city. Huber aptly calls Babylon 'a city without a bride' (Rev. 18:23),[44] which prepares the way for the jubilant presentation of the bride of the Lamb (19:7; 21:2, 9).

New Jerusalem: the holy temple city

The Apocalypse presents 'the holy city' as the present and future alternative to 'the great city' Babylon. Revelation 11:2 explains the nations 'will trample the holy city for forty-two months.' Elsewhere in Scripture 'the holy city' denotes Jerusalem (Neh. 11:1, 18; Isa. 48:2; 52:1; Dan. 9:24; Matt. 4:5; 27:53). Thus preterists interpret the nations trampling the city and the temple's outer court in Revelation 11:2 as a reference to Rome's sack of Jerusalem in AD 70 (cf. Luke 21:24).[45] Alternatively, dispensationalists understand Revelation 11:1–2 to prophesy a future temple rebuilt in Jerusalem during the end-time tribulation.[46] However, Revelation elsewhere consistently identifies 'the holy city' as 'the New Jerusalem' that comes down from heaven (21:2, 10; 22:19) and the 'temple' (*naos*) as the heavenly sanctuary (11:19; 14:15, 17; 15:5–6, 8; 16:1, 17) or God's presence among his

---

[43] Revelation more closely follows textual tradition preserved in Jer. 25:10 MT; the LXX substitutes 'a fragrance of perfume' for 'the grinding of the millstones'.

[44] Huber 2007: 185.

[45] Chilton 1990: 274–275; Campbell 2012: 130. While affirming a preterist dating of Revelation, Leithart (2018a: 422) does not identify the *naos* in 11:1 with the Jerusalem temple but with 'the spiritual temple of the church, the holy people that tabernacles in heaven'.

[46] Thomas 1995: 81–86.

people in the New Jerusalem (3:12; 7:15; 21:22).[47] Thus 'the holy city' in 11:2 'must refer to the initial form of the heavenly city, part of which is identified with believers living on earth'.[48]

The symbolic act of measuring God's temple, altar and worshippers in 11:1 recalls Ezekiel 40:3–14 and anticipates Revelation 21:15–17, where John measures the New Jerusalem with its walls and gates. Similar to sealing in 7:3, measuring signifies God's protection and ownership. The contrast between the measured temple (11:1) and the unmeasured 'outer court' (11:2) is frequently understood as distinguishing between groups of people: the church and unfaithful Israel, or the faithful and unfaithful church. More likely, this distinction indicates that 'the saints will suffer incredibly, but because God's protective hand is upon them, they will emerge triumphant'.[49] Significantly, 'the holy city' is trampled for 'forty-two months' (11:2), equivalent to Daniel's 'time, times, and half a time' (Dan. 7:25; 12:7).[50] This symbolic interval corresponds to the 1,260 days that the two witnesses prophesy (11:3) and the dragon and the beast wage war against the saints (12:6, 14; 13:5–7).[51] Revelation most likely interprets the Danielic three-and-a-half years figuratively for the church age, when God's people endure tribulation yet experience divine preservation as they await their inheritance in the 'New Jerusalem' (21:2).

Immediately following the white throne judgment in 20:11–15, John sees 'a new heaven and a new earth' and 'the holy city, New Jerusalem, coming down out of heaven from God' (21:1–2a). Fekkes rightly observes that the vision of *renewal* in 21:1 – 22:5 'can only be fully appreciated against the backdrop of the previous series of visions of *removal*'.[52] Babylon the great has fallen (18:2); the beast, false prophet and dragon have been hurled into the lake of fire (19:20; 20:10); and Death and Hades and unredeemed humanity follow suit (20:14–15). Further, 'the earth' and 'the sky' fled from God's presence (20:11). In contrast to Babylon, where the sights and sounds of life and delight are 'no more' (18:22–23), in the New Jerusalem there is 'no more' death, mourning, crying, or pain (21:4). These 'first things' (*ta prōta*) characterized the 'first heaven and the first earth' (*ho . . . prōtos ouranos kai hē prōtē gē*), which have all 'passed away' (21:1, 4).

[47] Bachmann 1994: 474–480.
[48] Beale 1999: 568.
[49] Osborne 2002: 413.
[50] See ch. 5, pp. 97–101.
[51] See Beale 1999: 646–647 ('The Background of the "Three and a Half Year Period"').
[52] Fekkes 1994: 226, emphasis original.

John's vision of the new creation and holy city draws extensively on the restoration prophecies of Isaiah and Ezekiel.[53] 'And I saw a new heaven and a new earth' (21:1) clearly alludes to Isaiah 65:17, where Yahweh announces that he creates 'new heavens' and 'a new earth' and will not remember the 'former things'. Revelation 21:2–4 follows the progression in Isaiah 65:19, where Yahweh repeatedly stresses that he 'will be glad over Jerusalem' and his people, while the sound of crying shall be 'no more'. John's precise reference to 'the holy city, the New Jerusalem' (*tēn polin tēn hagian Ierousalēm kainēn*) closely resembles Isaiah 52:1, 'Put on your beautiful garments, O Jerusalem, the holy city' (LXX, *Ierousalēm polis hē hagia*).[54] Several contextual parallels corroborate this allusion: both prophets stress that nothing unclean will enter the holy city (Isa. 52:1; Rev. 21:27) and summon God's people to 'come out' (*exerchomai*) from Babylon (Isa. 48:20; 52:11; Rev. 18:4).[55] The Apocalypse draws again from the Isaianic well in 21:4–6. The sweeping promises that God 'will wipe away every tear from their eyes, and death shall be no more' reiterates John's earlier vision in 7:17 and alludes to Isaiah 25:8, 'He will swallow up death for ever; and the Lord GOD will wipe away tears from all faces.' Likewise, the Alpha and Omega offers to freely satiate his thirsty people with springs of living water (Rev. 21:6), recalling the interlude vision in 7:16 and the prophecy of eschatological salvation in Isaiah 49:10: 'they shall not hunger or thirst, neither scorching wind nor sun shall strike them, for he who has pity on them will lead them, and by springs of water will guide them'. Moreover, the announcement from the throne 'Behold, I am making all things new' (*idou kaina poiō panta*; Rev. 21:5) recalls Yahweh's promise 'Behold, I am doing new things' (*idou poiō kaina*), in contrast to 'the former things' (Isa. 43:18–19 LXX). 'These Isaiah predictions again find their realization in the new creation.'[56]

In Revelation 21:10 the angel transports John in the Spirit 'to a great, high mountain' (*epi oros mega kai hypsēlon*) and reveals to him the glorious holy city. This transitional marker alludes to the opening of Ezekiel's famous vision of the restored temple, where the exiled prophet is set 'on a very high mountain' (*ep' orous hypsēlou sphodra*)

---

[53] For extended discussion of Rev. 21 – 22 in the light of early Jewish sources, see Lee 2001.

[54] Cf. Fekkes 1994: 230–231; Mathewson 2003b: 39–41.

[55] Abma (1997: 3–28) explores the motif of 'travelling from Babylon to Zion' in Isa. 49 – 55.

[56] Beale and McDonough 2007: 1151.

Table 8.2: The New Jerusalem and Ezekiel's temple

	Revelation 21 – 22	Ezekiel 40 – 48
God dwells among his people	21:3	43:7; 48:35
the prophet carried away in the Spirit	21:10	43:5
the prophet taken to a high mountain	21:10	40:2
the glory of God	21:11, 23	43:2, 5
twelve gates inscribed with the names of Israel's tribes	21:12	48:31–34
an angel's measuring rod	21:15 (golden)	40:3
perfect symmetry	21:16 (the city is cubic: 12,000 stadia long, wide and high)	45:2 (the sanctuary is 500 cubits square)
The water of life	22:1 (from God's throne)	47:1 (from below the temple's threshold)
Tree(s)	22:2 (tree of life on either side of the river yields fruit; leaves for the nations' healing)	47:12 (fruit trees on both banks; leaves for healing)

and beholds a city-like building (40:2). John's description of the holy city's features is broadly patterned after Ezekiel 40 – 48 (see Table 8.2. above).[57] Ezekiel explains that 'the gates of the city will be named after the tribes of Israel' (48:31 NIV); likewise, John sees a high wall with twelve gates inscribed with 'the names of the twelve tribes of the sons of Israel' (Rev. 21:12), while going beyond his predecessor in describing the wall's foundations with the names of the Lamb's apostles (v. 14).

John stresses that the holy city comes down 'from God' and has 'the glory of God' (21:10–11). In Ezekiel 43:1–5 the prophet dramatically depicts the glory of Yahweh coming from the east, entering the temple gate and filling the renewed temple. This parallels the glory of God filling the tabernacle (Exod. 40:35) and Solomon's temple (1 Kgs 8:10)

---

[57] Table adapted from Tabb 2015: 2623. Beale (2004: 351) presents a complementary assessment of parallels between Revelation and Ezekiel.

and dramatically reverses Ezekiel's earlier vision of God's glory departing from Jerusalem (10:22–23). Thus the awesome, radiant presence of God himself adorns and illuminates the New Jerusalem.

Like Ezekiel, John's revelatory angel has a measuring rod and measures 'the city and its gates and walls' (Rev. 21:15; cf. Ezek. 40:3, 5–6). In Revelation 'the city lies foursquare [*tetragōnos*], its length the same as its width' (21:16), which recalls the 'square' dimensions of the doorposts, the altar, the sanctuary and the whole city in Ezekiel's vision (41:21; 43:16; 45:2; 48:20). However, the holy city in Revelation 21:16 has a length, width and height of 12,000 stadia (roughly 1,380 miles), a massive expansion of the sanctuary (500 cubits square) and the city property (25,000 cubits square, roughly 62 stadia) in Ezekiel. The number 12,000 also recalls the symbolic counting of God's redeemed people in Revelation 7:5–8.[58] Significantly, the New Jerusalem is 'pure gold' (21:18), and its dimensions are a perfect cube, which uniquely recalls the Old Testament description of the most holy place in the temple: 'The length [*mēkos*] twenty cubits and twenty cubits the width [*platos*] and twenty cubits its height [*hypsos*], and he covered it with overlaid gold [*chrysiō*]' (1 Kgs 6:20 LXX). Thus Alexander writes:

> As golden cubes, the Holy of Holies and New Jerusalem are clearly connected. Since God dwells inside both of these structures, we may reasonably conclude that the entire New Jerusalem is an expanded Holy of Holies . . . By associating the temple with God, John appears to imply that the whole city is a sanctuary.[59]

The twelve jewels adorning the walls of the city in Revelation 21:19–20 substantially correspond to the twelve precious stones on the high priest's breastplate that corresponded to Israel's tribes (Exod. 28:17–21), with seven exact lexical parallels:

- jasper (*iaspis*)
- sapphire (*sapphiros*)
- emerald (*smaragdos*)
- chrysolite (*chrysolithos*)
- beryl (*bēryllos*)
- topaz (*topazion*)
- amethyst (*amethystos*).

---

[58] See the discussion on Rev. 7 in ch. 5, pp. 102–105.
[59] Alexander 2008: 20. Similarly, Beale 2004: 348, 370.

Ezekiel's lament over Tyre's king associates Eden, 'the garden of God', with precisely the twelve same stones as Exodus 28 (Ezek. 28:13–14).[60] Further, in Isaiah 54:11–12 LXX Yahweh promises to prepare Jerusalem's foundations with sapphires (*ta themelia sou sappheiron*), her battlements with jasper (*iaspin*), her gates with stones of crystal (*tas pylas sou lithous krystallou*) and her walled area with chosen stones.[61] The New Jerusalem's bejewelled beauty contrasts with Babylon's passing luxury.

While Ezekiel 40 – 48 envisions a rebuilt temple in the restored Jerusalem, John says, 'I saw no temple in the city, for its temple is the Lord God the Almighty and the Lamb' (Rev. 21:22). Some interpreters presume that the Old Testament prophecies of a physical temple must be fulfilled in a future millennial kingdom, not the New Jerusalem.[62] But the repeated allusions to Ezekiel 40 – 48 in Revelation's vision of the New Jerusalem and the absence of any reference to a physical temple in 20:1–10 make this position implausible and unwarranted. The New Jerusalem does not contain a *physical* sanctuary; rather, 'the equation of God and the Lamb with the temple approaches closely the essence of the Ezekiel vision, which is God's glorious presence itself'.[63] Yahweh stresses in Ezekiel 43:7 that he 'will dwell in the midst of the people of Israel for ever', and the book's closing verse states that the city's name shall be 'Yahweh Is There' (48:35). In Revelation 21,

> when temple gives way to city and throne, it is precisely because the full meaning of what a temple is and what it does has been realized in the direct and immediate presence of God that the covenant people enjoy the fullness of divine blessing.[64]

---

[60] Beale (2004: 79–80) argues convincingly that 'Eden is the archetypal temple sanctuary, upon which all of Israel's temples were based.' On Revelation's use of Gen. 2 – 3, see Table 9.1 on p. 188.

[61] Tob. 13.16 expands on Isaiah's vision of the restored Jerusalem: 'For Jerusalem will be built as his house for all ages. How happy I will be if a remnant of my descendants should survive to see your glory and acknowledge the King of heaven. The gates of Jerusalem will be built with sapphire and emerald, and all your walls with precious stones. The towers of Jerusalem will be built with gold, and their battlements with pure gold. The streets of Jerusalem will be paved with ruby and with stones of Ophir' (NRSV). Fekkes (1990: 280) reasons that the 'pearly gates' in Rev. 21:21 are 'a well-reasoned and comprehensive interpretation' of the Hebrew phrase *šĕ'ārayîk lĕ'abnê 'eqdoḥ* in Isa. 54:12.

[62] E.g. Thomas 1995: 474.

[63] Beale 2004: 348. Cf. ch. 9, pp. 195–198.

[64] Stevenson 2001: 306. Similarly, Lee 2001: 282; deSilva 2009b: 171.

Revelation 21:23–26 includes a series of allusions to Isaiah 60 when depicting the light, glory and security of the holy city. First, John explains that the city does not require the illumination of the sun or moon because 'the glory of God gives it light, and the Lamb is its lamp' (21:23; cf. 22:5). This recalls Isaiah 60:19: 'The sun will no more be your light by day, nor will the brightness of the moon shine on you, for Yahweh will be your everlasting light, and your God will be your glory.' In Isaiah 'light' is a potent image of salvation, revelation and new creation (cf. 2:5; 9:2; 42:6, 16; 49:6). The people 'hope for light, and behold, darkness' (59:9), but Yahweh's glorious, illuminating presence will bring an end to their mourning (60:20). Second, Revelation 21:24 depicts the response of nations and kings to this divine light in Isaianic terms. 'By its light will the nations walk' alludes to Isaiah 60:3: 'And nations shall come to your light', fulfilling the latter-day expectations of Isaiah 2:2–5. Revelation's vision of the earth's kings bringing the glory and honour of the nations into the city (21:24, 26) also recalls Isaiah 60:3, 5, 11. Third, the city's 'gates will never be shut by day – and there will be no night there', which alludes to Isaiah 60:11: 'Your gates will always stand open, they will never be shut, day or night.' While closed gates protected cities from foes, the perpetually open gates signal unending security and the welcome of the nations into the city of God.

New Jerusalem: the adorned bride

The New Jerusalem is a massive temple city where God's presence fills the new creation; it is also a radiant bride made ready for her covenant partner. In the Apocalypse 'the Bride' is a poignant designation for God's eternal *city* and his redeemed *people*, which serves as the antithesis of the seductive prostitute Babylon.[65] The drama of the divine marriage unfolds in several phases: the wedding is planned, publicized and prepared (Rev. 19:7–9); next the bride is revealed and 'a reciprocal covenant promise' is made (21:2–3); finally, the bejewelled bride is described (21:18–21).[66]

Revelation 12 depicts the people of God as a woman adorned 'in heaven' (v. 1) who is persecuted yet protected 'on earth' (v. 13–16).[67]

---

[65] Bauckham (1993b: 132–143) similarly considers the New Jerusalem as the place, people and presence of God.

[66] Fekkes 1990: 283. He notes that the terms *hetoimazō* (prepare [19:7; 21:2]) and *kosmeō* (adorn [21:2, 19]) link these three movements together.

[67] See ch. 5, pp. 105–107.

Similarly, the 'bride' is a corporate image for God's redeemed people in Revelation 19:7 (cf. 2 Cor. 11:2; Eph. 5:25–27). After the heavenly multitude rejoices over God's judgment of the great prostitute (19:1–3; cf. 18:20), John hears thunderous exultation at the announcement of the heavenly matrimony and the introduction of the chaste 'bride':

> 'Hallelujah! For the Lord our God the Almighty reigns. Let us rejoice and be glad and give him glory! For the wedding of the Lamb has come, and his bride has made herself ready. Fine linen, bright and clean, was given her to wear.' (Fine linen stands for the righteous acts of God's holy people.) Then the angel said to me, 'Write this: Blessed are those who are invited to the marriage supper of the Lamb!' (19:6–9a NIV)

The Old Testament frequently depicts Israel as the bride or wife of Yahweh. Ezekiel recounts how Yahweh 'clothed' his bride Jerusalem in fine linen and embroidered apparel, yet she 'played the whore' and made colourful shrines from her beautiful wedding garments (Ezek. 16:10, 16). However, the prophets envisioned a day when Yahweh would call back his wayward covenant partner and 'betroth' Israel to himself for ever 'in righteousness' (Hos. 2:14–20; Isa. 54:5–8). Isaiah in particular employs the metaphor of marriage to describe 'the *eschatological* relationship between God and his covenant people when he restores them from exile'.[68]

The introductory nuptial scene in Revelation 19 has several strong lexical and thematic links to Isaiah 61:10 – 62:5. First, the opening invitation 'Let us rejoice and *be glad* [*agalliōmen*]' (Rev. 19:7) recalls Isaiah 61:10 LXX, 'Let my soul *be glad* [*agalliasthō*] in the Lord' (NETS). Second, John parenthetically describes the bride's clothing as the saints' 'righteous acts' (*ta dikaiōmata*), which parallels Isaiah's repeated stress on the 'righteousness' or 'vindication' (*dikaiosynē*) of restored Jerusalem that will shine forth among the nations (Isa. 61:11 – 62:2).[69] The Apocalypse elsewhere employs the *dik-* word group to highlight the righteous acts and just judgments of God and Christ (cf. 15:3–4; 16:5–7; 19:11), though the proverbial expression 'let the righteous one still practise righteousness' (*ho dikaios dikaiosynēn*

---

[68] Mathewson 2003b: 46, emphasis original.

[69] Fekkes (1990: 273) notes the suggestive parallel between Rev. 19:8 and 'the robe of righteousness' in Isa. 61:10 MT. Beale (1999: 941–942) writes, 'Isaiah utilizes the metaphor consistently to refer to the *eschatological* relationship between God and his covenant people when he restores them from exile' (emphasis original).

poiēsatō eti) in 22:11 applies righteousness language to human acts (cf. Dan. 12:10).

In Revelation 19:8 the bride's radiant garments signify the church's enduring moral purity (cf. Eph. 5:27), in contrast to the harlot's 'fine linen, purple and scarlet', representing her fleeting wealth (Rev. 18:16; cf. 17:4; 18:12). Likewise, her 'righteous acts' (*ta dikaiōmata*; 19:8) are antithetical to Babylon's multitude of unrighteous acts (*ta adikēmata*; 18:5) and indicate that God vindicates his bride and executes vengeance on the harlot.[70] The divine passive *edothē autē* (19:8) signals that the bride's beautiful wedding dress 'has been granted to her as a gift in the first instance . . . Her faithlessness, persistent since remote times, is finally dissolved for ever in the chemistry of grace.'[71]

In Revelation 19:9 the imagery shifts from the bride's preparation to the guests' invitation to the marriage supper. The Apocalypse commonly employs multiple images to depict the same referent in a single passage and so too here: God's people are pictured as the Lamb's betrothed and the blessed guests are summoned to the feast.[72] Both images connote believers' corporate and individual joy, expectation and intimacy with Christ; the former image of the bride 'focuses on the corporate church', while the image of the guests emphasizes the calling and blessing of 'individual members'.[73] The motif of guests invited to a wedding feast (19:9) recalls Jesus' kingdom parable in Matthew 22:1–14. This parable distinguishes between the many guests called or invited (*kaleō*) to the feast and the 'chosen' few who actually attend; however, the Apocalypse calls those invited (*kaleō*) to the feast 'blessed' (*makarioi*), suggesting that these are called and chosen to partake (cf. Rev. 17:14).[74]

As noted earlier, the drama of eschatological marriage unfolds in several stages in the Apocalypse. While Revelation 19:7 announces that the Lamb's marriage has come and his bride has readied herself, she is not revealed and the marriage is not consummated until chapter 21. Koester aptly writes, 'Instead of coming directly to his marriage celebration, the Lamb is called away to battle.'[75] The anticipation of

---

[70] The saints' clothing in 19:8 may combine the notions of '*righteous acts by saints* and God's *righteous acts for saints*' according to Beale (1999: 941), emphases original.

[71] Ortlund 1996: 163–164.

[72] Koester 2014: 738; Osborne 2002: 675. Thomas (1995: 372) unconvincingly argues that the bride and the invited guests represent distinct groups.

[73] Beale 1999: 945. Rev. 12:17 similarly alternates between 'the woman' – the corporate people of God – and 'her offspring', individual members of the community.

[74] Beale 1999: 945.

[75] Koester 2014: 737.

the imminent wedding followed by the delay builds expectation and reassures the book's readers as they wait for the culmination of God's plans. Finally, after every enemy of God has been vanquished, John beholds 'the Bride, the wife of the Lamb' in her resplendent glory (21:9).

In Revelation 21:2 the 'holy city' is *likened* to a bride adorned for her husband, but 'in verses 9–10, the Bride appears *per se* and is equated with and identified as the new Jerusalem'.[76] Again John draws on Isaiah's prophecies of eschatological salvation as he describes the bride city. The simile 'like a bride adorned for her husband' (*hōs nymphēn kekosmēmenēn tō andri autēs*) in Revelation 21:2 alludes to Zion as 'adorned like a bride' (*hōs nymphēn katekosmēsen*) in Isaiah 61:10 LXX (cf. 62:5).[77] The New Jerusalem's adornment with jewels and gold reinforces the presentation of the temple city as a bride dressed for her wedding (Rev. 21:11, 18–21; cf. Isa. 49:18; 54:5, 11–12); once again, John deliberately contrasts the bride's enduring beauty with the harlot's borrowed bling (17:4; see Table 8.3 below).[78]

Table 8.3: Revelation's tale of two cities

Babylon the great	The New Jerusalem
the great prostitute (17:1) the great city of earth (17:18)	the wife of the Lamb (21:9) the holy city from heaven (21:2,10)
clothed with purple and scarlet (17:4)	clothed with bright, fine linen (19:8)
abominable deeds (18:4–6)	righteous deeds (19:8)
gold, jewels and pearls through corrupt commerce (17:4; 18:12, 16)	jewels, gold and pearls reflect God's glory (21:11, 18, 21)
the kings of the earth commit immorality and weep (18:9)	the kings of the earth bring their glory into the city (21:24)
a haunt for every unclean spirit, bird and beast (18:2)	nothing unclean will enter (21:27)
the nations deceived (18:23)	the nations healed (22:2)
torment and judgment (18:10)	blessing and life (22:14)
summons to come out (18:4)	summons to enter (22:14)

[76] Ortlund 1996: 168.

[77] Oswalt (1998: 574) explains that in Isa. 61:10 the prophet speaks as Zion.

[78] Table adapted from Tabb 2015: 2615. On Revelation's contrast between the harlot city and the bride city, see also Deutsch 1987: 123; Bauckham 1993b: 131–132; Beale 1999: 1117–1119; Mathewson 2003b: 49.

Thus in Revelation 21

> John mixes his metaphors, providing a richer understanding of the church triumphant as both the dwelling place of God and the beloved of the Lamb. The lines of expectation created by the fullness of Old Testament theology crowd into John's brief description of their final resolution.[79]

The New Jerusalem is the people of God and the place where God dwells with them for ever. The attractive picture of the Lamb's bejewelled bride works alongside the repulsive portrait of the imposter harlot to motivate Revelation's readers to remain faithful and true to their betrothed while resisting worldly pressures to compromise.[80]

Conclusion

The Apocalypse combines several significant biblical-theological motifs in describing and contrasting the harlot city and the bride city. The 'great city' embodies civilization that prizes human ambition, lust, wealth and power. Thus readers detect strands of Babylon, Tyre and Babel in John's tapestry. 'Babylon the great' is a glitzy, proud, seductive shell, which is empty and vain at the core because it seeks its own glory and opposes God and his people. Conversely, the 'holy city' stands for the place where God's glorious presence dwells and for the people whom God has redeemed and brought into covenant relationship with himself. This 'holy city' at present 'exists only in hiddenness and contradiction';[81] it is trampled and marginalized, a laughing stock and a gadfly in the world's eyes. Yet the Apocalypse discloses the true nature of reality and reveals that things are not as they might appear from humanity's perspective. 'Babylon the great' is a charlatan city clothed with stolen scarlet and glistening with fool's gold, whose designer make-up covers her ugly face. Babylon's powerful, prosperous political and economic edifice is really a house of cards with no future. Conversely, the humble 'holy city', whose light flickers at present, will one day shine like the sun with the radiant presence of God and the Lamb.

These two cities present Revelation's readers with an ultimate question of where their allegiance lies: with the Creator God and his

[79] Ortlund 1996: 168.
[80] Koester 2014: 804.
[81] Bauckham 1993b: 128.

people or with the world and all that it offers. In 18:4–5 a heavenly voice urges readers to respond to the news of Babylon's fall (v. 2): 'Come out of her, my people [*exelthate ho laos mou ex autēs*], lest you take part in her sins, lest you share in her plagues; for her sins are heaped high as heaven, and God has remembered her iniquities.' This warning recalls similar appeals by the prophets:[82]

> Go out from Babylon [LXX, *Exelthe ek Babylōnos*], flee from Chaldea, declare this with a shout of joy, proclaim it, send it out to the end of the earth; say, 'Yahweh has redeemed his servant Jacob!' (Isa. 48:20)

> Depart, depart, go out from there [LXX, *exelthate*]; touch no unclean thing; go out from the midst of her [LXX, *exelthate ek mesou autēs*]; purify yourselves, you who bear the vessels of Yahweh. (Isa. 52:11)

> Go out of the midst of her, my people [MT, *şĕ'û mittôkah 'ammî*]! Let every one save his life from the fierce anger of Yahweh! (Jer. 51:45)[83]

We have seen that 'Babylon' signifies the world's idolatrous, political economy, the city of humanity that opposes God. 'Babylon' is transhistorical and defies simple geographical identification with a single place on the map. John's readers may rightly see correspondence between 'Babylon' and Rome, but the 'great city' also resembles Babel, Sodom, Egypt, Tyre, Babylon and Golgotha. To 'come out of' Babylon does not require God's people to relocate physically or seclude themselves from the world but 'to take refuge in the living God' where they reside.[84] Revelation 11:3–10 presents the two witnesses – a symbol for the church – prophesying and dying on the streets of the 'great city' with earth dwellers looking on.[85] Likewise, Jesus summons embattled believers to 'be faithful unto death' (2:10), 'hold fast' (2:25; 3:11) and 'conquer' *in* Ephesus, Smyrna, Pergamum, Thyatira, Sardis, Philadelphia and Laodicea. Thus believers 'come out' by refusing to give in to 'the idolatrous allure of material affluence

---

[82] Cf. Jer. 50:8; 51:6–8.
[83] This verse is omitted from the LXX of Jeremiah.
[84] Augustine, *The City of God* 18.18.
[85] See further ch. 5, pp. 97–101.

and social acceptance'.[86] This means holding fast to the testimony of Jesus (12:11, 17) while enduring slander from synagogues (2:9), resisting the idolatrous compromise of the emperor cult and trade guilds (2:14–15, 20),[87] and shunning the seductive promise of affluence (3:17–18). There is a cost to coming out of Babylon – some may endure social pressure or economic disadvantage (13:17); others may face the sword (2:13; 13:10; 17:6). Yet God's people must 'come out' to avoid sharing in her plagues (18:4) and joining the chorus of bankrupted mourners who loved Babylon's lie (18:9–19).

The Apocalypse motivates God's people 'to resist the powerful allurements of Babylon' by unveiling 'an alternative and greater attraction' – the New Jerusalem, which 'belongs to the future, but . . . exercises its attraction already'.[88] Believers cannot yet enter by the city's pearly gates (22:14) but we eagerly await our place in it and are already considered 'the holy city' (3:12; 11:2). We have not yet experienced the full grandeur of the wedding day but have been redeemed by sacrificial love and betrothed to the Lamb (1:5; 19:7), and we must 'cultivate . . . an aching longing for the Bridegroom to come' for his Bride (22:17).[89] The saints may reside in Babylon's hostile territory but they belong to the city of God in the glorious new creation. 'There we shall be still and see; we shall see and we shall love; we shall love and we shall praise. Behold what will be, in the end, without end! For what is our end but to reach that kingdom which has no end?'[90]

---

[86] Johnson 2001: 339.
[87] On trade guilds see Beale 1999: 242, 249. According to Slater (1999: 253) the seven cities mentioned in Rev. 2 – 3 were each declared official centres for the imperial cult by the late first and early second century.
[88] Bauckham 1993b: 129.
[89] Ortlund 1996: 168.
[90] Augustine, *The City of God* 22.30.

Chapter Nine

All things new: a greater Eden

Then the angel showed me the river of the water of life, bright
as crystal, flowing from the throne of God and of the Lamb
through the middle of the street of the city; also, on either
side of the river, the tree of life with its twelve kinds of fruit,
yielding its fruit each month. The leaves of the tree were for
the healing of the nations. No longer will there be anything
accursed, but the throne of God and of the Lamb will be in
it, and his servants will worship him. They will see his face,
and his name will be on their foreheads. And night will be
no more. They will need no light of lamp or sun, for the Lord
God will be their light, and they will reign for ever and ever.
(Rev. 22:1–5)

C. S. Lewis concludes his classic novel *The Last Battle* with the
Pevensie children and their cousin Eustace taking in the new creation
and discussing whether or not it is like Aslan's country:

'If you ask me,' said Edmund, 'it's like somewhere in the Narnian
world.' . . .
   'I don't think *those* ones are so very like anything in Narnia,'
said Lucy. 'But look there . . . Those hills . . . the nice woody ones
and the blue ones behind – aren't they very like the Southern border
of Narnia?'
   'Like!' cried Edmond after a moment's silence. 'Why they're
exactly like.' . . .
   'And yet they're not like,' said Lucy. 'They're different. They have
more colours on them and they look further away than I
remembered and they're more . . . more . . . oh, I don't know . . .'
   'More like the real thing,' said the Lord Digory softly.[1]

The Apocalypse presents the glorious new creation as 'the real thing'
in 22:1–5.[2] Isaiah 43:19 prophesied that Yahweh would do new

[1] Lewis 1994: 73; emphasis original.
[2] Beynon 2010: 73.

187

things (LXX, *idou poiō kaina*), but in Revelation 21:5 God announces the comprehensive scope of his new creation activity: 'Behold, I am making *all* things new' (*idou kaina poiō panta*). The Apocalypse does not spell out the precise process of 'the first heaven and the first earth' passing away and 'a new heaven and a new earth' appearing (21:1). However, the syntax of 21:5 signals that God does not simply make *new things* to replace the old but makes all things *to be new*.[3] Middleton reasons that as Paul applies the language of cosmic renewal to the 'new creation' of believers in Christ (2 Cor. 5:17; cf. Isa. 43:18–19; 65:17), so 'the passing away of the present heaven and earth to make way for the new creation is also transformative and not a matter of destruction followed by replacement'.[4]

Revelation 22:1–5 builds on and develops John's previous description of the glorious new creation (particularly 21:3–5) in which God dwells with his people and brings consummate healing, redemption

Table 9.1: A new and greater Eden

Eden (Gen. 2 – 3)	New Jerusalem (Rev. 21 – 22)
a garden to till and keep (2:15)	a radiant, heavenly city (21:10–11)
river flowing from Eden (2:10)	river of the water of life flowing from God's throne (22:1)
gold and onyx nearby (2:11–12)	Pure gold, onyx and jewels (21:19–21)
command to rule and serve (1:26; 2:15)	serve as kings and priests (22:3, 5)
one man and woman (2:22–23)	the nations (22:2)
the serpent deceives and brings shame (3:1)	nothing unclean, shameful or deceitful (21:27)
exile away from God's presence (3:23–24)	God's presence endures for ever (21:3, 23)
lost access to the tree of life (3:22–24)	eternal access to the tree of life (22:2, 14)

---

[3] *Kaina* functions not as an attributive adjective but as a complement to the direct object *panta* in a double accusative construction. See Mathewson 2016: 286. The context of 21:5 suggests that the present tense form *poiō* ('I am making') is future referring, while the imperfective aspect portrays the action as it develops and unfolds. See Mathewson 2010: 73.

[4] Middleton 2014: 206. Beale (2011b: 299–302) argues convincingly that 2 Cor. 5:17 signals the initial fulfilment of Isaiah's prophecies of new creation.

and newness to the created order. Various features of this vision recall the original biblical account of paradise before humanity's sin brought curse, disorder, pain and death (see Table 9.1 on p. 188), while also drawing upon restoration prophecies in Ezekiel 47 and Zechariah 14.[5] Revelation does not simply anticipate a return to Eden or offer an analogy for the original paradise. Rather, 'John's new Jerusalem out-Edens Eden!'[6] In this glorious vision of the new creation, the tree of life and river of life flowing from the divine throne provide eschatological food and drink for God's multi-ethnic people, who will perfectly carry out humanity's original calling to rule and serve as priest-kings.

The tree of life

References to the tree of life in the midst of paradise in Genesis 2 – 3 and Revelation 22 create an inclusio framing the entire biblical story.[7] Genesis 2:9 introduces 'the tree of life . . . in the midst of the garden', and its significance comes into focus only after its access is restricted in Genesis 3:22, 24. Interpreters debate whether Adam and Eve ever partook of this tree's fruit before their transgression and expulsion from the garden. Blocher reasonably concludes:

> Since access to the tree of life was free (Gen. 2:16), Adam must have eaten of it daily; this signifies the constant renewal of life, body and soul, through fellowship with the LORD. But this renewal was incompatible with sinfulness (as indicated by the flaming sword), and so was lost at the fall.[8]

The prophets depict Israel's future restoration in Edenic terms.[9] Isaiah prophesies that Yahweh 'comforts Zion' and 'makes her wilderness like Eden' (Isa. 51:3; cf. Ezek. 36:35). Isaiah 65:22 LXX states that in the new creation the days of God's people shall be 'according to the

---

[5] Table adapted from Tabb 2015: 2626.

[6] Blount 2013: 397. Similarly, Leithart 2018b: 400.

[7] Lanfer 2009: 96.

[8] Blocher 2000: 375. Similarly, Augustine, *Guilt and Remission of Sins* 2.35. Alternatively Voss (1954: 38) argues, 'It appears from Gen 3:22, that man previous to his probation had not eaten of it . . . The tree was associated with the higher, the unchangeable, the eternal life to be secured through the probation.' Beale (2011b: 38–39) reasons that Gen. 3:22 suggests that Adam had not decisively or consummatively eaten from the tree of life.

[9] Rightly Gallusz 2014: 168–169.

days of the tree of life' (*hēmeras tou xylou tēs zōēs*).[10] Ezekiel depicts a river issuing from the restored temple and 'very many trees on the one side and on the other' (47:1, 7). The angelic figure explains:

And on the banks, on both sides of the river, there will grow all kinds of trees for food. Their leaves will not wither, nor their fruit fail, but they will bear fresh fruit every month, because the water for them flows from the sanctuary. Their fruit will be for food, and their leaves for healing. (v. 12)

Ezekiel's reference to trees 'for food' near the river recalls Eden (Gen. 2:9–10), and the prophecy highlights the trees' unending fruitfulness and healing quality due to their life-giving water supply from the sanctuary.

The Apocalypse scintillatingly describes the New Jerusalem as the climactic fulfilment of Old Testament prophecies of Edenic restoration. In Revelation 22:1–2 John sees

the river of the water of life shining like crystal, coming from the throne of God and of the Lamb. In the midst of the city's broad street and on either side of the river was the tree of life producing twelve fruits, giving its fruit according to each month; and the leaves of the tree were for the healing of the nations.[11]

'The tree of life' (*xylon zōēs*) clearly alludes to Genesis 2:9 (LXX, *to xylon tēs zōēs*), while the river flowing from the throne (*potamon . . . ekporeuomenon ek tou thronou*) closely parallels Genesis 2:10, 'a river flowed from Eden' (LXX, *potamos de ekporeuetai ex Edem*). These allusions to Eden are filtered through Ezekiel's temple vision, which describes waters 'flowing from the sanctuary', the healing leaves, trees on both banks of the river and plentiful fruit each month (47:12).[12]

The Apocalypse expands and reinterprets Ezekiel's prophecy in several ways. First, John refers to the river *of life*, likely influenced by Zechariah 14:8 ('living water'), linking this vision with Revelation 21:6.[13]

[10] This reflects an interpretive expansion of the Hebrew text, which reads, 'like *the days of a tree*' (*kîmê hā'eṣ*); noted also by Mathewson 2003b: 192.

[11] Translation from Mathewson 2016: 299.

[12] Wong (1998: 212) presents a similar list of correspondences between Ezek. 47:12 and Rev. 22:1–2, but unconvincingly concludes that these texts have different eschatological fulfilments in the millennium and eternity after the millennium, respectively.

[13] Mathewson 2003b: 188. Jauhiainen (2005: 123) considers Rev. 22:1 an 'echo' of Zech. 14:8, though 'John's vision both fulfils and surpasses Zechariah's vision'.

'The river of life' also accurately summarizes Ezekiel's remarkable image of the river flowing into the Dead Sea and 'healing' (*hygiazō*) the water such that formerly uninhabitable waters will be teeming with life as in Genesis 1:20–21: 'everything will live [*zēsetai*)] where the river goes' (Ezek. 47:8–9 LXX).[14] Second, the river proceeds *from the throne*, rather than the sanctuary, since the New Jerusalem's 'temple *is* the Lord God the Almighty and the Lamb' (21:22). Third, John describes 'the tree of life', rather than 'every tree' (Ezek. 47:12), to indicate renewed access to the ancient tree from Genesis 2 to 3. Fourth, if one follows the punctuation of the NA28 Greek text, Revelation 22:2 locates the tree 'in the midst' of the street and 'on either side' of the river.[15] Many commentators interpret *xylon* as a collective singular (as in Ezekiel), referring to many trees of life lining the river's banks.[16] Others explain that the Apocalypse transforms Ezekiel's forest of trees into a singular tree of life as in Eden, with roots extending to both banks.[17] Both readings are possible, but the latter is preferred given the clear allusion to Genesis 2:9 here and elsewhere in the Apocalypse. Fifth, John specifies that the tree of life provides *twelve* varieties of fruit, a number that signifies the Old Testament and New Testament people of God in the Apocalypse:

- 12,000 sealed from each of the twelve tribes (7:4–8)
- twelve stars, recalling Israel's sons (12:1; cf. Gen. 37:9)
- twelve pearly gates with the names of Israel's tribes (21:12, 21)
- twelve foundations of Jerusalem's walls with the names of the apostles (21:14).

Sixth, John specifies the eschatological purpose of the tree's leaves 'for the healing of the nations' (22:2).

Mathewson rightly cautions that John's chief aim is not to present 'a geographically consistent visualization' but to stress 'meanings conveyed by the symbols'.[18] Revelation 22:1–2 masterfully assimilates features of Ezekiel's restoration prophecy with an allusion to Genesis 2:9 'to present the eschatological restoration in terms of a restored

---

[14] Block 1998: 694–695.
[15] For discussion of the syntax of Rev. 22:2, see Mathewson 2016: 300.
[16] Giesen 1997: 474; Aune 1998b: 1177–1178; Beale 1999: 1106; Osborne 2002: 771–772; Smalley 2005: 562.
[17] Mathewson 2003b: 189–190; Koester 2014: 823.
[18] Mathewson 2003b: 191.

paradise'.[19] Thus the tree of life and the water of life 'together . . . represent the food and drink of eschatological life',[20] symbolic of the eternal life that comes from God.

This Edenic vision in Revelation 22 signals the fulfilment of Christ's promise to give conquerors 'to eat of the tree of life, which is in the paradise of God' (2:7). The prophets chided Israel for playing the whore 'under every shady tree' (Jer. 2:20; 3:6, 13; 2 Kgs 16:4; 17:10), and Revelation 2:7 may suggest a similar polemic against the idolatrous practices in Ephesus, where a tree-shrine played a central role in the worship of Artemis.[21] Coins in Ephesus represented the patron deity by a date palm, offering life and fertility for devotees.[22] However, only the risen Christ can deliver the promise of enduring life in paradise. Thus Macaskill writes:

> The life that is enjoyed by the occupants of the New Jerusalem is in no way separable from the presence of God. Nor is it in any way separable from the atoning work of Jesus, since it proceeds from the throne of the Lamb.[23]

Early interpreters frequently explained 'the tree of life' in the Apocalypse as a reference to Christ's cross. For example, Tyconius writes:

> Indeed, the tree of life is the wisdom of God, the Lord Jesus Christ, who hung on the cross. In the church and in the spiritual paradise, he gives to the faithful food of life and the sacrament of the celestial bread.[24]

This reading is attractive for several reasons. First, the tree as a symbol of the Lamb's triumph in paradise would reinforce the Apocalypse's emphasis on Christ's redemptive death. Further, *xylon* elsewhere in the New Testament often refers to the cross but rarely to a live tree.[25] Additionally, Revelation 2:7 may contrast the local practice of

[19] Ibid.
[20] Bauckham 1993b: 133.
[21] Hemer 1986: 44–51.
[22] For a picture of a coin depicting Ephesus' patron deity Artemis, see Tabb 2015: 2591.
[23] Macaskill 2010: 77.
[24] Cited in Weinrich 2005: 23.
[25] Cf. Acts 5:30; 10:39; 13:29; Gal. 3:13; 1 Peter 2:24. Jesus' enigmatic statement about the green wood in Luke 23:31 is an exception.

unrepentant criminals seeking asylum at the tree used in Artemis worship with sinners finding refuge in Christ.[26]

While intriguing, the identification of 'the tree of life' as a reference to the cross is exegetically tenuous. While the general term *xylon* often refers to the 'cross' in Christian literature, the expression 'the tree of life' unmistakably refers back to Genesis 2 – 3. Further, the description of the tree's fruit and leaves in Revelation 22 (alluding to Ezek. 47) suggests a living tree in paradise rather than the wooden cross.[27] 'In Revelation, Jesus promises access to the tree but is not himself the tree.'[28]

Thus the tree of life symbolizes eternal life in fellowship with God, which was lost after humanity's exile from Eden (Gen. 2:9; 3:22–24) but is restored in the new creation (Rev. 2:7; 22:2). 'What was taken from Adam due to his disobedience, and which has been guarded, is now open for the righteous to enter, so that they may eat of the tree of life.'[29] This tree embodies the glorious eschatological inheritance in the holy city for God's people who have been redeemed by Christ and hold fast to his word (22:14, 19).

No more curse or threats

The seer's glorious description of paradise continues in Revelation 22:3: 'No longer will there be any curse [*kai pan katathema ouk estai eti*]' (NIV). The rare term *katathema*, rendered 'curse' (NIV) or 'accursed thing' (ESV), occurs only here in the New Testament and nowhere in the LXX. Bauckham explains that *katathema* 'is the curse itself', not 'the thing which is cursed (placed under the ban)'.[30] Elsewhere John explains that nothing unclean, detestable or false will ever enter the holy city (21:27). Rather, the immoral and idolatrous are 'outside' the city and consigned to the lake of fire (21:8; 22:15), as is the ancient serpent who deceived Eve and received God's curse (Gen. 3:1–15; Rev. 20:10). Revelation 22:3 signals a further reversal of the catastrophic effects of Adam and Eve's transgression, which led God to curse the ground and subject humanity to painful toil (Gen. 3:17–18; 5:29).[31]

[26] Hemer 1986: 55. Cf. Osborne 2002: 124; Boxall 2006: 51–52.
[27] 'There is no need to find a reference beyond the Eden imagery of Ezek. 47:12 and Gen. 2:9 to the cross', according to Mathewson (2003b: 199).
[28] Koester 2014: 823.
[29] Mathewson 2003b: 194.
[30] Bauckham 1993a: 316. Cf. Mathewson 2003b: 202.
[31] Macaskill (2010: 78–79) similarly discerns 'an allusion to the comprehensive cursing of Genesis 3.14–19' in Rev. 22:3.

The Greek phrase *ouk estai eti* also echoes similar statements in Revelation 21:1, 4 and links the curse with the 'former things' – death, mourning, crying and pain – that pass away and shall not endure in the new creation. 'In the New Jerusalem the curse is removed because sin is gone and people now come to the tree of life.'[32]

Additionally, Revelation 22:3 alludes to the prophecy of Zechariah 14:11 LXX that Jerusalem 'will never again be accursed [*ouk estai anathema eti*]' but will be inhabited and secure. Elsewhere in the Old Testament, Daniel declared from exile that 'the curse [*katara*] and oath that are written in the Law of Moses the servant of God have been poured out upon us, because we have sinned against him' (9:11). Zechariah envisioned the full reversal of Israel's calamity and exile, when hostile nations would no longer oppress Israel but Yahweh would establish his reign 'over all the earth' and strike his enemies (14:9, 13).

While Zechariah focuses on the safety of Jerusalem, Revelation 22:3 universalizes the removal of the curse and links it closely to the nations' healing in verse 2.[33] The nations are no longer hostile foes but redeemed servants who walk by the light of the Lamb and bring their glory into the holy city (21:24; cf. Zech. 14:16). Zechariah envisions some survivors from the nations coming to Jerusalem to observe the feast of booths, but Revelation presents people from all nations as God's servants who minister in the New Jerusalem.[34] 'There will be no form of curse in the new Jerusalem because God's consummate, ruling presence will fill the city.'[35]

John employs the formula *ouk estai eti* to state that 'the sea' (*hē thalassa*) and 'night' (*nyx*) will have no place in the new creation (21:1; 22:5). Unlike other 'former things' that pass away and will exist no longer – death, mourning, crying, pain and curse – the sea and night do not explicitly result from humanity's fall into sin but are present in God's original creation (Gen. 1:5, 10). Elsewhere the Apocalypse identifies the sea as the source of the blasphemous beast (13:1; cf. Dan. 7:3), the realm of the dead (20:13) and the principal locale for Babylon's idolatrous commercial activity (18:17, 19). Further, Revelation 12:12 pronounces 'woe' on the earth and the sea – together representing the former creation as a synecdoche – because the devil exerts his great wrath there for a short

---

[32] Koester 2014: 824.
[33] Mathewson 2003b: 202–203; Jauhiainen 2005: 125–126.
[34] Jauhiainen 2005: 126.
[35] Beale 1999: 1113.

while.[36] Thus the sea has negative connotations of evil power and ungodly activity, and its absence in the new creation signals the removal of every danger and trial for God's people.[37] The sea may also recall the paradigmatic scene of judgment and salvation at the exodus, where Yahweh parted the waters for his people but 'threw the Egyptians into the midst of the sea' (Exod. 14:22, 27).[38] Mathewson writes, 'More than signifying some change in the cosmological landscape, the removal of the sea expresses the hope of God's people in the final removal of all things that threaten and hinder them from full experience of salvation.'[39]

Further, 'night' is associated with darkness and the absence of light. Darkness features prominently in the plagues against Egypt (Exod. 10:21–22) and in Revelation's cycles of judgment, culminating in 16:10, where the beast's kingdom becomes darkened.[40] In Revelation 21:23–25 the absence of night relates to three realities. First, the radiant divine light of the New Jerusalem renders the former creation's light sources obsolete (v. 23; cf. Isa. 60:19; *T. Levi* 18.4). Second, John explains that the nations will walk by this light, signalling the establishment of a God-honouring moral order for all peoples (v. 24; cf. Isa. 60:3). Third, the gates of the holy city remain open because (*gar*) 'there will be no night there' (v. 25; cf. Isa. 60:11). The open gates highlight the removal of all hostile threats and the city's complete safety and security.

God with us

Having expelled every enemy and eradicated the earth of any vestige of sin, curse and death, God and the Lamb take up their glorious reign over their renewed creation for the eternal benefit and enjoyment of the saints. John explains:

> No longer will there be anything accursed, but the throne of God and of the Lamb will be in it, and his servants will worship him. They will see his face, and his name will be on their foreheads. And

---

[36] For a similar summary of usage, see Beale 1999: 1042.

[37] Middleton (2014: 169) writes, 'The disappearance of the sea in Revelation 21:1 . . . is not making the point that no one goes swimming in the new creation . . . The point is that the forces of evil and chaos will be eradicated.'

[38] For further reflections on the new-exodus motif in Rev. 21:1, see Mathewson 2003a: 243–258. Cf. ch. 7, pp. 158–160.

[39] Mathewson 2003a: 258.

[40] Cf. ch. 7, pp. 153–158.

night will be no more. They will need no light of lamp or sun, for the Lord God will be their light, and they will reign for ever and ever. (Rev. 22:3–5)

This stunning scene expands on John's previous description of the magnificent temple city filled with the illuminating, life-giving presence of God and the Lamb.

As discussed earlier, the Apocalypse's temple city fulfils and transforms the prophet Ezekiel's expansive vision of a restored temple in Jerusalem.[41] The New Jerusalem's gates marked with Israel's tribes, its cubic dimensions, the river flowing through the city and the healing tree of life on each bank all recall Ezekiel 40 – 48. Strikingly, John does not see a physical temple in the holy city, 'for its temple is the Lord God the Almighty and the Lamb' (Rev. 21:22). Beale writes:

> Whereas the container for the divine glory in the Old Testament was often an architectural building, in the new age this old physical container will be shed like a cocoon and the new physical container will be the entire cosmos. The ultimate essence of the temple is the glorious divine presence.[42]

In Ezekiel 43:7 Yahweh asserts that he 'will dwell in the midst of the people of Israel for ever', recalling the restoration promises of 37:26–28. Ezekiel's prophecy concludes fittingly in 48:35, 'And the name of the city from that time on shall be, Yahweh Is There.' This is precisely the point of Revelation 21:3: 'Behold, the dwelling place of God is with man. He will dwell with them, and they will be his people, and God himself will be with them as their God.' The voice from the throne recalls Old Testament promises that God would permanently dwell among his people (cf. Lev. 26:11–12; Jer. 32:38; Ezek. 37:27) and signals their ultimate fulfilment in the glorious temple city defined by the glorious tabernacling presence of God and the Lamb.[43] John sees no temple building, yet what he describes is 'more like the real thing'.[44]

---

[41] See ch. 8, pp. 174–180, and ch. 9, pp. 188–193.
[42] Beale 2005: 29.
[43] For further biblical-theological reflections on God's presence with his people, see Beale and Kim 2014.
[44] Lewis 1994: 73.

The Old Testament repeatedly presents God's ruling over the created world from his heavenly throne (Pss 11:4; 103:19; Isa. 6:1; 66:1), and the divine throne is the central feature of John's vision of heaven in Revelation 4 – 5. However, Revelation's concluding vision pictures God's throne no longer in heaven but in the holy city as 'the focal point of the new creation'.[45] Middleton writes, 'The center of God's governance of the cosmos from now on will be permanently established on a renewed earth.'[46] The Apocalypse presents the throne of God and the Lamb as the source of the water of life (22:1), signalling that God himself is 'the life of the new creation'[47] and will abundantly save, sustain and satisfy his thirsty people for ever (7:16; 21:6; cf. Isa. 49:10). Jesus announced in Revelation 3:21 that he 'conquered and sat down with my Father on his throne', and John states twice in the book's concluding vision that God and the Lamb jointly occupy the divine throne in the holy city (22:1, 3; cf. 5:6; 7:17).[48] Strikingly, Revelation 22:3–4 refers to the throne's *joint* occupants four times using the *singular* pronoun: '*his* servants will worship *him*' and 'will see *his* face, and *his* name will be on their foreheads'. The singular here does not designate only God or only the Lamb but signals their profound unity.[49]

'They will see his face' signals a new level of intimate knowledge and access to God not previously experienced by his people (22:4). Moses requested, 'Please show me your glory.' Yahweh agreed to pass by Moses but he hid his servant in the cleft of the rock and allowed him to see his back but not his face (Exod. 33:18–23). The Old Testament priests blessed the Israelites by praying, 'Yahweh make his face shine on you and be gracious to you; Yahweh turn his face toward you and give you peace,' and thereby put his name on the sons of Israel (Num. 6:25–27). This famous blessing inspired the faithful to pray for God's face to shine on his people and save them (Pss 31:16; 67:1; 80:3, 7, 19; 119:135). According to John, 'No one has ever seen God' (John 1:18; cf. Exod. 33:20), yet Jesus' disciples 'beheld his glory, glory as of the only Son from the Father, full of grace and truth' (John 1:14; cf. 14:7). Finally, in the holy city 'the upright will see his face' (Ps. 11:7), gaze upon his beauty (Ps. 27:4) and be transformed by this glorious sight (Rev. 22:4; cf. Matt. 5:8; 1 John 3:2; *4 Ezra* 7.98; *T. Zeb.* 9.8).

---

[45] Gallusz 2014: 170.
[46] Middleton 2014: 170.
[47] Bauckham 1993b: 133.
[48] Gallusz 2014: 170.
[49] Beale 1999: 1113.

God's redeemed people will experience the glorious presence and unending reign of God and the Lamb (Rev. 21:3; 22:3). God and the Lamb will be the source of everlasting life and perpetual light for the saints (22:1, 5). In the new creation every threat and barrier to uninhibited fellowship between God and his people is eliminated, and they will see his face and worship him for ever as priestly kings (22:3–5).

The creation mandate fulfilled

The presence of the tree of life and the elimination of every curse and threat in the New Jerusalem indicate a recovery of what was lost due to humanity's sin and exile from Eden. John's vision of cosmic renewal also establishes an enduring identity and vocation for the saints that recall humanity's calling and role as priests and rulers in the first creation account.

In Genesis 2:15 God puts the man he created in paradise 'to work it and keep it'. The Hebrew verb '*bd*, rendered 'work' here and throughout Genesis 2 – 4, denotes cultivating the earth (Gen. 2:5; 3:23; 4:2, 12). However, the combination of '*bd* and *šmr* in the Old Testament refers to Israel's responsibility to 'serve' God and 'keep' his commands (Deut. 13:4; Josh. 22:5) or to Israel's priests who 'keep guard' and 'minister' in the tabernacle (Num 3:7–8; 8:26).[50] Thus Genesis 2:15 presents Adam as 'the archetypal priest who served in and guarded . . . God's first temple'.[51] His work in the garden constitutes priestly activity maintaining and protecting the first sanctuary. When Adam disobeys God's command not to eat of the restricted tree (2:17; 3:17), he is sent out of the garden 'to work [*'bd*] the ground', and God installs cherubim 'to guard [*šmr*] the way to the tree of life'. Thus Adam failed to carry out his priestly duties and so was barred from the garden-temple he had been charged with protecting.

Revelation envisions restored access to the tree of life that symbolizes the life-giving presence of God and re-establishes redeemed humanity as ministers in God's Edenic sanctuary. John writes, 'The throne of God and of the Lamb will be in it, and his servants will worship [*latreusousin*] him' (Rev. 22:3). This reiterates the earlier scene in 7:15, where the multitude clothed in white 'are before the throne

---

[50] Beale 2004: 67. Cf. Wenham 1987: 67.
[51] Beale 2004: 68.

of God, and serve [*latreuousin*] him day and night in his temple; and he who sits on the throne will shelter them with his presence'. This vision of God's people serving as priests in the eschatological temple city fulfils Isaiah's prophecy that Israel 'shall be called the priests of Yahweh' and 'the ministers of our God' (Isa. 61:6).[52] However, the Apocalypse does not limit the priesthood to a single nation (Israel) or tribe (Levites); those serving as priests in God's temple (7:15) are the multitude from every tribe and tongue who have been redeemed by the Lamb and clothed in white (7:9, 14). Thus John combines the expectation of Isaiah 61:6 with 56:6–7, where the prophet identifies foreigners as God's servants who perform priestly ministry in God's house of prayer. Revelation 21:3 reiterates this expansive multi-ethnic vision: 'they will be his *peoples* [*laoi*], and God himself will be with them as their God'. God frequently promises in the Old Testament that Israel will be his *people* (Lev. 26:12; Jer. 32:38; Ezek. 37:27), but the plural *peoples* signals that all nations will benefit from God's saving activity and will share in his eschatological banquet (Isa. 25:6).[53] As anticipated in the multi-ethnic throng of worshippers in Revelation 5:9, 'those who are citizens of the new earth will be drawn from all the ethnic groups of this earth'.[54]

According to 22:4, the saints will behold God's face 'and his name will be on their foreheads'. This remarkable description highlights the intimate relationship between God and his people and also further signals their identity as priests of God and the Lamb.[55] Exodus 28:36–38 prescribed that Israel's high priest had to wear an engraved plate with the words 'Holy to Yahweh' on his forehead (LXX, *epi tou metōpou*), and Revelation 14:1 portrays the 144,000 having the Lamb's name 'and his Father's name written on their foreheads'. In contrast to the unredeemed, who serve the beast and receive its mark (13:16; 14:9), the redeemed bear the divine name on their foreheads, indicating their ultimate allegiance to the true God and their calling as priests in the New Jerusalem (3:12).

In Revelation 22:5 John concludes his final vision by returning again to the saints' vocation in the new creation: 'they will reign for ever and ever'. The book's opening doxology identified believers as 'a kingdom' and 'priests' (Rev. 1:6; cf. Exod. 19:6), and the heavenly worshippers declare that the redeemed 'reign' (*basileuousin*) or 'will

---

[52] Beale 1999: 1113.
[53] Middleton 2014: 174. Cf. Bauckham 1993a: 311.
[54] Alexander 2008: 163.
[55] Beale 1999: 1114.

reign' (*basileusousin*) on the earth (5:10).[56] In 20:6 John declares that those who share in the first resurrection 'will be priests of God and of the Messiah and will reign [*basileusousin*] with him for a thousand years' (cf. 20:4). Interpreters have long debated the nature and timing of the saints' millennial reign. Whether John's vision in chapter 20 depicts the present experience of deceased believers who come to life spiritually and reign with Christ in heaven until his return, or future resurrection and earthly reign of believers after Jesus' return, the qualifier 'for a thousand years' (however understood) in 20:4, 6 indicates that this reign is *temporary* and *provisional*, in contrast to believers' *ultimate* and *enduring* reign in the new creation (22:5).

The eternal reign of God's people in the new Eden brings the original creation mandate to its eschatological goal. After making man and woman in his image and likeness, God blessed them and commanded them to fill and subdue the earth and exercise dominion over the created order (Gen. 1:26–28). God's command for human beings to exercise dominion follows from their identity as divine image bearers. Beale explains:

> They were to reflect God's kingship by being his vice-regents on earth. Because Adam and Eve were to subdue and rule 'over all the earth', it is plausible to suggest that they were to extend the geographical boundaries of the garden until Eden covered the whole earth . . . God's ultimate goal in creation was to magnify his glory throughout the earth by means of his faithful image-bearers inhabiting the world in obedience to the divine mandate.[57]

Of course, Adam and Eve spectacularly failed to carry out this mandate and were put outside the garden (Gen. 3:24). Revelation presents the glory of God filling and illuminating the new creation (21:10, 23), with the redeemed enjoying unbridled intimacy with the sovereign Creator (22:4) and exercising dominion as faithful priest-kings (22:3, 5). The redemptive drama of Revelation 5 serves as the bridge linking Adam's failure and the saints' future. Jesus the Lion of Judah is found 'worthy' and has 'conquered' because, as the slain Lamb, he ransomed people for God and made them 'a kingdom' (5:5, 9–10).[58] Jesus thus fulfils Adam's commission to image God rightly by

---

[56] For discussion of the textual variant in Rev. 5:10, see ch. 5, pp. 91–92.
[57] Beale 2004: 81–82.
[58] See ch. 3, pp. 59–61.

ruling over the world.[59] Revelation 11:15 states that Christ 'shall reign for ever and ever' (*basileusei eis tous aiōnas tōn aiōnōn*), and 22:5 says precisely the same about Christ's people: 'they shall reign for ever and ever' (*basileusousin eis tous aiōnas tōn aiōnōn*). 'But there is no tension in the biblical worldview between God's sovereign rule . . . and human rule' by God's image bearers.[60] In Danielic terms Jesus is 'given dominion and glory and a kingdom' and then grants those who conquer a share in his unending messianic kingdom (Dan. 7:14, 18).[61]

Conclusion

Osborne writes, 'The New Jerusalem will not only be the final holy of Holies (21:9–27) but also the final Eden (22:1–5). It will be more than a restored or regained Eden – it will be a transformed Eden. All that the original garden could have been is expanded and intensified.'[62] The denouement of John's vision unknots all the vestiges of Adam's sin and expulsion from Eden and unfolds the glorious *telos* of salvation: God's enduring, life-giving presence with his redeemed people in his new creation. No longer will human beings face temptation, threat or trouble; with singular allegiance and supreme satisfaction they will behold God's face and fulfil their calling as royal priests. 'To live in the New Jerusalem is to experience life in all its fullness and vitality.'[63]

The risen Christ concludes each message to the seven churches in Revelation 2 – 3 by highlighting various aspects of the inheritance in the new creation that God has prepared for believers who 'overcome' (see Table 9.2. on p. 202).[64] To the church at Ephesus Jesus promises that the one who conquers will 'eat of the tree of life' (2:7), which alludes to the loss of Eden and anticipates the life-giving, healing tree at the centre of paradise in 22:2.

To Smyrna Christ assures victorious believers that they 'will not be hurt by the second death' (2:11). The 'second death' is the lake of fire and sulphur, the place of eternal punishment for unbelievers and idolaters who have no portion in the New Jerusalem (21:8; 22:15). The

---

[59] Schreiner 2013: 629.
[60] Middleton 2014: 175.
[61] See ch. 3, pp. 55–59.
[62] Osborne 2002: 776.
[63] Alexander 2008: 156.
[64] Cf. ch. 5, pp. 108–110. Table adapted from Tabb 2015: 2624.

Table 9.2: The promised inheritance in the new creation

End-time blessing	Old Testament background	Promises to the seven churches	New creation fulfilment
access to the tree of life	Gen. 2:9	Rev. 2:7	Rev. 22:2, 14, 19
hidden manna, entrance to the messianic supper	Exod. 16:31–34; Isa. 25:6	Rev. 2:17	Rev. 19:9
ruling the nations with an iron rod	Ps. 2:9	Rev. 2:26–27; 3:21	Rev. 22:5
given the morning star (Christ)	Num. 24:17	Rev. 2:28	Rev. 22:16
clothed with pure garments	Isa. 52:1; 61:10	Rev. 3:5	Rev. 19:7–8; 21:2
name written in book of life	Dan. 12:1	Rev. 3:5	Rev. 21:27
included in God's temple	Isa. 56:5	Rev. 3:12	Rev. 21:22–27
new identity and citizenship	Isa. 62:2; 65:15	Rev. 3:12	Rev. 21:2, 10; 22:4

second death has no power over those who come to life and reign with Christ during the millennium and will reign for ever in the new creation (20:6; 22:5).

To Pergamum the risen Lord promises 'hidden manna' and 'a white stone, with a new name written on the stone that no one knows except the one who receives it' (2:17). The hidden manna recalls the omer of bread preserved in the ark of the covenant to remind future generations how God fed his people in the wilderness (Exod. 16:32–35). For this church tempted by idolatrous Roman feasts (Rev. 2:14) Christ's words hold out hope of the eschatological feast for those invited to the messianic banquet (Rev. 19:9; cf. Isa. 25:6). The symbolism of the 'white stone' is enigmatic but may represent favourable judgment and honour or admission to the marriage supper of the Lamb.[65] The 'new name' points to the saints' enduring identity and status in restored relationship with God (Rev. 22:4; cf. Isa. 62:2; 65:15).[66]

[65] For the former, see Koester 2014: 290. For the latter, see Mounce 1997: 83.
[66] For additional discussion of the 'new name' see Beale 1999: 253–258.

To Thyatira the Son of God promises participation in his messianic reign: 'to him I will give authority over the nations, and he will rule them with a rod of iron' (2:26–27). Employing the language of Psalm 2:9, Christ shares his authority, victory and kingdom rule with his people, who will reign for ever in the New Jerusalem (Rev. 22:5; cf. 1:6; 20:4).[67] Jesus will also give him 'the morning star' (2:28), a messianic symbol that refers to Christ himself (22:16; cf. Num. 24:17). The promise to Laodicea that conquerors will share Christ's throne (3:21) draws attention to the throne of God and the Lamb that gives light and life to the new creation, where God's people will serve as priest-kings (22:3).

To Sardis Christ promises that victorious believers 'will be clothed thus in white garments' (3:5), in contrast to those with soiled garments (3:4). This anticipates the bright and pure clothing of the church as the bride adorned for her husband (19:8; 21:2; cf. Isa. 61:10). Further, Jesus stresses that he 'will never blot his name out of the book of life' (3:5). This complements the promise to Smyrna in 2:11 and highlights God's sovereign choice to redeem and give everlasting life to true believers while protecting them from Satan's spiritual deception (13:8; 17:8; 20:12; 21:27; cf. Dan. 12:1; Luke 10:20).

The promise to the church in Philadelphia offers the most explicit and extensive connection to the book's consummate vision of the New Jerusalem. Jesus states in Revelation 3:12:

> The one who conquers, I will make him a pillar in the temple of my God. Never shall he go out of it, and I will write on him the name of my God, and the name of the city of my God, the New Jerusalem, which comes down from my God out of heaven, and my own new name.

This multifaceted promise highlights different aspects of believers' eschatological fellowship and identification with the Lord.[68] Victorious believers will never be excluded from God's presence but will permanently dwell in the temple city (21:2–4; cf. 7:15) and will behold God's face and minister before him (22:3–4).[69] Further, the saints will be marked by the name of God, his city and his Son, stressing their new identity as God's holy people and their enduring citizenship in the city defined by God's presence (Ezek. 48:35). Christ's words in

[67] See ch. 5, pp. 90–95.
[68] Beale 1999: 293.
[69] On believers as pillars in the temple, see Beale 2004: 328–330.

3:12 recall the 'new name' mentioned in 2:17 and prepare for the interlude vision of the 144,000 on Mount Zion with the name of the Lamb and his Father on their foreheads (14:1) and the culminating vision of believers marked by 'his name' in 22:4.

The Apocalypse stresses 'the one who conquers will inherit these things' (*ho nikōn klēronomēsei tauta* [21:7]). Christ's promises in Revelation 2 – 3 and the denouement of the new creation in chapters 21–22 offer confidence, awe, hope and motivation for embattled believers to resist Babylon's seduction, endure the beast's onslaught and hold fast to the testimony of Jesus (12:17; 19:10).[70] In Revelation 22:1–5 John masterfully paints the scene of ultimate paradise with the colours of Genesis, Ezekiel and Zechariah. This vision of new creation satisfies believers' longings for full redemption from the effects of Adam's sin in Genesis 3, for an enduring home in the city of God and for an ultimate vocation as priests and vice-regents of God and the Lamb. Schreiner aptly states:

> What makes the new universe so dazzling is not gold or jewels but rather the presence of God. The whole world is his holy of holies. . . . The goal of all of redemptive history will be obtained: 'They will see his face' (22:4). They will see the King in his beauty.[71]

---

[70] DeSilva (2009b: 220) explains that John arouses 'confidence in connection with the behaviors and commitments he promotes'.

[71] Schreiner 2013: 629.

Part IV:
The word of God

Chapter Ten

The unsealed scroll:
the trustworthy words of God

> And the angel said to me, 'Write this: Blessed are those who
> are invited to the marriage supper of the Lamb.' And he said
> to me, 'These are the true words of God.' ... Then I saw
> heaven opened, and behold, a white horse! The one sitting
> on it is called Faithful and True, and in righteousness he
> judges and makes war. (Rev. 19:9, 11)

> And he said to me, 'Do not seal up the words of the prophecy
> of this book, for the time is near.' (Rev. 22:10)

The Old Testament repeatedly celebrates the divine characteristics
and effects of the Law of Yahweh. It is perfect, sure, right, pure, true,
incomparably valuable and desirable; it gives life, wisdom and illumination; it warns the errant and promises reward for adherents (Ps.
19:7–10). The divine words are considered completely true and reliable
because they come from Yahweh and reflect his revealed character
(Exod. 34:6; Deut. 7:9).[1] The Apocalypse similarly stresses its own
authority and authenticity as the ultimate revelation of the exalted
Christ, who is himself the trustworthy and true divine Word (Rev.
1:1–2; 19:11).

This chapter considers Revelation's multifaceted presentation of
itself as the word of God. First, the opening verses present the book's
contents as 'the testimony of Jesus' and characterize John as an
eyewitness to Christ's supreme revelation (Rev. 1:1–2). Second, Revelation presents itself as a 'book of prophecy' (22:7, 19), faithfully
recorded by a true prophet who writes with divine authority and
authorization (1:3, 11). Third, the command not to seal up the words
of the prophecy reverses the command that Daniel seal his scroll until
the end and signals the imminent fulfilment of its words (22:10; cf.
Dan. 12:9). Fourth, the prohibition against adding to or taking from
the book's words recalls a series of warnings in Deuteronomy and

---

[1] See below, pp. 220–223.

portrays the Apocalypse as authoritative Scripture for the people of God. Finally, the character of God and Christ as 'trustworthy and true' serves as the basis for the complete veracity of the written words of the book (Rev. 3:14; 19:9; 21:5; 22:6; cf. Isa. 65:16). The chapter concludes with reflections on the blessing for those who hear and keep the words of this book of prophecy (1:3).

The testimony of Jesus and John

In the prologue of the book John presents himself as Christ's servant, 'who testified [*emartyrēsen*] to the word of God and to the testimony of Jesus Christ, even to all that he saw' (Rev. 1:2 NASB). Here John offers crucial explanation of the content and communication of 'the revelation of Jesus Christ' (1:1).[2]

First, the seer characterizes this revelation as 'the word of God' (*ton logon tou theou*). Many of the Old Testament prophetic books begin by saying that 'the word of the Lord' or 'the word of God' came to the prophet.[3] Elsewhere in the New Testament 'the word of God' denotes the Old Testament Scriptures (Matt. 15:6; John 10:35) and the divine message of salvation in Christ that the apostles and others boldly proclaimed and faithfully taught (Acts 4:31; 2 Cor. 2:17; Col. 1:25; Heb. 13:7). By calling the revelation he receives 'the word of God' (Rev. 1:2), John stresses the divine origin and authority of this book of Christian prophecy.[4]

Second, John presents this prophecy as 'the testimony of Jesus Christ' (*tēn martyrian Iēsou Christou*). The shortened phrase 'the testimony of Jesus' recurs five times in the book (1:9; 12:17; 19:10 [twice]; 20:4), and has been interpreted in multiple ways: (1) Jesus' testimony in his life and death, (2) believers' proclamation or confession about Jesus, (3) believers' witness to Jesus that leads to death, (4) both Jesus' own testimony and believers' testimony about Jesus and (5) the testimony of the risen Jesus in the Apocalypse.[5] In 1:2 'the testimony of Jesus Christ' parallels the divine 'word' and receives further definition as what John 'saw' and 'testified to'. The book's epilogue further stresses the exalted Christ's testimony.

---

[2] For discussion of *apokalypsis* in 1:1, see ch. 1, pp. 4–8.

[3] See e.g. Isa. 1:10; Jer. 1:2; Ezek. 1:3; Hos. 1:1; Jon. 1:1; Mic. 1:1; Zeph. 1:1; Hag. 1:1; Zech. 1:1; Mal. 1:1. Jeremiah refers sixty-nine times to 'the word of Yahweh' (MT, *děbar-yhwh*), more than any other OT book; for discussion, see Shead 2012: 44–47.

[4] Rowland 1993: 57; Dixon 2017: 141.

[5] This summarizes the comprehensive survey by Dixon 2017: 2–3.

Reiterating the chain of communication in 1:1–2, Jesus says in 22:16 that he sent his angel 'to testify [*martyrēsai*] to you about these things for the churches'. In 22:18 Christ prefaces his warning against adding to or taking from the words of this book with an 'oath' or 'witness formula', *martyrō egō*.[6] Finally, in 22:20 Christ reiterates that he is 'the one who testifies to these things' (*ho martyrōn tauta*). Here *tauta* includes not merely the immediately preceding verses but the whole revelation communicated to John (22:8) by Jesus' angel (22:6, 16).[7] Thus the prologue and epilogue together emphasize that this prophetic book is the testimony from the exalted Christ himself.[8]

'Testimony' and related terms have legal connotations.[9] The Law specifies that charges in court must be established on the evidence of two or more witnesses (Num. 35:30; Deut. 17:6; 19:15; cf. 2 Cor. 13:1). In Isaiah Yahweh calls the heavens and earth as witnesses against his people for their sinful deeds (1:2) and then designates his people as his 'witnesses' in the cosmic courtroom who give evidence that he is the true God (43:9–10). In the Apocalypse Jesus introduces himself as 'the Amen, the faithful and true witness' (Rev. 3:14; cf. 1:5), a title that identifies him with 'the God of truth' (Isa. 65:16) and stresses the veracity and dependability of his testimony. Because the exalted Christ is 'faithful and true', the testimony he gives to John is also completely trustworthy (Rev. 22:6).[10]

Third, 1:2 recounts that John himself bears witness (*emartyrēsen*) to what he has seen (*hosa eiden*). The explanatory phrase *hosa eiden* ('even to all that he saw') clarifies that John receives the revelatory testimony from Jesus in heavenly visions. John receives these visions 'in the Spirit' (1:10) as a true prophet, and Christ commands him to 'write . . . the things that you have seen' (1:19).[11] Thus John writes what he sees as an obedient servant of Christ and eyewitness to this revelation from Christ.[12] Like the angel sent by Jesus 'to testify' (22:16; cf. 1:1), 'John takes his place in the chain of transmission, continuing to pass on the testimony that belongs to Jesus.'[13] The

---

[6] Aune 1998b: 1229–1230; Smalley 2005: 582–583. For discussion of the speaker in 22:18, see below, pp. 216–217.

[7] Alternatively, Blount (2013: 414–415) understands *tauta* to refer only to Jesus' professions in 22:12–19.

[8] Similarly, Dixon 2017: 32–33.

[9] See ch. 3, pp. 53–55.

[10] See further below, pp. 220–223.

[11] See ch. 4, pp. 71–74.

[12] John 19:35 employs similar language to depict the beloved disciple's eyewitness testimony.

[13] Dixon 2017: 139.

churches access 'the testimony of Jesus Christ' only through John's faithful testimony in this book of prophecy.

This book of prophecy

While Revelation combines elements of multiple genres, the introduction and epilogue emphatically stress the book's prophetic quality and contents:

> Blessed is the one who reads aloud the words of *this prophecy*. (1:3)

> Blessed is the one who keeps the words of *the prophecy of this book*. (22:7)

> Do not seal up the words of *the prophecy of this book*, for the time is near. (22:10)

> I warn everyone who hears the words of *the prophecy of this book*: if anyone adds to them, God will add to him the plagues described in this book, and if anyone takes away from the words of the book of *this prophecy*, God will take away his share in the tree of life and in the holy city, which are described in this book. (22:18–19)

As true prophecy, Revelation informs and instructs, challenges and consoles. It discloses future realities, such as the return of Christ, the final judgment and the restoration of all things, and brings the divine word to bear on the churches' present situation to motivate God's people to resist sin and false teaching and endure hardship.

John is instructed to 'write' twelve times in the Apocalypse, including twice in his initial vision of the risen Christ:

> *Write* [*grapson*] what you see in a book and send it to the seven churches, to Ephesus and to Smyrna and to Pergamum and to Thyatira and to Sardis and to Philadelphia and to Laodicea. (1:11)

> *Write* [*grapson*] therefore the things that you have seen, those that are and those that are to take place after this. (1:19)

Following these summary commands, Jesus directs John to 'write' messages to the angels of each church (2:1, 8, 12, 18; 3:1, 7, 14). John must 'write' specific promises of blessing in 14:13 and 19:9. The final directive comes from the one seated on the throne: 'Write [*grapson*], for these words are trustworthy and true' (21:5). John speaks of his prophetic message as 'revelation' (1:1) and 'testimony' (1:2), but employs 'the words of this prophecy' (1:3) and similar phrases to refer to 'its concrete form as a book'.[14] John is both seer and scribe, who receives divine visions and carefully recounts Christ's revelation 'in a book' (1:11).[15]

Shead argues that the prophets – particularly Jeremiah – write down the words they receive from God that they may remain into the future 'to bear witness to the truth and faithfulness of God when his words come to be fulfilled'.[16] Isaiah 30:8 illustrates this aim as the Lord commands Isaiah to write down a prophetic oracle 'that it may be for the time to come as a witness for ever'. Similarly, Jeremiah must 'write in a book' (*grapson . . . epi bibliou*) all the words he receives because God will restore his people's fortunes and return them to their land (Jer. 30:2–3 [37:2–3 LXX]), and Habakkuk must write his vision on a tablet because 'the vision awaits its appointed time' (Hab. 2:2–3). Like the Old Testament prophets, John writes what he sees and hears so that gathered believers may read and hear 'the testimony of Jesus' in John's absence (Rev. 1:2–3) and so that these trustworthy words may endure until their consummate fulfilment.

John alludes extensively to the Old Testament prophetic books, signalling his conscious dependence on and place within this tradition. John also writes as a Christian prophet who has uniquely received 'revelation' and 'testimony' from the risen Christ (1:1–2). This book thus brings clarity and completion to the previous prophetic writings by disclosing the comprehensive fulfilment of the divine mystery revealed to his forebears (10:7).[17] The book's opening verse alludes to Daniel 2:28–30 in expressing its revelatory, symbolic nature and eschatological contents.[18] While Daniel's prophecy reveals 'the things that must take place *at the end of days*' (*ha dei genesthai ep' eschatōn tōn hēmerōn* [2:28 LXX]), Revelation discloses 'the things that must take place *quickly*' (*ha dei genesthai en tachei* [1:1; 22:6]). This modification signals the proximity and perspicuity of the book's prophetic message.

---

[14] Ibid. 145.
[15] Spellman 2016: 48.
[16] Shead 2012: 236.
[17] Bauckham 1993b: 5.
[18] See ch. 1, pp. 11–12; Beale 1999: 50–52, 181–182.

John's prophetic commissioning and experience in the Spirit deliberately recall the ministry of Ezekiel.[19] In Revelation 10:8–10 John symbolically eats an open scroll to show that he is a genuine prophet like Ezekiel, called by God to deliver a true yet difficult message.[20] God instructs Ezekiel to 'speak my words' to the rebellious house of Israel regardless of whether they hear (Ezek. 2:7). The prophet then receives a scroll with 'words of lamentation and mourning and woe' written on both sides, and then consumes the scroll, which tastes 'sweet as honey' (2:10; 3:3). This symbolic meal prepares for Ezekiel's charge to speak the words of God to his stubborn, rebellious people (3:4–11). When John eats the scroll, it is 'sweet as honey' in his mouth yet 'bitter' in his belly (Rev. 10:10).

Scholars debate the precise connotation of the scroll's sweetness and bitterness. Beale reasons that the scroll's sweetness conveys the delight and joy of God's life-giving words (cf. Jer. 15:16; Pss 19:10; 119:103), while the enduring bitterness signifies John's distress over the message of judgment he must announce.[21] Alternatively, Koester takes the sweetness and bitterness to represent the sweet promise of redemption and the challenge of suffering for the Christian community.[22] Boxall suggests that the divine word is bitter in a twofold sense: 'It is bitter for the prophet, who must be prepared to suffer for it . . . It is also bitter for those who hear, for it is a word of judgement no less than salvation.'[23] On balance, the scroll's bitterness likely stresses the word of judgment that John must bring, which parallels Ezekiel's message of mourning and woe (Ezek. 2:10) and recalls the bitterness that the third trumpet brings in Revelation 8:11.

While God does not send Ezekiel 'to many peoples of obscure speech and strange language' who would listen to the prophet's words (Ezek. 3:6), John must prophesy 'about many peoples and nations and languages and kings' (Rev. 10:11). The seer's summons to prophesy again anticipates the two witnesses' prophetic ministry among many peoples, nations and languages in 11:3, 9.[24] John prophesies about (*epi*) many peoples (10:11), but records these

---

[19] See ch. 4, pp. 71–74.
[20] The scroll John takes in Rev. 10:10 is probably the same scroll that Jesus has unsealed and opened in 6:1 – 8:1.
[21] Beale 1999: 550–552.
[22] Koester 2014: 483.
[23] Boxall 2006: 158.
[24] For discussion of the two witnesses in Rev. 11, see ch. 5, pp. 97–101.

words of prophecy 'for the churches' (*epi tais ekklēsiais* [22:16; cf. 1:3–4]).

The unsealed scroll

The opening verses of the epilogue stress the veracity of the book's message, the imminence of its fulfilment and the blessing promised to the one who 'keeps' its prophetic words (Rev. 22:6–7; cf. 1:1, 3). In 22:10 the revealing angel commands John, 'Do not seal up the words of the prophecy of this book, for the time is near.'[25] This important verse develops the book's extensive use of seal imagery and contains a significant allusion to Daniel 12:4.

Within the Apocalypse, seals signify safekeeping, security or secrecy. First, people are sealed on their foreheads to signal that they belong to God, not the beast (Rev. 7:2–3; 20:4).[26] As in Ezekiel 9:4–6, those marked out by God are kept safe and spared when God executes his judgment (Rev. 9:4).

Second, an angel shuts and seals (*esphragisen*) the pit where the dragon is held to prevent him from deceiving the nations (Rev. 20:3). The seal over the dragon signals the complete security of his confinement, analogous to Darius sealing the lion's den (Dan. 6:17) and the Roman guards sealing Jesus' tomb (Matt. 27:66).

Third, scrolls or books are 'sealed' to signal the secrecy of their contents. John sees a mysterious scroll secured with seven seals in 5:1. Official copies of ancient documents such as a royal edict, property deed or marriage contract were closed with wax seals – often in the presence of witnesses – to prevent tampering and demonstrate their authenticity (Esth. 8:8; Jer. 32:10–11; Tob. 7.14). This heavenly scroll with writing 'within and on the back' recalls the double-sided scroll in Ezekiel 2:9–10. The scroll in 5:1 is sealed until the Lamb takes the scroll and opens each of its seven seals in 6:1 – 8:1. The scroll 'open' in the angel's hand in 10:2 also alludes to Ezekiel 2:8 – 3:3, which suggests that the scroll John takes and eats is the same scroll

---

[25] Giesen (1997: 484) understands Christ to be the speaker in 22:10–11 and reads these verses together with vv. 12–16. Charles (1920, 2: 212–213) likewise considers Christ as the speaker in 22:10, though he claims that the sayings in the epilogue have been defectively transmitted and proposes a significant 'reconstruction'. However, a majority of commentators interpret vv. 10–11 as the words of the revealing angel who speaks in vv. 6, 9. Cf. Thomas 1995: 501; Mounce 1997: 405; Aune 1998b: 1216; Smalley 2005: 570; Koester 2014: 840. On the organization of the epilogue, see Osborne 2002: 778.

[26] Cf. ch. 5, pp. 103–104; *NIDNTTE*, 4: 415 (*sphragis*).

that Jesus unsealed.[27] The scroll is concealed and inscrutable until the Lamb dramatically breaks its seals to reveal its divine contents. The prophet then internalizes the scroll's message and makes it known to many peoples (Rev. 10:8–11).

The imperative 'seal up' (*sphragison*) in 10:4 is of particular significance for understanding the prohibition 'do not seal up' (*mē sphragisēs*) in 22:10. In 10:1–3 John sees a mighty angel and hears his lion-like voice and the sounding of seven thunders.[28] As the prophet prepares his pen, he hears a heavenly voice instruct him to 'seal up what the seven thunders have said, and do not write it down' (10:4). John evidently hears what the thunders say, yet he does not write down their message for the benefit of his readers. The content of the thunders is sealed in that it is kept hidden and not revealed. Elsewhere revelation is 'sealed' after it is written on a scroll or tablet (Isa. 29:11; Dan. 12:4; Rev. 5:1), but in 10:4 John must 'seal up' the message and thereby keep it secret by *not* writing it down.[29] It is not the seven thunders but the scroll in the angel's hand that contains the prophetic message John must reveal (10:2, 8–10).[30]

Daniel 12:4 offers crucial biblical-theological background for interpreting the angel's directive in Revelation 22:10. Daniel receives a revelation concerning 'the time of the end' (11:40), in which God's people will experience great distress followed by deliverance and resurrection life (12:1–2). The angel then directs Daniel to 'shut up the words and seal the book [*emphraxon tous logous kai sphragison to biblion*], until the time of the end' (12:4 TH, my tr.). Baldwin explains, '*Shut up the words* implies keeping them safely until the time when they will be needed ... *Seal the book* has the double sense of authenticating and of preserving intact.'[31] The commands 'shut up' and 'seal' do not mean that the words of Daniel's prophecy are kept secret or hidden from those desiring to read them. Rather, though the

---

[27] Mazzaferri 1989: 279; Bauckham 1993a: 243–257; Beale 1999: 527–528; Koester 2014: 476–477; Leithart 2018a: 397. Dixon (2017: 66) goes one step further and equates the scroll in 5:1 and 10:2 with the entire 'revelation of Jesus Christ' given to John (1:1). Interpreters who resist identifying the scrolls in 5:1 and 10:2 include Thomas 1995: 62–63; Mounce 1997: 202.

[28] Beale (1999: 525) argues that the mighty angel in Rev. 10:1 'is the divine Angel of the Lord, as in the OT, who is to be identified with Christ himself'. While this interpretation is possible, the Apocalypse elsewhere consistently distinguishes Jesus from the angels, and 'the mighty angel' in 5:2 is clearly distinct from the Lamb in 5:6. See Stuckenbruck 1995: 229–232; Fee 2013: 140–141; Koester 2014: 476.

[29] Bauckham 1993a: 260.

[30] Ibid.

[31] Baldwin 1978: 227, emphases original.

prophecy is written down it cannot be fully understood or grasped by Daniel's generation.[32] The prophet acknowledges that even he does not comprehend the things revealed to him (Dan. 12:8; cf. 8:27), and the angel instructs him to go his way 'for the words are shut up and sealed until the time of the end' (12:9; cf. 8:26). Daniel is not like the seers and prophets in Isaiah 29:10–12 who cannot understand 'sealed' prophetic visions because of their own spiritual obduracy. Rather, Daniel does not grasp exactly when or how these prophetic words will come to pass, because they concern a future time.

The imperative 'do not seal' in Revelation 22:10 signals a reversal from Daniel's situation. Daniel shut up and sealed his visions because they concerned the distant future, but words of John's book of prophecy must remain unsealed because they relate to 'what must soon take place' (22:6) and 'the time is near' (22:10). Beale explains the redemptive-historical significance of this development: 'What Daniel prophesied can now be understood because the prophecies have begun to be fulfilled and the latter days have begun.'[33] The closing words of 22:10 – 'for the time is near' (*ho kairos gar engys estin*) – establish the reason why John's prophecy must not be sealed and recall the same pronouncement in 1:3: 'Blessed is the one who reads aloud the words of this prophecy, and blessed are those who hear, and who keep what is written in it, *for the time is near*' (*ho gar kairos engys*). Thus 22:10 presents the Apocalypse of Jesus Christ as an unsealed book of genuine prophecy that discloses what was previously kept secret and announces the imminent fulfilment of its revelatory message.

The new law code

The closing verses of the Apocalypse contain a stern warning to the book's hearers:

> I warn everyone who hears the words of the prophecy of this book: if anyone adds to them, God will add to him the plagues described in this book, and if anyone takes away from the words of the book

---

[32] Collins (1993: 341–342) reasons that the sealing of the book in Dan. 8:26 and 12:4, 9 'is necessitated by the convention of pseudepigraphy' and the hundreds of years between when Daniel purportedly received his prophetic visions in the Babylonian and Persian periods and when they were composed in the second century BC. For a critique of Collins's position, see Hill 2008: 156.
[33] Beale 1999: 1130.

of this prophecy, God will take away his share in the tree of life and in the holy city, which are described in this book. (Rev. 22:18–19)

Scholars debate whether Jesus or John is the first-person speaker (*egō*) in verse 18. In 1:9 the prophet introduces himself *Egō Iōannēs*, and Christ employs a similar self-reference in 22:16 (*Egō Iēsous*). Many interpreters understand the speaker in 22:18–19 to be the seer John, who testifies regarding the truthfulness, authority and binding nature of the book of prophecy he has written.[34] Alternatively, Mounce reasons, 'The solemnity of the injunction suggests that the speaker is Christ himself.'[35] The identity of *egō* is ambiguous in the initial phrase of verse 18 and does not substantially affect the theological significance and rhetorical impact of the warning, particularly since the opening verses of the Apocalypse present the book's contents as the revelatory 'testimony' of the exalted Christ, which is mediated to readers through the written witness of the prophet (1:1–2, 11).

Nevertheless, 22:18–19 most likely presents Jesus as the speaker for at least two reasons. First, this interpretation fits the immediate context, which includes a series of first-person statements by the exalted Christ:

And behold, *I am coming* [*erchomai*] soon. Blessed is the one who keeps the words of the prophecy of this book. (22:7)

Behold, *I am coming* [*erchomai*] soon, bringing my recompense with me, to repay each one for what he has done. *I* [*egō*] am the Alpha and the Omega, the first and the last, the beginning and the end. (22:12–13)

I [*egō*], Jesus, have sent my angel to testify to you about these things for the churches. *I* [*egō*] am the root and the descendant of David, the bright morning star. (22:16)

He who testifies to these things says, 'Surely *I am coming* [*erchomai*] soon.' (22:20)

---

[34] Those favouring this interpretation include Beale 1999: 1154; Smalley 2005: 582–583; Boxall 2006: 319.

[35] Mounce 1997: 410. Similarly, Giesen 1997: 492; Koester 2014: 844; Dixon 2017: 146.

The first-person saying in verse 7 refers to 'the words of the prophecy of this book', which anticipates the warning against adding to or taking from these words in verses 18–19. Further, Christ employs testimony language in verse 20 (*ho martyrōn*), which follows closely on the heels of his testimony (*martyrō*) in verse 18.[36] Second, *martyrō egō* in verse 18 carries the force of an oath or legal testimony.[37] Koester notes similar language at the conclusion of ancient wills that specify the beneficiaries of an inheritance. 'Since Revelation speaks of retaining or losing a share in God's city (Rev. 22:19), it is fitting that Jesus has stated his name (22:16) and now attests the contents.'[38]

The most significant interpretive question in 22:18–19 concerns the precise meaning of prohibition against adding to (*epitithēmi*) or taking away (*aphaireō*) from the words of this prophetic book. Interpreters have taken these verses in at least three ways: (1) a prohibition against tampering with the text of the book, (2) a restriction on further prophetic activity or (3) a warning against falsifying the message by errant teaching or conduct.

First, Aune argues that the 'integrity formula' employed in these verses stresses the book's sacredness and completeness and warns against tampering with the written text.[39] He suggests that this warning is motivated by John's concern that rival prophets in the churches might modify or explain away this revelation, and observes that in Deuteronomy 12:32 – 13:5 warnings against false prophets follow immediately after the prohibition against adding to or taking from God's commandments.[40] The *Letter of Aristeas* reflects a similar concern with tampering and unauthorized revisions to the Greek translation of the Jewish law. After the translation is complete, the priests and elders 'commanded that a curse should be laid, as was their custom, on anyone who should alter the version by any addition or change to any part of the written text, or any deletion either' in order to ensure that the words were preserved fully (*Letter of Aristeas* 311). Thus the warning in Revelation 22:18–19 'acts as a kind of copyright' and also signals John's divine authorization and commissioning to

[36] Hieke and Nicklas 2003: 69.
[37] Aune 1998b: 1229–1230; Smalley 2005: 582–583.
[38] See Koester 2014: 844 for extensive references to Greek papyri.
[39] Aune 1998b: 1231–1232. Hieke and Nicklas (2003: 72–82) explain that the text-securing formula ('Textsicherungsformel') in these verses protects the integrity of the divine revelation, which cannot be amended.
[40] Aune 1998b: 1232. Royalty (2004: 298) takes this interpretation further, calling Rev. 22:18–19 an 'attack on John's opponents'.

write this sacred book.[41] However, while these verses have implications for faithfully preserving the text of Revelation, they directly address not copyists but congregants who hear its words (22:18; cf. 1:3).[42]

Alternatively, Thomas reasons that the warnings in 22:18–19 do not primarily concern tampering with the written text of the Apocalypse or restricting false prophecy only. Rather, he interprets 22:18–19 as a divine prohibition against any further prophetic activity.[43] Thomas conjectures that John might have concluded that the termination of all prophecy was necessary after his previous warnings against false prophets like Jezebel continued to influence the churches.[44] He argues that John employs the 'canonization-formula' in Deuteronomy 4 to claim scriptural authority for his book of prophecy, thereby prohibiting any further exercise of the gift of prophecy.[45]

While Thomas rightly observes the close relationship of Revelation 22:18–19 to Deuteronomy 4, he mistakenly concludes that these verses require the cessation of all prophetic activity. The epilogue of Revelation refers to 'the spirits of the prophets' and 'your brothers the prophets' (22:6, 9),[46] which seems oddly out of place if the risen Christ expressly prohibits the gift of prophecy a few verses later. Deuteronomy's prohibitions against adding to or taking from the divine word do not proscribe future divine revelation or prophetic activity; rather, the biblical law 'provides the theological norm against which to assess the validity of any prophetic utterance'.[47] Moreover, the immediate context of the warning in Deuteronomy 4:2 and 12:32 (13:1 MT, LXX) refers to the dangers and disastrous consequences of following after deceptive prophets. In 4:3 Moses recalls the Baal-Peor incident, when a plague destroyed thousands of Israelites who followed Balaam's advice and engaged in idolatry and immorality (Num. 25:1–9; 31:16). The parallel admonition against adding to or taking from God's commands in Deuteronomy 12:32 leads into calls to reject the words of prophets or dreamers who entice the people to serve other gods and rebel against Yahweh (13:1–3).[48]

---

[41] Blount 2013: 414.

[42] Morris 1987: 249.

[43] Thomas 1989: 210.

[44] Ibid. 210–211.

[45] Thomas 1995: 517. Similarly, MacArthur 2000: 310.

[46] 'Your brothers the prophets' likely designates a circle of Christian prophets, as explained by Koester (2014: 91, 840).

[47] Shead 2012: 154–155.

[48] Thompson (2008: 192) writes, 'In the Hebrew Bible chapter 13 begins with 12:32, which provides a suitable introduction to the case of the false prophet.'

Finally, Beale persuasively argues that in Revelation 22:18–19 '"adding and taking away" refers not to mere, general disobedience to the divine word, but to false teaching about the inscripturated word and following such deceptive teaching.'[49] He explains that these verses allude to a series of warnings in Deuteronomy and depict the Apocalypse 'as a new law code to a new Israel.'[50] Most commentators recognize that the combination of hearing, adding and taking in 22:18–19 recall Deuteronomy 4:1–2:

> And now, O Israel, listen [*akoue*] to the statutes and the rules that I am teaching you, and do them, that you may live, and go in and take possession of the land that Yahweh, the God of your fathers, is giving you. You shall not add [*prosthēsete*] to the word that I command you, nor take [*apheleite*] from it, that you may keep the commandments of Yahweh your God that I command you.[51]

As noted above, Moses' instructions here and in the parallel passage in 12:32 relate closely to warnings against the insidious influence of false prophets who would lead Israel to serve other gods (4:3; 13:1–5). Moreover, the threat of 'the plagues written in this book' (*tas plēgas tas gegrammenas en tō bibliō toutō*) in Revelation 22:18 alludes to Deuteronomy 29:20–21 LXX, where Moses warns that 'all the curses written in the book of this law' (*pasai hai arai tēs diathēkēs tautēs hai gegrammenai en tō bibliō tou nomou toutou*) will attach to any person who proudly turns away from Yahweh to serve the gods of the nations. The Jewish apocalypse *1 Enoch* similarly relates altering and taking away from the seer's words (104:11) to speaking evil words, inventing fictions and praising idols (104:9–10).[52] Thus 'In a context in which John's opponents accommodate idolatry (Rev. 2:2, 14, 20), this passage warns against deviating from Revelation's call for teaching and a manner of life that are faithful to God.'[53]

The repetition of 'add' and 'take away' in 22:18–19 signals that the punishment fits the crime. Those who 'add to' or 'take away' from the book's words by distorting or disregarding its authoritative message will be exposed to divine judgment and excluded from divine

---

[49] Beale 2011a: 8. Similarly, Smalley 2005: 583–584.
[50] Beale 2011a: 7.
[51] 'Add to' renders *epitithēmi* in Rev. 22:18 and *prostithēmi* in Deut. 4:2 and 13:1 LXX (12:32 ET), but the terms have overlapping senses (see L&N 59.72).
[52] Beale 1999: 1151–1152. Cf. Josephus, *Against Apion* 1.42–43.
[53] Koester 2014: 845.

blessing: God will 'add' to them the plagues of his wrath (cf. 15:1) and will 'take away' their share in the tree of life and holy city (22:18–19), leaving them 'outside' with the immoral, idolaters and 'everyone who loves and practices falsehood' (22:15). In contrast, those who hear and heed its trustworthy and true words are promised lavish blessing with God in the New Jerusalem (22:7, 14). The threefold repetition of 'the words of the prophecy of this book' in the epilogue (22:7, 18–19) underscores the unity of the Apocalypse while emphasizing the ultimate consequences to those who respond faithfully or unfaithfully to its message.[54]

By invoking Deuteronomy's warning against adding to or taking from the words of the Law in 22:18–19, Jesus boldly asserts that 'the authority of the book of Revelation parallels and exceeds that of the Torah'.[55] Both Moses and Christ warn about the consequences of denying or distorting the words of God; while the former speaks of the land beyond the Jordan that he has seen but cannot enter (Deut. 3:25 – 4:1), the latter testifies concerning the saints' eschatological inheritance in the Edenic city of God (Rev. 22:18–19; cf. 22:1–3). Moreover, the verses immediately preceding and following Jesus' warning anticipate his imminent 'coming' (22:17, 20), which further heightens the urgency and finality of his message to the churches. Thus the stakes could not be higher for hearing and heeding the testimony of the exalted Christ inscribed in this book of prophecy.

Trustworthy and true

The Apocalypse characterizes the exalted Christ as 'faithful and true' (*pistos kai alēthinos*) and applies the same description to the words he reveals to John. Jesus presents himself to the unfaithful Laodicean church in 3:14 as 'the Amen, the faithful and true witness' (*ho amēn, ho martys ho pistos kai alēthinos*). In 19:11 John depicts Jesus as a victorious king, who is seated on a white horse and 'is called Faithful and True' (*pistos kai alēthinos*). Additionally, the revealing angel and God himself stress to John in 21:5 and 22:6 that 'these words are trustworthy and true' (*houtoi hoi logoi pistoi kai alēthinoi*).

The Old Testament Scriptures repeatedly stress that God and his works are 'true' and 'faithful'. The foundational presentation of the

---

[54] Spellman 2016: 49.
[55] Ibid. Cf. Beale 2011a: 3.

Lord's name and character in Exodus 34:6 LXX depicts him as 'true' (*alēthinos*).[56] According to Deuteronomy 7:9 LXX, the Lord is 'the faithful God' (*theos pistos*), who keeps his covenant and mercy for a thousand generations. Moses combines the divine descriptions 'true' and 'faithful' in his famous song: 'God – his works are true [*alēthina*], and all his ways are justice. A faithful [*pistos*] God, and there is no injustice, a righteous and holy Lord' (Deut. 32:4 LXX).[57] Isaiah asserts that 'the Holy One of Israel is faithful [*pistos*]' (49:7) and twice refers to him as 'the true God' (*ho theos ho alēthinos*) in 65:16 LXX, rendering the Hebrew phrase *'ĕlōhê 'āmēn*.

The Old Testament similarly stresses the truthfulness and trustworthiness of God's revealed words. David responds to God's promise to establish his royal house by declaring, 'You are God, and your words are true [*alēthinoi*]' (2 Sam. 7:28). Similarly, the widow of Zarephath affirms that the Lord's word in Elijah's mouth is 'true' (LXX; *alēthinon*) after witnessing him raise her son (1 Kgs 17:24). The psalmist lauds the Lord's testimony as 'sure' (*pistē*) and his judgments as 'true' (*alēthina*) in Psalm 19:7, 9 (18:8, 10 LXX). Psalm 111:7 (110:7 LXX) stresses that 'truth and justice' are the works of God's hands, while his commandments are all 'trustworthy' (*pistai*).

John's book of prophecy applies to Christ and his revelation these very labels 'faithful' and 'true' that throughout the Old Testament depict the perfect character and communication of the God of Israel. In particular, Revelation 22:6 closely parallels Daniel 2, where Daniel interprets the king's dream and stresses its veracity:

> There is a God in heaven revealing mysteries who has made known to King Nebuchadnezzar what must happen in the last days [*ha dei genesthai ep' eschatōn tōn hēmerōn*] . . . The great God has made known to the king what must happen after these things, and the vision is true [*alēthinon*], and its interpretation is trustworthy [*pistē*]. (Dan. 2:28, 45 [TH], my tr.)

> And he said to me, 'These words are trustworthy and true [*pistoi kai alēthinoi*]. And the Lord, the God of the spirits of the prophets, has sent his angel to show his servants what must soon take place [*ha dei genesthai en tachei*].' (Rev. 22:6)

---

[56] Num. 14:18 and Ps. 86:15 (85:15 LXX) allude to Exod. 34:6 and likewise refer to God as *alēthinos*.

[57] Similarly, 3 Macc. 2.11 extols God as faithful (*pistos*) and true (*alēthinos*).

This allusion signals the imminent fulfilment of mysteries that would come 'in the last days'; it also stresses that God is the ultimate source of these mysteries, which Jesus reveals in this book of prophecy (1:1).[58]

In Revelation 3:14 Christ's self-disclosure as 'the Amen, the faithful and true witness' likely alludes to Isaiah 65:16 and identifies the exalted Jesus with 'the God of Amen'.[59] His total trustworthiness contrasts with the Laodicean church's treachery and unfaithfulness. In his vision of Jesus' return as conquering king, John reiterates that Jesus is called 'faithful and true' and discloses that his name is 'The Word of God' (Rev. 19:11, 13). The Fourth Gospel famously refers to Jesus as *ho logos*, the eternally existing divine agent of creation who became flesh and revealed his glory as the only Son of God (John 1:1–3, 14). Jesus the divine 'Word' has personally made known the true God as 'God's ultimate self-disclosure' (1:18).[60] In Revelation the glorious Christ embodies God's trustworthy Word by justly judging the nations with the sword coming from his mouth (19:15, 21; cf. 1:16; 2:16).

Significantly, these designations of Christ's identity as 'Faithful and True' and 'the Word of God' immediately follow the revealing angel's affirmation 'These are the true words of God' (*houtoi hoi logoi alēthinoi tou theou eisin* [19:9]). Jesus is the true *Logos*, and it follows that the *logoi* he reveals to his servant John are similarly trustworthy and true. 'The message and the message giver are described in the same terms.'[61] John's enigmatic explanation that 'the testimony of Jesus is the spirit of prophecy' (19:10) recalls the identification of John's revelatory visions from Christ as 'the testimony of Jesus' in 1:2.[62] The 'testimony of Jesus' that John receives and faithfully records in this book is authentic prophecy, which believers should heed as authoritative communication from God. These words offer a genuine alternative to the counterfeit prophecies circulating in the churches that distract and deter people from worshipping God alone (2:14–15, 20).

In 19:9 and 21:5 an affirmation of the truthfulness and divine source of 'these words' accompanies the command 'Write this'. In the latter text the connective *hoti* (for) in 21:5 indicates that the prophet

---

[58] Gladd 2016: 160.
[59] See ch. 3, pp. 54–55. For extensive discussion of the OT background of Rev. 3:14, see Beale 1996: 133–152.
[60] Carson 1991: 116.
[61] Dixon 2017: 138.
[62] See further ch. 4, pp. 76–80.

must put pen to parchment precisely because the revelation he receives is 'trustworthy and true'. The ultimate basis for the trustworthiness of this book of prophecy is the absolute perfection and reliability of the character and actions of God and Christ, whose revealed words are likewise faultless and faithful.[63] John testifies to all that he saw as a true prophet and servant of Christ. John writes down these genuine divine messages to safeguard their enduring witness until the exalted Christ comes (22:7) and the divine mystery is fulfilled (10:7). The revelation is written down to ensure that 'the churches' may profit from the words of this prophecy (22:16) by receiving the grace and peace they communicate (1:4; 22:21) and laying hold of the 'blessing' promised to all who keep the trustworthy words of God (1:3; 22:7).

Conclusion: blessed is the reader

The beatitudes in Revelation 1:3 and 22:7 invite and urge readers to respond faithfully to the book's message:

> Blessed is the one who reads aloud the words of this prophecy, and blessed are those who hear, and who keep what is written in it, for the time is near. (1:3)

> And behold, I am coming soon. Blessed is the one who keeps the words of the prophecy of this book. (22:7)

The initial beatitude 'sets a positive direction for the book as a whole',[64] while the saying in 22:7 restates 1:3 to reinforce its foundational offer of divine favour for those who 'keep' these words. These beatitudes summon readers to hear this book as genuine prophecy, to heed its urgent appeals for endurance and to understand their place in redemptive history.

First, believers must rightly 'hear' the Apocalypse as authentic prophecy revealed by the exalted Christ. Each of the seven messages to the churches includes the refrain 'He who has an ear, let him hear what the Spirit says to the churches' (2:7, 11, 17, 29; 3:6, 13, 22). This formula has close parallels in the Gospels and the Old Testament prophets, where 'ears' refer metaphorically to people's spiritual capacity to respond properly to the divine Word.[65] Those with 'an

---

[63] This summarizes the detailed argument in Beale 2011a: 1–22.
[64] Koester 2014: 131.
[65] See ch. 4, pp. 80–84.

ear' rightly grasp that the Spirit of God and the exalted Christ address the churches in and through this book of prophecy. They also test the spirits and resist the siren song of the false prophet and its emissaries such as Balaam and Jezebel (2:14, 20; 16:13–14). In 3:20 Jesus addresses the complacent church of Laodicea and presents himself standing at the door and knocking, which may suggest the return of a master to his servants (Luke 12:36) or a husband to his bride (Song 5:2).[66] He then promises to come in and commune with anyone who 'hears my voice and opens the door'. Thus 'Christ's voice is mediated. The readers hear Christ's voice through John's text.'[67] Each believer who hears the Saviour's voice in and through the Apocalypse must respond to his invitation for intimate fellowship.

Second, proper hearing of Spirit-inspired prophecy necessarily entails heeding its message. In 1:3 and 22:7 divine blessing is offered to 'the one who keeps' (*tērōn*) the divine words. John's Gospel stresses the importance of keeping Jesus' word. Jesus promises eternal life to those who keep his word (John 8:51–52), and explains that whoever loves him will keep his word (14:23; cf. 1 John 2:5). In the messages to the seven churches the exalted Christ commends Philadelphian believers for keeping his word concerning endurance and promises to 'keep them' in turn (Rev. 3:8, 10). Conversely, the congregation at Sardis must remember and keep what they have received from Christ, which involves repenting and waking up from their spiritual slumber (3:3). Keeping God's commands is an essential characteristic of the woman's offspring in 12:17 and of the saints in 14:12. While this book of prophecy discloses 'the things that must soon take place' (1:1), it promises favour not to one who decodes its predictions but who does what it says (1:3). Revelation thus has 'has an ultimate ethical aim' and, in keeping with the biblical prophetic tradition, summons God's covenant people to hear and heed the divine Word.[68]

Third, the concluding words of 1:3, 'for the time is near' (*ho gar kairos engys*), establish the eschatological orientation of the book and explain the basis for the earlier offer of divine blessing for those who hear and heed the prophetic word. This phrase recurs in 22:10: 'Do not seal up the words of the prophecy of this book, for the time is near' (*ho kairos gar engys estin*). Jesus similarly declares at the outset of his earthly ministry, 'The time [*ho kairos*] is fulfilled, and the kingdom of God has come near [*ēngiken*]' (Mark 1:15 NRSV). Daniel

---

[66] See, respectively, Bauckham 1993a: 107–108; Osborne 2002: 212.
[67] Koester 2014: 340.
[68] Beale and Campbell 2015: 37. Cf. deSilva 2009b: 10–11.

prophesies about the 'time' (*ho kairos*) when the saints shall possess the kingdom (7:22) and receives visions concerning 'the time of consummation' (*heōs kairou synteleias*), when 'all these things shall be finished' (12:7 LXX, my tr.; cf. 8:19; 11:35). Until this time Daniel is instructed to 'shut up the words and seal the book' (12:4). Daniel presents this appointed time as far off, but in the Apocalypse 'the time is near' (Rev. 1:3). Daniel's scroll remained sealed for a future generation, but John must not seal up his prophetic words (22:10). Revelation dramatically recounts that Jesus receives the sealed scroll from the Ancient of Days and opens the seven seals (5:7; 6:1), revealing God's previously hidden purposes to save his people, judge his foes and consummate his kingdom. Thus, now that the Christ has conquered and sat down on his Father's throne, there are no more sealed scrolls (3:21; 5:5).

Like 1:3 Revelation's other six beatitudes have a distinctly eschatological thrust. They promise divine favour for those who die in the Lord (14:13), who remain dressed and ready for Christ's coming (16:15), who are invited to the Lamb's marriage feast (19:9), who share in the first resurrection and reign with Christ (20:6) and who wash their robes and access the tree of life and the New Jerusalem (22:14). In 22:7 the blessing follows Christ's declaration 'And behold, I am coming soon.' Similar to Jesus' famous macarisms in Matthew 5:3–11 and Luke 6:20–22, the divine offer of present blessing to struggling saints anticipates the consummate bliss and well-being that they will experience when God sets his world aright. Paul writes, 'In Revelation, being a disciple is about living in the "now" as well as the "not yet" of expectation, with the former decisively shaped by the latter.'[69]

[69] Paul 2018: 48.

Chapter Eleven

Conclusion

And he who was seated on the throne said, 'Behold, I am making all things new.' Also he said, 'Write this down, for these words are trustworthy and true.' (Rev. 21:5)

Worship God. (Rev. 22:9)

The Apocalypse is the capstone of canonical prophecy: it discloses divine mysteries and brings decisive clarity and closure to the biblical story in the already-not-yet reign of Christ and the glorious new creation. We have seen throughout this study that John's prophetic letter to the seven churches weaves together various prophecies and patterns from the Old Testament – particularly the Prophets – into a glorious tapestry.

The book's foundational depiction of God on his throne flanked by heavenly worshippers (Rev. 4) recalls and develops the great throne-room visions of Isaiah, Ezekiel and Daniel. The book's various divine designations such as 'him who is and who was and who is to come' (1:4), 'the Alpha and the Omega' and 'the Almighty' (1:8) all allude to the Old Testament and cumulatively stress the utter supremacy, centrality and self-sufficiency of the true God who is enthroned in heaven as the Creator, Ruler and Judge of all (see ch. 2).

John remarkably describes 'the seven Spirits' that burn as torches before God's heavenly throne (1:4; cf. 4:5), endow the Lamb with divine insight and go forth into all the earth as the illumining, empowering presence of God (5:6), distinctively synthesizing imagery from Zechariah and Isaiah. John casts his visionary experience 'in the Spirit' and his prophetic commission to eat the scroll in terms reminiscent of Ezekiel (see chs. 4 and 10).

From the opening title *Apokalypsis Iēsou Christou* (1:1) to the final exclamation 'Amen. Come Lord Jesus!' (22:20), the risen Christ takes centre stage in this book of prophecy. John's foundational vision of 'one like a son of man' in 1:12–20 applies features of the Ancient of Days (Dan. 7) and the heavenly man (Dan. 10) to Jesus Christ and stresses his transcendent authority over and penetrating knowledge of the seven churches. The Apocalypse presents Jesus as the true messianic king who fulfils Old Testament expectation as 'firstborn', 'Lion of Judah', 'Root of David' and one who rules the nations with an iron rod. Christ's messianic kingship is inaugurated as he sits on the heavenly throne and opens the secret scroll, and will be consummated at the end of the age when he comes as 'King of kings and Lord of lords' (19:16). The Apocalypse's signature designation for Christ is 'the Lamb', which stresses his sacrificial death. The Lamb saves and shepherds his people and sits down on the exclusive throne of God as sharer in the divine essence and executor of divine judgment, redemption and restoration (see ch. 3).

These trustworthy words of prophecy clarify the true identity, present challenges and eschatological destiny of God's redeemed people (see ch. 5). Drawing upon Zechariah 4, Christ's churches are 'lampstands' (Rev. 1:20; 11:4), whose light shines in a dark world through their faithful testimony. Revelation 7 presents the church as both the 144,000 sealed from Israel's tribes and the innumerable crowd saved from every nation. The saints inhabit the great city of this world but must not share in its sins, since they are betrothed to the Lamb and are heirs of the city of God. Believers share 'in the tribulation' (1:9), follow the slaughtered Lamb (14:4) and overcome the ancient adversary by faithful witness (12:10–11). Christ the greater Passover Lamb has purchased people from every people to be priests and a kingdom (5:9–10), fulfilling Israel's calling in Exodus 19. While this ministerial vocation will be fully realized when God makes all things new (22:3, 5), the church presently discharges its duties as a royal priesthood by offering true worship to God and the Lamb while resisting the usurping claims of other lords (see ch. 6). Thus the worship and witness of believers from every tribe 'points representatively to the acknowledgment of the true God by all the nations, in the universal worship for which the whole creation is destined'.[1]

Revelation reminds readers that this God alone is true, good and worthy of our worship and trust. It also stirs the saints to recognize and resist the deceptive and deadly siren song of the world played by Babylon's band (see ch. 6). Moreover, this apocalyptic prophecy presents an alternative perspective on the world as it really is in the light of God's present rule and eschatological purposes. It forces the church to evaluate whether we love, long for and live for 'the world or the things in the world' (1 John 2:15) or Christ and his kingdom.

---

[1] Bauckham 1993b: 161.

Johnson writes, 'Whenever Revelation works on us as God intends it to, we trust, love, and fear Jesus more.'[2]

Readers of Revelation thus face a crucial choice of allegiance and adoration. Who is worthy to rule: the Lamb or the beast? Who speaks for God: John or 'Jezebel'? The city of man and the city of God alike promise security and prosperity. But the Apocalypse exposes Babylon's blessings as fleeting and flawed. Combining prophetic critiques of Babylon and Tyre, the climax of prophecy discloses that the world's great city is a glorious house of cards that will collapse in ruin. The New Jerusalem may seem like a distant dream for believers hounded by hardships, but its glory will never fade and its light never flicker because God and the Lamb will dwell among their people for ever (21:3; see ch. 8). Every rival will be defeated, every tear dried, every longing fulfilled as the saints will gaze upon God and the Lamb and gladly serve as priests and kings (21:4; 22:3–5). Those with ears to hear must hold fast to the trustworthy and true words of this prophecy and align with the host of heaven by offering true worship to God alone (7:11; 22:9).

> Love divine, all loves excelling,
> joy of heav'n, to earth come down,
> fix in us Thy humble dwelling;
> all Thy faithful mercies crown.
> Jesus, Thou art all compassion;
> pure, unbounded love Thou art;
> visit us with Thy salvation;
> enter ev'ry trembling heart.
>
> Finish then Thy new creation;
> pure and spotless let us be.
> Let us see Thy great salvation
> perfectly restored in Thee.
> Changed from glory into glory,
> till in heav'n we take our place,
> till we cast our crowns before Thee,
> lost in wonder, love, and praise.[3]

---

[2] Johnson 2001: 340.
[3] Wesley 2017: 205.

Bibliography

(2009), *Revised Common Lectionary*, Bellingham, Wash.: Faithlife.

Abma, R. (1997), 'Travelling from Babylon to Zion: Location and Its Function in Isaiah 49–55', *JSOT* 22: 3–28.

Adams, E. (2006), 'The "Coming of God" Tradition and Its Influence on New Testament Parousia Texts', in M. A. Knibb, C. Hempel and J. Lieu (eds.), *Biblical Traditions in Transmission: Essays in Honour of Michael A. Knibb*, JSJSup 111, Leiden: Brill, 1–19.

Alexander, T. D. (2008), *From Eden to the New Jerusalem: Exploring God's Plan for Life on Earth*, Nottingham: Inter-Varsity Press.

Allen, L. C. (1990), *Ezekiel 20–48*, WBC 29, Dallas: Word.

Augustine (2003), *Concerning the City of God Against the Pagans*, tr. H. Bettenson, Penguin Classics, New York: Penguin.

Aune, D. E. (1997), *Revelation 1–5*, WBC 52A, Nashville: Thomas Nelson.

——— (1998a), *Revelation 6–16*, WBC 52B, Nashville: Thomas Nelson.

——— (1998b), *Revelation 17–22*, WBC 52C, Nashville: Thomas Nelson.

Bachmann, M. (1994), 'Himmlisch: der "Temple Gottes" von Apk 11.1', *NTS* 40: 474–480.

Baldwin, J. G. (1978), *Daniel: An Introduction and Commentary*, TOTC 23, Downers Grove: InterVarsity Press.

Bandstra, A. J. (1992), '"A Kingship and Priests": Inaugurated Eschatology in the Apocalypse', *CTJ* 27: 10–25.

Bandy, A. S. (2009), 'The Layers of the Apocalypse: An Integrative Approach to Revelation's Macrostructure', *JSNT* 31: 469–499.

——— (2010a), 'The Hermeneutics of Symbolism: How to Interpret the Symbols of John's Apocalypse', *SBJT* 14: 46–58.

——— (2010b), *The Prophetic Lawsuit in the Book of Revelation*, NTM 29, Sheffield: Sheffield Phoenix.

——— (2011), 'Patterns of Prophetic Lawsuits in the Oracles to the Seven Churches', *Neot* 45: 178–205.

—— (2013), 'Persecution and the Purpose of Revelation with Reference to Roman Jurisprudence', *BBR* 23: 377–398.

Bandy, A. S., and B. L. Merkle (2015), *Understanding Prophecy: A Biblical-Theological Approach*, Grand Rapids: Kregel.

Bauckham, R. (1976), 'Martyrdom of Enoch and Elijah: Jewish or Christian?', *JBL* 95: 447–458.

—— (1993a), *The Climax of Prophecy: Studies on the Book of Revelation*, Edinburgh: T&T Clark.

—— (1993b), *The Theology of the Book of Revelation*, NTT, Cambridge: Cambridge University Press.

—— (2001a), 'Prayer in the Book of Revelation', in R. N. Longenecker (ed.), *Into God's Presence: Prayer in the New Testament*, Grand Rapids: Eerdmans, 252–271.

—— (2001b), 'Revelation', in J. Barton and J. Muddiman (eds.), *The Oxford Bible Commentary*, Oxford: Oxford University Press, 1287–1306.

Beale, G. K. (1984a), 'The Influence of Daniel upon the Structure and Theology of John's Apocalypse', *JETS* 27: 413–423.

—— (1984b), *The Use of Daniel in Jewish Apocalyptic Literature and in the Revelation of St. John*, Lanham, Md.: University Press of America.

—— (1985), 'The Origin of the Title "King of Kings and Lord of Lords" in Revelation 17.14', *NTS* 31: 618–620.

—— (1992), 'The Interpretative Problem of Rev 1:19', *NovT* 34: 360–387.

—— (1994), 'Review Article: J. W. Mealy After the Thousand Years', *EvQ* 66: 229–249.

—— (1996), 'The Old Testament Background of Rev 3.14', *NTS* 42: 133–152.

—— (1999), *The Book of Revelation: A Commentary on the Greek Text*, NIGTC, Grand Rapids: Eerdmans.

—— (2004), *The Temple and the Church's Mission: A Biblical Theology of the Dwelling Place of God*, NSBT 17, Leicester: Apollos; Downers Grove: InterVarsity Press.

—— (2005), 'Eden, the Temple, and the Church's Mission in the New Creation', *JETS* 48: 5–31.

—— (2006), 'The Purpose of Symbolism in the Book of Revelation', *CTJ* 41: 53–66.

—— (2008), *We Become What We Worship: A Biblical Theology of Idolatry*, Downers Grove: IVP Academic.

———— (2010), *The Use of Daniel in Jewish Apocalyptic Literature and in the Revelation of St. John*, repr., Eugene: Wipf & Stock.

———— (2011a), 'Can the Bible Be Completely Inspired by God and Yet Still Contain Errors? A Response to Some Recent "Evangelical" Proposals', *WTJ* 73: 1–22.

———— (2011b), *A New Testament Biblical Theology: The Unfolding of the Old Testament in the New*, Grand Rapids: Baker Academic.

———— (2012), *Handbook on the New Testament Use of the Old Testament: Exegesis and Interpretation*, Grand Rapids: Baker Academic.

Beale, G. K., and D. H. Campbell (2015), *The Book of Revelation: A Shorter Commentary*, Grand Rapids: Eerdmans.

Beale, G. K., and B. L. Gladd (2014), *Hidden But Now Revealed: A Biblical Theology of Mystery*, Downers Grove: InterVarsity Press.

Beale, G. K., and M. Kim (2014), *God Dwells Among Us: Expanding Eden to the Ends of the Earth*, Downers Grove: InterVarsity Press.

Beale, G. K., and S. McDonough (2007), 'Revelation', in G. K. Beale and D. A. Carson (eds.), *Commentary on the New Testament Use of the Old Testament*, Grand Rapids: Baker Academic, 1081–1161.

Beynon, G. (2010), *Last Things First: Living in the Light of the Future*, Nottingham: Inter-Varsity Press.

Biguzzi, G. (2006), 'Is the Babylon of Revelation Rome or Jerusalem?', *Bib* 87: 371–386.

Blocher, H. A. G. (2000), 'Adam and Eve', in *NDBT*, 372–376.

Block, D. I. (1992), 'Beyond the Grave: Ezekiel's Vision of Death and Afterlife', *BBR* 2: 113–141.

———— (1998), *The Book of Ezekiel, Chapters 25–48*, NICOT, Grand Rapids: Eerdmans.

Blomberg, C. L. (2006), *From Pentecost to Patmos: An Introduction to Acts through Revelation*, Nashville: B&H Academic.

———— (2013), 'Why I Am a Historic Premillennialist', *CTR* 11: 71–87.

Blomberg, C. L., and S. W. Chung (eds.) (2009), *A Case for Historic Premillennialism: An Alternative to "Left Behind" Eschatology*, Grand Rapids: Baker Academic.

Blount, B. K. (2013), *Revelation: A Commentary*, NTL, Louisville: Westminster John Knox.

Bock, D. L. (2012), 'Did Jesus Connect Son of Man to Daniel 7? A Short Reflection on the Position of Larry Hurtado', *BBR* 22: 399–402.

Bøe, S. (2001), *Gog and Magog: Ezekiel 38–39 as Pre-Text for Revelation 19,17–21 and 20,7–10*, WUNT 2.135, Tübingen: Mohr Siebeck.

Borchert, G. L. (2000), 'Light', in *NDBT*, 644–646.

Boxall, I. (2006), *The Revelation of Saint John*, BNTC 18, Peabody: Hendrickson.

Bruce, F. F. (1973), 'The Spirit in the Apocalypse', in B. Lindars and S. S. Smalley (eds.), *Christ and Spirit in the New Testament: Studies in Honour of Charles Francis Digby Moule*, Cambridge: Cambridge University Press, 333–344.

Caird, G. B. (1984), *A Commentary on the Revelation of St. John the Divine*, 2nd edn, BNTC, London: A&C Black.

——— (1997), *The Language and Imagery of the Bible*, Grand Rapids: Eerdmans.

Campbell, W. G. (2012), *Reading Revelation: A Thematic Approach*, Cambridge: James Clarke.

Carson, D. A. (1991), *The Gospel According to John*, PNTC, Grand Rapids: Eerdmans.

——— (2004), 'Mystery and Fulfillment: Toward a More Comprehensive Paradigm of Paul's Understanding of the Old and the New', in D. A Carson (ed.), *The Paradoxes of Paul*, Justification and Variegated Nomism 2, Tübingen: Mohr Siebeck; Grand Rapids: Baker, 393–436.

Carson, D. A., and D. J. Moo (2005), *An Introduction to the New Testament*, 2nd edn, Grand Rapids: Zondervan.

Casey, J. (1987), 'The Exodus Theme in the Book of Revelation against the Background of the New Testament', in B. van Iersel, A. G. Weiler and M. Lefébure (eds.), *Exodus, a Lasting Paradigm*, Edinburgh: T&T Clark, 34–43.

Charles, R. H. (1920), *A Critical and Exegetical Commentary on the Revelation of St. John*, ICC 44, 2 vols., New York: Charles Scribner's.

Charlesworth, J. H. (ed.) (1983–5), *The Old Testament Pseudepigrapha*, 2 vols, Garden City: Doubleday.

Chilton, D. (1990), *The Days of Vengeance: An Exposition of the Book of Revelation*, Fort Worth, Tex.: Dominion.

Collins, A. Y. (1976), *The Combat Myth in the Book of Revelation*, HDR 9, Missoula: Scholars Press.

Collins, J. J. (1979), 'Introduction: Towards the Morphology of a Genre', *Semeia* 14: 1–20.

——— (1993), *Daniel: A Commentary on the Book of Daniel*, Hermeneia, Minneapolis: Fortress.

————— (2010), 'Apocalypse', in J. J. Collins and D. C. Harlow (eds.), *The Eerdmans Dictionary of Early Judaism*, Grand Rapids: Eerdmans, 341–345.

Dalrymple, R. (2011), *Revelation and the Two Witnesses: The Implications for Understanding John's Depiction of the People of God and His Hortatory Intent*, Eugene: Wipf & Stock.

Davies, J. A. (2004), *A Royal Priesthood: Literary and Intertextual Perspectives on an Image of Israel in Exodus 19.6*, JSOTSup 395, London: T&T Clark.

Dehandschutter, B. (1980), 'The Meaning of Witness in the Apocalypse', in J. Lambrecht (ed.), *L'Apocalypse johannique et l'apocalyptique dans le Nouveau Testament*, BETL 53, Louvain: Louvain University Press.

Dempster, S. G. (2003), *Dominion and Dynasty: A Biblical Theology of the Hebrew Bible*, NSBT 15, Leicester: Apollos; Downers Grove: InterVarsity Press.

DeRouchie, J. S. (2013), 'The Blessing-Commission, the Promised Offspring, and the Toledot Structure of Genesis', *JETS* 56: 219–247.

deSilva, D. A. (2008), 'The Strategic Arousal of Emotion in John's Visions of Roman Imperialism: A Rhetorical-Critical Investigation of Revelation 4-22', *Neot* 42: 1–34.

————— (2009a), 'An Example of How to Die Nobly for Religion: The Influence of 4 Maccabees on Origen's Exhortatio ad Martyrium', *JECS* 17: 337–355.

————— (2009b), *Seeing Things John's Way: The Rhetoric of the Book of Revelation*, Louisville: Westminster John Knox.

Deutsch, C. (1987), 'Transformation of Symbols: The New Jerusalem in Rv 21:1–22:5', *ZNW* 78: 106–126.

Dickens, C. (1999), *A Tale of Two Cities*, repr., Mineola, N.Y.: Dover.

Dixon, S. S. U. (2017), *The Testimony of the Exalted Jesus in the Book of Revelation*, LNTS 570, London: Bloomsbury T&T Clark.

Dow, L. K. F. (2012), 'Commentaries on Revelation', in E. J. Schnabel and S. E. Porter (eds.), *On the Writing of New Testament Commentaries: Festschrift for Grant R. Osborne on the Occasion of His 70th Birthday*, TENTS 8, Leiden: Brill, 421–448.

Draper, J. A. (1983), 'The Heavenly Feast of Tabernacles: Revelation 7:1–17', *JSNT* 19: 133–147.

Duff, P. B. (2001), *Who Rides the Beast? Prophetic Rivalry and the Rhetoric of Crisis in the Churches of the Apocalypse*, Oxford: Oxford University Press.

Edwards, J. (1723), *Apocalyptic Writings*, WJE Online 5, <http://edwards.yale.edu>.

Ellul, J. (1977), *Apocalypse: The Book of Revelation*, New York: Seabury.

Estelle, B. D. (2017), *Echoes of Exodus: Tracing a Biblical Motif*, Downers Grove: InterVarsity Press.

Fee, G. D. (2013), *Revelation: A New Covenant Commentary*, New Covenant Commentary Series 18, Cambridge: Lutterworth.

Fekkes III, J. (1990), '"His Bride Has Prepared Herself": Revelation 19–21 and Isaian Nuptial Imagery', *JBL* 109: 269–287.

—— (1994), *Isaiah and Prophetic Traditions in the Book of Revelation: Visionary Antecedents and their Development*, JSNTSup 93, Sheffield: JSOT Press.

Fokkelman, J. P. (2004), *Narrative Art in Genesis: Specimens of Stylistic and Structural Analysis*, 2nd edn, Eugene: Wipf & Stock.

Ford, J. M. (1975), *Revelation: Introduction, Translation, and Commentary*, AB 38, New Haven: Yale University Press.

France, R. T. (1998), *Jesus and the Old Testament*, repr., Vancouver: Regent College.

Friesen, S. J. (2005), 'Satan's Throne, Imperial Cults and the Social Settings of Revelation', *JSNT* 27: 351–373.

—— (2006), *Imperial Cults and the Apocalypse of John: Reading Revelation in the Ruins*, Oxford: Oxford University Press.

Gallusz, L. (2014), *The Throne Motif in the Book of Revelation*, LNTS 487, London: Bloomsbury T&T Clark.

Gentry Jr, K. L. (1998), 'A Preterist View of Revelation', in C. M. Pate (ed.), *Four Views on the Book of Revelation*, Grand Rapids: Zondervan, 35–92.

Gentry, P. J. (2013), 'The Meaning of "Holy" in the Old Testament', *BSac* 170: 400–417.

—— (2017), *How to Read and Understand the Biblical Prophets*, Wheaton: Crossway.

Giblin, C. H. (1974), 'Structural and Thematic Correlations in the Theology of Revelation 16–22', *Bib* 55: 487–504.

—— (1994), 'Recapitulation and the Literary Coherence of John's Apocalypse', *CBQ* 56: 81–95.

Giesen, H. (1997), *Die Offenbarung des Johannes*, RNT, Regensburg: F. Pustet.

Gladd, B. L. (2016), 'An Apocalyptic Trinitarian Model: The Book of Daniel's Influence on Revelation's Conception of the Trinity', in B. Crowe and C. Trueman (eds.), *The Essential Trinity: New*

Testament Foundations and Practical Relevance, London: Apollos, 156–174.

Glenny, W. E. (2009), *Finding Meaning in the Text: Translation Technique and Theology in the Septuagint of Amos*, VTSup 126, Leiden: Brill.

Goldingay, J. (1989), *Daniel*, WBC 30, Dallas: Word.

Gorman, M. J. (2011), *Reading Revelation Responsibly: Uncivil Worship and Witness: Following the Lamb into the New Creation*, Eugene: Cascade.

Grabiner, S. (2015), *Revelation's Hymns: Commentary on the Cosmic Conflict*, LNTS 511, London: Bloomsbury T&T Clark.

Gradl, H.-G. (2012), 'Buch und Brief: Zur motivischen, literarischen und kommunikativen Interdependenz zweier medialer Typen in der Johannes-Offenbarung', in J. Frey, J. Kelhoffer and F. Tóth (eds.), *Die Johannesapokalypse: Kontexte – Konzepte – Rezeption*, WUNT 287, Tübingen: Mohr Siebeck, 413–433.

Gurtner, D. M. (2013a), *Exodus: A Commentary on the Greek Text of Codex Vaticanus*, Septuagint Commentary Series, Leiden: Brill.

——— (2013b), 'Noncanonical Jewish Writings', in J. B. Green and L. M. McDonald (eds.), *The World of the New Testament: Cultural, Social, and Historical Contexts*, Grand Rapids: Baker Academic, 291–309.

Hamilton, J. M. (2010), *God's Glory in Salvation Through Judgment: A Biblical Theology*, Wheaton: Crossway.

——— (2014), *With the Clouds of Heaven: The Book of Daniel in Biblical Theology*, NSBT 32, Nottingham: Apollos; Downers Grove: InterVarsity Press.

Hamilton, V. P. (1995), *The Book of Genesis, Chapters 18–50*, NICOT, Grand Rapids: Eerdmans.

Hamstra, S. (1998), 'An Idealist View of Revelation', in C. M. Pate (ed.), *Four Views on the Book of Revelation*, Grand Rapids: Zondervan, 93–132.

Hannah, D. D. (2011), 'The Elect Son of Man of the Parables of Enoch', in L. W. Hurtado and P. Owen (eds.), *'Who Is This Son of Man?' The Latest Scholarship on a Puzzling Expression of the Historical Jesus*, LNTS 390, London: T&T Clark, 130–158.

Hays, R. B. (1989), *Echoes of Scripture in the Letters of Paul*, New Haven: Yale University Press.

——— (2012), 'Faithful Witness, Alpha and Omega: The Identity of Jesus in the Apocalypse of John', in S. Alkier and R. B. Hays (eds.),

Revelation and the Politics of Apocalyptic Interpretation, Waco: Baylor University Press, 69–83.

Heil, J. P. (1993), 'The Fifth Seal (Rev 6,9–11) as a Key to the Book of Revelation', *Bib* 74: 220–243.

——— (2014), *Book of Revelation: Worship for Life in the Spirit of Prophecy*, Eugene: Cascade.

Hemer, C. J. (1986), *The Letters to the Seven Churches of Asia in their Local Setting*, Sheffield: JSOT Press.

Hendriksen, W. (1998), *More Than Conquerors: An Interpretation of the Book of Revelation*, repr., Grand Rapids: Baker.

Hieke, T. (2012), 'The Reception of Daniel 7 in the Revelation of John', in S. Alkier and R. B. Hays (eds.), *Revelation and the Politics of Apocalyptic Interpretation*, Waco: Baylor University Press, 47–67.

Hieke, T., and T. Nicklas (2003), *'Die Worte der Prophetie dieses Buches': Offenbarung 22, 6–21 als Schlussstein der christlichen Bibel Alten und Neuen Testaments*, Biblisch-theologische Studien 62, Neukirchen-Vluyn: Neukirchener Verlag.

Hill, A. E. (2008), 'Daniel–Malachi', in T. Longman III and D. E. Garland (eds.), *Daniel–Malachi*, Revised Expositor's Bible Commentary 8, Grand Rapids: Zondervan, 20–212.

Holtz, T. (1962), *Die Christologie der Apokalypse des Johannes*, Berlin: Akademie-Verlag.

Hopkins, K. (2000), *A World Full of Gods: The Strange Triumph of Christianity*, New York: Free.

Huber, K. (2012), 'Jesus Christus – der Erste und der Letzte: Zur Christologie der Johannesapocalypse', in J. Frey, J. Kelhoffer and F. Tóth (eds.), *Die Johannesapokalypse : Kontexte – Konzepte – Rezeption*, WUNT 287, Tübingen: Mohr Siebeck, 435–472.

Huber, L. R. (2007), *Like a Bride Adorned: Reading Metaphor in John's Apocalypse*, Emory Studies in Early Christianity 10, New York: T&T Clark.

Hurtado, L. W., and P. Owen (eds.) (2011), *'Who Is This Son of Man?' The Latest Scholarship on a Puzzling Expression of the Historical Jesus*, LNTS 390, London: T&T Clark.

Inwood, B. (2007), *Seneca: Selected Philosophical Letters: Translated with Introduction and Commentary*, Clarendon Later Ancient Philosophers, Oxford: Oxford University Press.

Jauhiainen, M. (2005), *The Use of Zechariah in Revelation*, WUNT 2.199, Tubingen: Mohr Siebeck.

Jeske, R. L. (1985), 'Spirit and Community in the Johannine Apocalypse', *NTS* 31: 452–466.

Johns, L. L. (2003), *The Lamb Christology of the Apocalypse of John: An Investigation into Its Origins and Rhetorical Force*, WUNT 2.167, Tübingen: Mohr Siebeck.

Johnson, D. E. (2001), *Triumph of the Lamb: A Commentary on Revelation*, Phillipsburg: P&R.

Kaiser, W. C. (2008), 'Exodus', in T. Longman III and D. E. Garland (eds.), *Genesis–Leviticus*, Revised Expositor's Bible Commentary 1, Grand Rapids: Zondervan, 335–562.

Karrer, M. (2017), *Johannesoffenbarung (Offb. 1,1–5,14)*, EKKNT 24.1, Göttingen: Vandenhoeck & Ruprecht.

Keener, C. S. (2000), *Revelation*, NIVAC, Grand Rapids: Zondervan.

Kline, M. G. (1975), 'First Resurrection', *WTJ* 37: 366–375.

Koester, C. R. (2001), *Revelation and the End of All Things*, Grand Rapids: Eerdmans.

—————— (2005), 'Revelation and the Left Behind Novels', *WW* 25: 274–282.

—————— (2014), *Revelation: A New Translation with Introduction and Commentary*, AB 38A, New Haven: Yale University Press.

Köstenberger, A. J. (2007), 'John', in G. K. Beale and D. A. Carson (eds.), *Commentary on the New Testament Use of the Old Testament*, Grand Rapids: Baker Academic, 415–512.

Köstenberger, A. J., L. S. Kellum and C. L. Quarles (2016), *The Cradle, the Cross, and the Crown: An Introduction to the New Testament*, 2nd edn, Nashville: B&H Academic.

Köstenberger, A. J., and R. D. Patterson (2011), *Invitation to Biblical Interpretation: Exploring the Hermeneutical Triad of History, Literature, and Theology*, Grand Rapids: Kregel.

Kowalski, B. (2004), *Rezeption des Propheten Ezechiel in der Offenbarung des Johannes*, SBB 52, Stuttgart: Katholisches Bibelwerk.

Kraft, H. (1974), *Die Offenbarung des Johannes*, HNT 16A, Tübingen: Mohr Siebeck.

Kraybill, J. N. (1996), *Imperial Cult and Commerce in John's Apocalypse*, JSNTSup 132, Sheffield: Sheffield Academic Press.

Ladd, G. E. (1972), *A Commentary on the Revelation of John*, Grand Rapids: Eerdmans.

Lanfer, P. T. (2009), 'Allusion to and Expansion of the Tree of Life and Garden of Eden in Biblical and Pseudepigraphal Literature', in C. A. Evans and H. D. Zacharias (eds.), *Early Christian Literature and Intertextuality*, vol. 1: *Thematic Studies*, LNTS 391, London: T&T Clark, 96–108.

Lee, M. V. (1998), 'A Call to Martyrdom: Function as Method and Message in Revelation', *NovT* 40: 164–194.

Lee, P. (2001), *The New Jerusalem in the Book of Revelation: A Study of Revelation 21–22 in the Light of Its Background in Jewish Tradition*, WUNT 2.129, Tübingen: Mohr Siebeck.

Leithart, P. J. (2018a), *Revelation 1–11*, T&T Clark International Theological Commentary, London: Bloomsbury T&T Clark.

——— (2018b), *Revelation 12–22*, T&T Clark International Theological Commentary, London: Bloomsbury T&T Clark.

Levey, S. H. (1987), *The Targum of Ezekiel*, ArBib 3, Wilmington: Glazier.

Lewis, C. S. (1961), *An Experiment in Criticism*, Cambridge: Cambridge University Press.

——— (1994), *The Last Battle*, repr., The Chronicles of Narnia, New York: HarperCollins.

Lincoln, A. T. (2000), *Truth on Trial: The Lawsuit Motif in the Fourth Gospel*, Peabody: Hendrickson.

Litwak, K. D. (1998), 'Echoes of Scripture? A Critical Survey of Recent Works on Paul's Use of the Old Testament', *CurBR* 6: 260–288.

Lucas, E. C. (2002), *Daniel*, AOTC 20, Leicester: Apollos; Downers Grove: InterVarsity Press.

MacArthur, J. (1999), *Revelation 1–11*, Chicago: Moody.

——— (2000), *Revelation 12–22*, Chicago: Moody.

Macaskill, G. (2010), 'Paradise in the New Testament', in M. Bockmuehl and G. G. Stroumsa (eds.), *Paradise in Antiquity: Jewish and Christian Views*, Cambridge: Cambridge University Press, 64–81.

McComiskey, T. E. (1992), 'Zechariah', in T. E. McComiskey (ed.), *The Minor Prophets: An Exegetical and Expository Commentary*, Grand Rapids: Baker, 1003–1244.

McDonough, S. M. (1999), *YHWH at Patmos: Rev. 1:4 in Its Hellenistic and Early Jewish Setting*, WUNT 2.107, Tübingen: Mohr Siebeck.

——— (2000), 'Of Beasts and Bees: The View of the Natural World in Virgil's Georgics and John's Apocalypse', *NTS* 46: 227–244.

McKane, W. (1986), *A Critical and Exegetical Commentary on Jeremiah*, vol. 1, ICC, Edinburgh: T&T Clark.

McNicol, A. J. (2011), *Conversion of the Nations in Revelation*, LNTS 438, London: T&T Clark.

Maier, G. (1981), *Die Johannesoffenbarung und die Kirche*, WUNT 25, Tübingen: Mohr Siebeck.

Malone, A. S. (2017), *God's Mediators: A Biblical Theology of Priesthood*, NSBT, Nottingham: Apollos; Downers Grove: InterVarsity Press.

Mangina, J. L. (2010), *Revelation*, Brazos Theological Commentary on the Bible, Grand Rapids: Brazos.

—— (2012), 'God, Israel, and Ecclesia in the Apocalypse', in S. Alkier and R. B. Hays (eds.), *Revelation and the Politics of Apocalyptic Interpretation*, Waco: Baylor University Press, 85–103.

Marriner, K. T. (2016), *Following the Lamb: The Theme of Discipleship in the Book of Revelation*, Eugene: Wipf & Stock.

Mathewson, D. (1992), 'Revelation in Recent Genre Criticism: Some Implications for Interpretation', *TJ* 13: 193–213.

—— (2003a), 'New Exodus as a Background for "the Sea Was no More" in Revelation 21:1C', *TJ* 24: 243–258.

—— (2003b), *A New Heaven and a New Earth: The Meaning and Function of the Old Testament in Revelation 21.1–22.5*, JSNTSup 238, Sheffield: Sheffield Academic Press.

—— (2010), *Verbal Aspect in the Book of Revelation: The Function of Greek Verb Tenses in John's Apocalypse*, Linguistic Biblical Studies 4, Leiden: Brill.

—— (2016), *Revelation: A Handbook on the Greek Text*, Baylor Handbook on the Greek New Testament, Waco: Baylor University Press.

Mazzaferri, F. D. (1989), *The Genre of the Book of Revelation From a Source-Critical Perspective*, BZNW 54, Berlin: de Gruyter.

Mealy, J. W. (1992), *After the Thousand Years: Resurrection and Judgment in Revelation 20*, JSNTSup 70, Sheffield: Sheffield Academic Press.

Menn, J. (2013), *Biblical Eschatology*, Eugene: Wipf & Stock.

Michaels, J. R. (1991), 'Revelation 1:19 and the Narrative Voices of the Apocalypse', *NTS* 37: 604–620.

—— (1997), *Revelation*, IVP New Testament Commentary, Downers Grove: InterVarsity Press.

Middleton, J. R. (2014), *A New Heaven and a New Earth: Reclaiming Biblical Eschatology*, Grand Rapids: Baker.

Morris, L. (1987), *Revelation: An Introduction and Commentary*, TNTC 20, Downers Grove: InterVarsity Press.

Mounce, R. H. (1997), *The Book of Revelation*, rev. ed., NICNT, Grand Rapids: Eerdmans.

Moyise, S. (1995), *The Old Testament in the Book of Revelation*, JSNTSup 115, Sheffield: Sheffield Academic Press.

———— (2004), 'The Psalms in the Book of Revelation', in S. Moyise and M. J. J. Menken (eds.), *The Psalms in the New Testament*, The New Testament and the Scriptures of Israel, London: T&T Clark, 231–246.

Naylor, M. (2010), 'The Roman Imperial Cult and Revelation', *CurBR* 8: 207–239.

Nicklas, T. (2012), 'The Apocalypse in the Framework of the Canon', in S. Alkier and R. B. Hays (eds.), *Revelation and the Politics of Apocalyptic Interpretation*, Waco: Baylor University Press, 143–153.

Oecumenius (2011), 'Commentary on the Apocalypse', in W. C. Weinrich (ed.), *Greek Commentaries on Revelation*, Ancient Christian Texts, Downers Grove: IVP Academic, 1–108.

Ortlund, R. C. (1996), *God's Unfaithful Wife: A Biblical Theology of Spiritual Adultery*, NSBT 2, Leicester: Apollos; Downers Grove: InterVarsity Press.

Osborne, G. R. (2002), *Revelation*, BECNT, Grand Rapids: Baker Academic.

Oswalt, J. N. (1998), *The Book of Isaiah, Chapters 40-66*, NICOT, Grand Rapids: Eerdmans.

Pate, C. M. (1998), 'A Progressive Dispensationist View of Revelation', in C. M. Pate (ed.), *Four Views on the Book of Revelation*, Grand Rapids: Zondervan, 133–176.

Paul, I. (2000), 'The Use of the Old Testament in Revelation 12', in S. Moyise (ed.), *The Old Testament in the New Testament: Essays in Honour of J. L. North*, JSNTSup, Sheffield: Sheffield Academic Press, 256–276.

———— (2001), 'The Book of Revelation: Image, Symbol and Metaphor', in S. Moyise (ed.), *Studies in the Book of Revelation*, Edinburgh: T&T Clark, 131–148.

———— (2018), *Revelation*, TNTC 20, London: Inter-Varsity Press.

Paulien, J. (1988), 'Elusive Allusions: The Problematic Use of the Old Testament in Revelation', *BR* 33: 37–53.

Peterson, B. N. (2016), 'The Sin of Sodom Revisited: Reading Genesis 19 in Light of Torah', *JETS* 59: 17–31.

Peterson, D. G. (1992), *Engaging with God: A Biblical Theology of Worship*, Downers Grove: InterVarsity Press.

Petterson, A. R. (2015), *Haggai, Zechariah and Malachi*, AOTC 25, Nottingham: Apollos; Downers Grove: InterVarsity Press.

Phillips, R. D. (2017), *Revelation*, Reformed Expository Commentary, Phillipsburg: P&R.

Porter, S. E. (1997), 'The Use of the Old Testament in the New: A Brief Comment on Method and Terminology', in J. A. Sanders and C. A. Evans (eds.), *Early Christian Interpretation of the Scriptures of Israel: Investigations and Proposals*, SSEJC 5, Sheffield: Sheffield Academic Press, 79–96.

———— (2008), 'Allusions and Echoes', in S. E. Porter and C. D. Stanley (eds.), *As It Is Written: Studying Paul's Use of Scripture*, Atlanta: Society of Biblical Literature, 29–40.

Quek, T.-M. (2009), '"I Will Give Authority Over the Nations": Psalm 2.8–9 in Revelation 2.26–27', in C. A. Evans and Z. H. Daniel (eds.), *Early Christian Literature and Intertextuality*, vol. 2: *Exegetical Studies*, LNTS 392, London: T&T Clark, 175–187.

Riddlebarger, K. (2003), *A Case for Amillennialism: Understanding the End Times*, Grand Rapids: Baker.

Rissi, M. (1972), *The Future of the World: An Exegetical Study of Revelation 19.11–22.15*, SBT 23, London: SCM.

Roberts, A. J., and A. Wilson (2018), *Echoes of Exodus: Tracing Themes of Redemption through Scripture*, Wheaton: Crossway.

Rowland, C. (1993), *Revelation*, Epworth Commentaries, London: Epworth.

Royalty, R. M. (2004), 'Don't Touch This Book! Revelation 22:18–19 and the Rhetoric of Reading (in) the Apocalypse of John', *BibInt* 12: 282–299.

Rusten, E. M. (1977), 'A Critical Evaluation of Dispensational Interpretations of the Book of Revelation', PhD diss., New York University.

Rutledge, F. (2017), *The Crucifixion: Understanding the Death of Jesus Christ*, Grand Rapids: Eerdmans.

Schnabel, E. J. (2002), 'John and the Future of the Nations', *BBR* 12: 243–271.

Schreiner, T. R. (2013), *The King in His Beauty: A Biblical Theology of the Old and New Testaments*, Grand Rapids: Baker.

Schüssler Fiorenza, E. (1977), 'Composition and Structure of the Book of Revelation', *CBQ* 39: 344–366.

———— (1998), *The Book of Revelation: Justice and Judgment*, 2nd edn, Philadelphia: Fortress.

Schweizer, E. (1964), 'πνεῦμα, πνευματικός', in *TDNT* 6: 333–451.

Shaw, D. A. (2013), 'Converted Imaginations? The Reception of Richard Hays's Intertextual Method', *CurBR* 11: 234–245.

Shead, A. G. (2012), *A Mouth Full of Fire: The Word of God in the Words of Jeremiah*, NSBT 29, Nottingham: Apollos; Downers Grove: InterVarsity Press.

Slater, T. B. (1985), '"King of Kings and Lord of Lords" Revisited', *NTS* 39: 159–160.

—— (1999), 'On the Social Setting of the Revelation to John', *NTS* 44: 232–256.

Smalley, S. S. (2005), *The Revelation to John: A Commentary on the Greek Text of the Apocalypse*, Downers Grove: InterVarsity Press.

Smidt, J. C. de (1994), 'The Holy Spirit in the Book of Revelation – Nomenclature', *Neot* 28: 229–244.

Smith, B. D. (2016), 'The Identification of Jesus with YHWH in the Book of Revelation: A Brief Sketch', *CTR* 14: 67–84.

Smith, R. L. (1984), *Micah–Malachi*, WBC 32, Waco: Word.

Spellman, C. (2016), 'The Scribe Who Has Become a Disciple: Identifying and Becoming the Ideal Reader of the Biblical Canon', *Them* 41: 37–51.

Steinmann, A. E. (1992), 'The Tripartite Structure of the Sixth Seal, the Sixth Trumpet, and the Sixth Bowl of John's Apocalypse (Rev 6:12–7:17, 9:13–11:14, 16:12–16)', *JETS* 35: 69–79.

Stevenson, G. (2001), *Power and Place: Temple and Identity in the Book of Revelation*, BZNW 107, Berlin: de Gruyter.

Stone, M. E. (1994), *Fourth Ezra: A Commentary on the Book of Fourth Ezra*, Hermeneia, Minneapolis: Fortress.

Storms, C. S. (2013), *Kingdom Come: The Amillennial Alternative*, Fearn: Mentor.

Stuart, D. K. (1987), *Hosea–Jonah*, WBC 31, Waco: Word.

Stuckenbruck, L. T. (1995), *Angel Veneration and Christology: A Study in Early Judaism and in the Christology of the Apocalypse of John*, WUNT 2.70, Tübingen: Mohr.

Swete, H. B. (1906), *The Apocalypse of St. John*, 2nd edn, New York: Macmillan.

Tabb, B. J. (2011), 'Johannine Fulfillment of Scripture: Continuity and Escalation', *BBR* 21: 495–505.

—— (2015), 'Revelation', in D. A. Carson (ed.), *NIV Zondervan Study Bible*, Grand Rapids: Zondervan, 2580–2626.

—— (2016), 'Persecution of the Early Church', in J. D. Barry (ed.), *The Lexham Bible Dictionary*, Bellingham, Wash.: Lexham.

—— (2017), *Suffering in Ancient Worldview: Luke, Seneca, and 4 Maccabees in Dialogue*, LNTS 569, London: Bloomsbury T&T Clark.

——— (2018), 'Review of S. Dixon, *The Testimony of the Exalted Jesus in the Book of Revelation*', *Them* 43: 111–112.

Thomas, R. L. (1989), 'The Spiritual Gift of Prophecy in Rev 22:18', *JETS* 32: 201–216.

——— (1992), *Revelation 1–7: An Exegetical Commentary*, Chicago: Moody.

——— (1993), 'The Structure of the Apocalypse: Recapitulation or Progression?', *Master's Seminary Journal* 4: 45–66.

——— (1995), *Revelation 8–22: An Exegetical Commentary*, Chicago: Moody.

——— (1998), 'A Classical Dispensationalist View of Revelation', in C. M. Pate (ed.), *Four Views on the Book of Revelation*, Grand Rapids: Zondervan, 177–230.

Thompson, J. A. (1980), *The Book of Jeremiah*, NICOT, Grand Rapids: Eerdmans.

——— (2008), *Deuteronomy: An Introduction and Commentary*, repr., TOTC 5, Downers Grove: IVP Academic.

Trites, A. A. (1977), *The New Testament Concept of Witness*, SNTSMS 31, Cambridge: Cambridge University Press.

Vanhoye, A. (1962), 'L'utilisation du livre d'Ézéchiel dans l'Apocalypse', *Bib* 43: 436–476.

Victorinus (2011), 'Commentary on the Apocalypse', in W. C. Weinrich (ed.), *Latin Commentaries on Revelation*, Ancient Christian Texts, Downers Grove: IVP Academic.

Vogelgesang, J. M. (1985), 'The Interpretation of Ezekiel in the Book of Revelation', PhD diss., Harvard University.

Voss, G. (1954), *Biblical Theology: Old and New Testaments*, Grand Rapids: Eerdmans.

Waddell, R. (2006), *The Spirit of the Book of Revelation*, Blandford: Deo.

Wall, R. W. (2006), *Revelation*, NIBCNT 18, Peabody: Hendrickson.

Wallace, D. B. (1996), *Greek Grammar Beyond the Basics: An Exegetical Syntax of the New Testament*, Grand Rapids: Zondervan.

Walvoord, J. F. (1966), *The Revelation of Jesus Christ: A Commentary*, Chicago: Moody.

——— (1985), 'Revelation', in J. F. Walvoord and R. B. Zuck (eds.), *The Bible Knowledge Commentary: New Testament*, Wheaton: Victor, 925–991.

Waymeyer, M. (2016), *Amillennialism and the Age to Come: A Premillennial Critique of the Two-Age Model*, The Woodlands, Tex.: Kress Biblical Resources.

Webster, D. D. (2014), *Follow the Lamb: A Pastoral Approach to The Revelation*, Eugene: Cascade.

Weinrich, W. C. (2005), *Revelation*, ACCS 12, Downers Grove: InterVarsity Press.

Wellum, S. J. (2016), *God the Son Incarnate: The Doctrine of Christ*, Foundations of Evangelical Theology, Wheaton: Crossway.

Wenham, G. J. (1987), *Genesis 1–15*, WBC 1, Waco: Word.

—— (1993), *Genesis 16–50*, WBC 2, Waco: Word.

Wesley, C. (2017), 'Love Divine, All Loves Excelling', in S. Aniol (ed.), *Hymns to the Living God*, Fort Worth, Tex.: Religious Affections Ministries, 205.

White, J. R. (2013), 'The 144,000 in Revelation 7 and 14: Old Testament and Intratextual Clues to Their Identity ', in D. M. Gurtner and B. L. Gladd (eds.), *From Creation to New Creation: Biblical Theology and Exegesis: Essays in Honor of G. K. Beale*, Peabody: Hendrickson, 179–197.

Wilcock, M. (1975), *I Saw Heaven Opened: The Message of Revelation*, BST, Leicester: Inter-Varsity Press.

Williamson, P. S. (2015), *Revelation*, Catholic Commentary on Sacred Scripture, Grand Rapids: Baker Academic.

Wilson, M. W. (1994), 'Revelation 19:10 and Contemporary Interpretation', in M. W. Wilson (ed.), *Spirit and Renewal: Essays in Honor of J. Rodman Williams*, Sheffield: Sheffield Academic Press, 191–202.

Winter, B. W. (2015), *Divine Honours for the Caesars: The First Christians' Responses*, Grand Rapids: Eerdmans.

Wise, M. O., M. G. Abegg and E. M. Cook (1996), *The Dead Sea Scrolls: A New Translation*, San Francisco: HarperSanFrancisco.

Witetschek, S. (2006), 'Der Lieblingspsalm des Sehers: die Verwendung von Ps 2 in der Johannesapokalypse', in M. A. Knibb (ed.), *The Septuagint and Messianism*, BETL 195, Leuven: Leuven University Press, 407–502.

Witherington III, B. (2003), *Revelation*, The New Cambridge Bible Commentary, Cambridge: Cambridge University Press.

Wong, D. K. K. (1997), 'The Two Witnesses in Revelation 11', *BSac* 154: 344–354.

—— (1998), 'The Tree of Life in Revelation 2:7', *BSac* 155: 211–226.

Wright, N. T. (2003), *The Resurrection of the Son of God*, Christian Origins and the Question of God 3, Minneapolis: Fortress.

Index of authors

Index of Scripture references

Titles in this series:

An index of Scripture references for all the volumes may be found at http://www.thegospelcoalition.org/article/new-studies-in-biblical-theology